AIDS:
THE LITERARY
RESPONSE

AIDS:
THE LITERARY RESPONSE

edited by
EMMANUEL S. NELSON

Twayne Publishers • NEW YORK
Maxwell Macmillan Canada • TORONTO
Maxwell Macmillan International •
NEW YORK   OXFORD   SINGAPORE   SYDNEY

Copyright © 1992 by Twayne Publishers

Twayne Publishers   Maxwell Macmillan Canada, Inc.
Macmillan Publishing Company   1200 Eglinton Avenue East
866 Third Avenue   Suite 200
New York, New York 10022   Don Mills, Ontario M3C 3N1

Macmillan Publishing Company is part of the Maxwell Communication Group
of Companies.

LIBRARY OF CONGRESS CATALOGING-IN-PUBLICATION DATA

AIDS—the literary response / edited by Emmanuel S. Nelson.
    p.   cm.
    Includes bibliographical references and index.
    ISBN 0-8057-9029-2 : $28.95. — ISBN 0-8057-9032-2 : $12.95
    1. Literature, Modern—20th century—History and criticism.
2. AIDS (Disease) in literature.   3. Gays in literature.
I. Nelson, Emmanuel S. (Emmanual Sampath), 1954–
PN771.A64   1992
809'.93356—dc20   92-8155
                                              CIP

10 9 8 7 6 5 4 3 2 1

PRINTED IN THE UNITED STATES OF AMERICA

There was neither death nor immortality then. There was no distinguishing sign of night nor of day. That one breathed, windless, by its own impulse. Other than that there was nothing beyond.

—Násadiya (Creation Hymn), *The Rig Veda*

Contents

Acknowledgments

Introduction

EMMANUEL S. NELSON

A medical disaster of global dimensions and wide-ranging cultural consequences, AIDS made its formal entry into public consciousness in 1981. Since then discourses on AIDS from a variety of perspectives have proliferated at a pace as daunting as the epidemic itself. A significant body of imaginative literature too has emerged since the mid-eighties in response to the impact of AIDS on individuals and on communities—homosexual as well as heterosexual—both here in the United States and internationally. The central objective of this collection of critical essays is to understand and to define the literary response to AIDS through examinations of representative texts and their contexts.

The primary focus of this volume is on the creative response of gay male artists: several of the chapters that follow the introduction are concerned largely or exclusively with the works of gay writers. Such a focus is inevitable, since much of the literature of AIDS has been created by gay men; but it is also morally and politically necessary. Certainly quite a few heterosexual writers have explored AIDS thematically in their texts, sometimes with considerable sensitivity and imaginative strength. Yet it is the artistic response of gay men to their individual and collective sorrow and terror, their anger and helplessness—for it is gay men, at least in the western nations, who have been disproportionately traumatized by AIDS—that has resulted in the most poignant and enduring texts of the AIDS era. After all, the reaction of gay artists to AIDS is bound to differ, even fundamentally so, from that of nongay writers: AIDS, to gay men, is a gravely personal issue. It is too real to be easily metaphorized or elegantly aestheticized. Many of them do not have to imagine the horror, for they live in the midst of a holocaust.

Indeed, much of the energy of gay writing since the mid-eighties has been directed at formulating responses to the crisis that AIDS has generated. When the epidemic broke out in the early eighties, the initial reaction of gay writers was stunned, confused silence. Since the mid-eighties, however, writers have begun to register their responses in a variety of ways. Some continue to explore a wide range of issues unrelated to AIDS, while acknowledging the threatening presence of the contagion—either by merely alluding to it or by rendering its menacing shadow integral to the tone and mood of their works. Some others, despite the problems inherent in achieving artistic distance from themes that are distressingly personal, have attempted direct, full-scale confrontation with the plague. A few others have seized the urgency of the moment to create a defiant literature of resistance. And some others have at least temporarily abandoned their usual modes of creative expression and have opted for the more direct medium of contemplative essays or journalistic reports. Even when a contemporary gay writer consciously eschews thematizing AIDS—because he is unwilling or unable to do so—he no longer can write with the innocent certainties that his pre-AIDS counterparts could take for granted. His personal vision cannot disregard the insistent reality of the unceasing epidemic.

The intensely personal nature of the catastrophe that gay writers have to confront in their lives and in their literature is one of the central sources of tension that informs much of their AIDS-related writing. What is testimonial and what is fictive in their literary constructions, for example, collide—sometimes resulting in works of fierce authenticity and haunting eloquence. And there are formidable political burdens that this new literature has to bear. Though gay writing in general, like the counter-hegemonic sexualities of its creators, has existed largely in an ideologically problematic space, the entry of AIDS into gay literary discourse has made the political ramifications even more troublesome. The advent of AIDS, for example, has literally made the body of the gay male an object of massive public curiosity and relentless cultural inquiry. His body is now widely perceived as a site of mysterious and fatal infections—a perception that has prompted its radical (re)othering and (re)medicalizing. The body has emerged as a supertext, a territory over which a bewildering number of competing medical, political, and cultural fictions seek domination. Contemporary gay writers, then, have to reappropriate their bodies from the unprecedented ongoing textual abuse in order to give voice to the realities of their endangered lives. In this moment of crisis in gay cultures everywhere, the gay artists—who themselves are being decimated at an alarming pace and in a gruesome manner—face the added burden of managing in their art the collective mood of emergency. They have to devise ways of finding some redemptive meaning in the senseless nightmare; of re-creating pain but framing it in a transcendent vision; of articulating a resistant, activist consciousness instead of merely helpless, paralyzing angst.

One is tempted, of course, to compare the literature of AIDS to other literatures of crisis: to literatures of genocides and holocausts, for example, or to prison writing. One is tempted to compare the memoirs of AIDS to the slave narratives of the nineteenth century—those sacred texts of African-

American culture that defiantly testify to the humanity and dignity of an enslaved people in the face of brutal realities. But I wish to resist those comparisons—even though I recognize some formal similarities, ideological affinities, and spiritual connections among them—because I wish to insist on the uniqueness of the literature of AIDS. AIDS writing is produced in response to a puzzling and unmanageable medical catastrophe, primarily by individuals on the sexual margins who have been most profoundly affected. It is a diverse body of literature that documents, disrupts, testifies, protests, even celebrates. Its quality may be uneven but its authenticity, especially when its creators are men whose lives are in peril and whose communities are under threat, can rarely be contested. And much of the literature of AIDS constitutes a feverish elegy, written collectively during the closing decades of the twentieth century, to a generation dying young.

The sixteen essays that follow interpret aspects of AIDS literature from a variety of critical perspectives. The authors' approaches range from the historical to the pedagogical, from practical criticism to cultural analysis to deconstructive reading. Such diversity in the contributors' theoretical stances and interpretive strategies enables this collection of essays to serve a key purpose: to offer not only multiple but also conflicting perspectives on the topic under consideration.

Laurel Brodsley's opening essay, "Defoe's *The Journal of the Plague Year:* A Model for Stories of Plagues," locates contemporary literature of AIDS in a broad historical context. She finds in Daniel Defoe's pioneering text on the bubonic plague of the seventeenth century a central paradigm for subsequent works of fiction as well as nonfiction that deal with catastrophic contagions. Defoe's objective was explicitly didactic: using a fictional format, Defoe the journalist, who was at once a witness as well as a survivor, sets out to educate his audience. Rather than merely report on the unfolding events of the plague, Defoe—through his fictional first-person narrator—offers a series of stories, digressions, anecdotes, and analyses which, collectively, project a complex, nearly complete picture of the devastation. He not only deals with the medical and social management of the plague but also provides insights into the collective psychology of a troubled people imperiled by the contagion. In such narrative, Brodsley argues, Defoe "suggests a structure for plague literature which has been revived in contemporary works . . . on AIDS." Using Paul Monette's *Borrowed Time* and Randy Shilt's *And the Band Played On*, she points to the stylistic and strategic similarities these texts share with Defoe's innovative novelistic documentation of an earlier plague.

But Joseph Dewey, in his essay that follows Brodsley's, asserts that the traditional genre of plague literature offers no stable models for thematizing AIDS. Even Defoe's *The Journal of the Plague Year*, he argues, provides no sustaining paradigm for the postmodern artists of the AIDS era: Defoe's absolute faith in God enables him to impose a reassuring logic on an incoherent world out of control; such faith, however, seems anachronistic, even illusory, in the contemporary context of secularity. The journals of our plague years, therefore, differ fundamentally from Defoe's. Dewey then proceeds to analyze three such "journals": Alice Hoffman's *At Risk*, Robert Ferro's *Second Son*, and George Whitmore's *Nebraska*. While he concedes that Hoffman's best-seller is at times a poignant work, he faults it for its "radical failure of nerve." By centering her narrative on an "innocent victim" and by locating that protagonist within the confines of a safely middle-class suburban nuclear family, Hoffman manages to sanitize AIDS and makes the epidemic "reader-friendly." In its eagerness to accommodate the sensitivities of the heterosexual mainstream, Hoffman's narrative is "unpleasantly exploitative as it summons the images of the epidemic without grappling with its essential definition." Unlike Hoffman's novel, Ferro's *Second Son* offers what Dewey calls "a most dramatic journal of [the] plague." With unflinching directness it "confronts mortality as well as the more complicated questions of love and sexuality raised by the fact of AIDS." Dewey concludes his essay with an intriguing reading of Whitmore's *Nebraska*, a text that is set in the pre-AIDS era, as the "most significant journal of our plague years." *Nebraska*, he argues, is an "affirming testament for the AIDS decade," consciously intended by its author to counter the complex new rationale for shame, denial, and repression faced by young gay men now coming of age in the midst of the contagion.

While Dewey dismisses Hoffman's *At Risk* as a "most elaborate dodge," Judith Laurence Pastore in her essay following Dewey's, offers a more sympathetic reading of the novel. She acknowledges the novel's suburban bias, its heterosexual context, and its centralizing of an "innocent victim." But she also points to the essentially realistic core of the text: AIDS, after all, has indeed infiltrated the seemingly safe suburbs and has invaded the lives of more than a few children and heterosexual adults. Furthermore, Pastore carefully examines the political significance of a bisexual adult male character in the novel: Brian, dying of AIDS, plays a healing role in the lives of Amanda, the protagonist, and Ivan, her father. The presence of Brian in the novel, according to Pastore, is a vital part of Hoffman's attempt to reconstitute "our vision of the self and its relationship to the Other." *At Risk* exposes the heartlessness of educated and affluent white adults who convert "one of their own—a white, middle-class child—into a fearful Other: marginalized gays, IV-drug users, and Haitians." By doing so the novel "opens up the possibility for greater compassion by first showing AIDS in the known and then shifting briefly to the 'Other' who even in an attenuated, sanitized version still has the potential of enabling people to make the necessary imaginative leap."

Les Wright's "Gay Genocide as Literary Trope" offers a thoughtful and sophisticated reading of the paranoid gay political fantasies that shape the "underlying discourses behind 'Silence = Death,' symbolized by the superimposed triangle of Hitler's death camps. Gay resistance equates American homophobes (literal Christian fundamentalists) with Nazis (figural evil) and post-Stonewall American gays with homosexual, and by extension, Jewish victims of the concentration camps." First, Wright maps this tropological bias in a pre-AIDS novel, *Project Lambda*, and then proceeds to demonstrate how the emergence of AIDS into this sensational politics of imaginary gay genocide further reinforces cultural mythologies nurtured by a segment of American gay activists in two AIDS novels of the eighties: Geoff Mains's *Gentle Warriors* and Marty Rubin's *Boiled Frog Syndrome*. The plot of Mains's novel, for example, "predicates on the conclusion that AIDS *was* a government plot." The novel evokes, in an atmosphere charged with leathersexual energy, fantastic images of a conspiratorial right-wing government determined to exterminate gays and heroic leathermen planning violent counter-conspiracies. In *Boiled Frog Syndrome*, another gay cautionary tale, America yet again emerges as a fascist territory where AIDS, a government invention, is used as an excuse to send gay men to death camps. Such fantasies, Wright acknowledges, are understandable products of a complex interplay of political and psychological forces in the collective psyche of a marginalized and mistreated minority group. But he also voices a note of caution: "The gay movement's adoption of Jewish persecution at the hands of Nazis is a specious argument and reveals dangerous epistemological slippage. And the production of discourses about AIDS by gay men has assured posterity that it will be remembered as a gay disease in spite of our every effort to resist that valorization."

If AIDS can grant potency to literary fantasies of government-orchestrated gay genocide, in the works of a few writers the epidemic barely makes its menacing appearance—as Myles Weber points out in his commentary on the absence of AIDS panic in Peter Cameron's fiction. Though much of Cameron's fiction is set in the 1980s, a decade in which AIDS became a fundamental fact of life and death, the epidemic is hardly a matter of serious concern for many of the characters. Weber argues that this absence of fear is a conscious strategy Cameron employs to assert an often unacknowledged truth: "that the gay population is not monolithic—that, in fact, the behavior, sexual and otherwise, of male homosexuals is as various as that of heterosexuals." Cameron counters the widely held myth that all gay men are sexually promiscuous—a myth that feeds the still lingering assumption that AIDS is a specifically gay disease. While promiscuity was certainly viewed by many urban gay men in the 1970s as a celebratory assertion of sexual self-determination, the younger gay men who came of age in the eighties—many of Cameron's characters fit this category—did not always feel such compelling need for sexual rebellion. Monogamy, once dismissed by quite a few gay men as an inconvenience, became a rather reasonable option for many who reached their sexual maturity in the plague-ridden 1980s. The absence of AIDS panic in Cameron's fiction, then, is not a sign of the author's indifference to the grim reality of AIDS; instead, it is a strategy designed to familiarize his readers with "one segment of one generation of that larger category known as gay men, thereby helping to provide a more accurate and complete picture of contemporary gay life and, in turn, drawing a clearer distinction between the officially recognized AIDS risk group and those persons actually at great risk." It is a way of quietly asserting what is frequently obscured in public discourses on AIDS: there are no high-risk groups, only high-risk behaviors.

Barbara Browning's "Babaluaiyé: Searching for the Text of a Pandemic" engages absence of a different kind: the lack of a pan-African text of the AIDS phenomenon. By using Ishmael Reed's *Mumbo Jumbo*, published in 1972, as a pre-text, Browning begins her fascinating deconstruction of the absent AIDS text. *Mumbo Jumbo* does indeed offer an ingenious point of departure for such a reading: it is an experimental novel that recounts the movement of a fictional plague in the 1920s that begins in New Orleans, a city strongly influenced by Haitian culture, and gradually moves up north and invades New York. Called Jes Grew, it is a mysterious pandemic not unlike AIDS. By interpreting the complex African spiritual belief systems encoded in Reed's text and by recontextualizing his 1972 novel by situating it in the midst of the devastated urban black and latino communities that are increasingly becoming the epicenters of AIDS in the United States, Browning "reads" the text that is yet to be constructed by a "collective, politicized pan-African community, including women."

Absence is also one of the concerns of Gert Hekma's brief essay on the literary response to AIDS in the Netherlands—an absence that might surprise many non-Dutch readers. Dutch gay artists, who are viewed by many gays and lesbians around the world as inhabitants of a sexually liberated space, have hardly created a significant body of literature in response to the AIDS crisis. Writers such as Gerard Reve and Gerrit Komrij have not yet even alluded to the epidemic in their works; other well-established gay writers, such as Jaap Harten, A. Moonen, Boudewijn Büch, and Hans Warren remain, for the most part, silent. Hekma explains this absence of response in the context of these writers' personal detachment from the "blossoming of gay and lesbian cultures in the eighties" as well as their largely assimilationist politics. Even the only major Dutch novel that deals with AIDS, Frans Kellendonk's *The Mystical Body*, is a generally unsympathetic treatment of the subject. Hekma suggests that Kellendonk's novel might be a symptom that a "free space to live and think for gays and lesbians is more difficult to attain, even in the Netherlands, than is generally assumed."

In the lengthier essay that follows Hekma's, David Wetsel offers a detailed commentary on the emerging literature of AIDS in France. Initially dismissed as a curious figment of paranoid American imagination, AIDS did not sink deeply into the consciousness of French gay men until the mid-eighties. The literary response, too, was a belated one: only in 1987 were the first significant works dealing with the epidemic published in France. Wetsel focuses his discussion on six major texts and places them in the immediate contexts of Parisian gay culture and sensibilities as well as in the larger context of French literary tradition. Emmanuel Dreuilhe's *Corps à Corps: journal du sida (Mortal Embrace: Living with AIDS)*, which exemplifies the use of elaborate martial metaphors in AIDS writing in general, was the first AIDS memoir to be published in France. Guibert's *A l'ami qui ne m'a pas sauvé la vie (To the Friend Who Did Not Save My Life)* is an autobiographical AIDS novel in which many of the writer's friends and enemies appear thinly disguised as fictional characters; the text provides Guibert with a literary forum to settle old scores. Copi's *La Visite inopportune (The untimely visit)* is a brilliantly tasteful farce on the AIDS crisis, but Dominique Fernandez's *La Gloire du paria (The glory of the outcast)* strikes a somber note in its relentless critique of the widespread denial of the epidemic among French gay men until the late eighties when the reality of AIDS became unmistakable in their panic-stricken communities. Guy Hocquenghem's *Eve*, Wetsel concludes, is perhaps the finest AIDS novel to be published in France. He argues that "*Eve* sets the problem of suffering within the context of the founding myths of European culture" by transcending the "autobiographical constraints limiting so much of the new literature of AIDS" and by "reviving a long-defunct genre in French literature: philosophical allegory."

International cinematic responses to AIDS is the subject of Kevin J. Harty's essay. In his detailed survey of significant AIDS films, Harty argues that the movie industry's reaction to the epidemic is still largely incommensurate with the magnitude of the crisis spawned by the epidemic. Included in his discussion are a variety of films: American, British, and German productions; low-budget films by gay producers; telemovies that are geared for "mainstream" consumption; and films that focus on "innocent victims." While Harty acknowledges that some of these works are indeed sensitive film treatments of the many complex issues that AIDS raises, he concludes that theater, rather than the movie industry, has taken the lead in handling AIDS-related issues thoughtfully and honestly. Hollywood, with its profit motives and its general unwillingness to offend "mainstream" sensitivities, still remains largely apathetic.

The theater, given its public and congregational nature, does indeed provide a powerful forum for artistic examination of the impact of AIDS. The stage provides space for re-presentation of everyday terrors and sorrows for calmer, more structured contemplation. Moreover, the political value of the public stage has traditionally proved particularly useful in contexts of compelling social urgency. Two of the best-known American AIDS plays— Hoffman's *As Is* and Kramer's *The Normal Heart*—are the focus of Joel Shatzky's essay, which tracks the entry of AIDS into American theater. Shatzky argues that these two plays "established the basic approaches to the dramatization of the AIDS epidemic: personal reaction and public outrage."

His survey of the critical responses to these two plays in the "mainstream" media—plays that offer uncompromisingly gay perspectives on the AIDS crisis—reveals the ambivalence inherent in the delicate task of criticizing the aesthetics and the politics of AIDS texts. Such ambivalence is evident in Shatzky's own cautious comparison of AIDS plays to theatrical treatments of the Holocaust.

Similar to Shatzky, D. S. Lawson views Hoffman's *As Is* and Kramer's *The Normal Heart* as embodiments of two divergent responses to the epidemic: remembrance and rage—responses that inform many American AIDS plays produced subsequent to these two early works. The dominant mood of *As Is* is one of nostalgia, of wistful longing for the innocence and sexual abundance of the pre-AIDS era. Lawson identifies this recollective mood as the defining characteristic of Fierstein's *Safe Sex*, Bumbalo's *Adam and the Experts*, van Itallie's *Ancient Boys*, and Lucas's *Prelude to a Kiss*. Kramer's *The Normal Heart*, on the other hand, is the prototypical rage play. Reminiscences of ancient frolics do surface, of course, but the dominant mood is anger: anger at the criminal apathy of those in power. This sense of outrage pervades several other dramatic texts that followed Kramer's work: Bowne's *Beirut*, Pintauro's *Raft of the Medusa*, and Cachianes's *Everybody Knows Your Name*, for example. Lawson's survey of the plays of rage and plays of remembrance is enriched by his insightful analyses of the dramaturgical and ideological attributes of each text.

Gregory Woods, in his "AIDS to Remembrance: The Uses of Elegy," locates AIDS poetry in the larger context of the elegiac tradition in English poetry. To the poet who wants to lament the death of a loved one or to mourn the passing of an entire era, the elegy serves as an apt vehicle of expression. And the characteristic shift in mood that occurs within an elegy—from an acknowledgment of grief to a reaffirmation of hope—holds out the potential for personal transcendence. Memorializing the dead in elegies may not be precisely the kind of stridently interventionist cultural practice that some AIDS activists, such as Douglas Crimp, have called for. But Woods identifies in at least some AIDS elegies the seeds of resistance, of defiance, of action. The poignancy that the poetry evokes "may, in fact, be a pad from which action may be launched; it is, at least, a *reaction*, all the better than a turning away." Woods concludes, "Every elegy must bear a caveat: tears alone make a soggy memorial."

The next three essays address one of the key issues in AIDS discourse: the problematic of representing AIDS. In his provocative essay, "The Repression of the Returned: AIDS and Allegory," James Morrison vigorously challenges some of the leading theorists of AIDS literature by identifying a collusive relationship between representations of AIDS in popular American culture and poststructuralist critical interventions that claim "to recover [from such representations] the reality of AIDS." The collusion, Morrison points out, occurs in their shared reliance on allegorical obliqueness. Because the representations of AIDS in popular culture are shaped by the definitions and conventions of public discourse authorized by the dominant power structure, they depend on a "rhetoric of indirection, a style of metaphoric thinking." That which is repressed resurfaces in allegorical forms. Similar recourse to indirection and metaphorical manipulation is evident in the works of many poststructuralist discourses on AIDS—Morrison cites the works of Douglas Crimp, Paula Treichler, Leo Bersani, Lee Edelman, and Steven Seidman as examples—which create "a version of AIDS that defines it as radically *other* in crucial ways: a disease of *others*, and a disease that is *something other*, that must be understood by means of figures, extended tropes, free-playing semiosis— something to be looked at, examined from a distance, a *spectacle* of represen- tation." And since both popular culture and poststructuralist discourse "operate in the sphere of allegory in their efforts to construct and understand the intense problematics of AIDS, they are potentially complicitous in stigmatizing those who suffer from the disease."

David Bergman's analysis of the rhetoric of Larry Kramer—one of the loudest and most confrontational AIDS activists in the United States since the early eighties—also engages the larger problem of "finding a language" to speak about AIDS. If Kramer at times sounds like an "enraged child" or a "guilt-inducing mother" or an intentionally "humiliating father," it is not merely because of his ambivalence toward sex or his internalized homopho- bia; it is primarily because of the difficulty in constructing a gay-identified rhetoric of AIDS "that is urgent without being oppositional." Bergman concludes that the Quilt exhibited by the NAMES Project offers the most powerful and poignant piece of AIDS rhetoric. It integrates art with activism, mourning with militancy, and it articulates "the type of statement gay writers are only beginning to stitch together with words."

Certainly the Quilt is the most spectacular work of art that has emerged from the AIDS crisis; massive, colorful, and made up of thousands of individual panels, it has been displayed by the NAMES Project in cities across the United States. Judith Elsley offers in her essay a brilliant reading of the meaning and significance of this elaborate text(ile). Each panel in the Quilt commemorates a loved one who has died of AIDS. The survivors inscribe their love and loss in their handmade textile memorials; their act of quilting the panels also becomes in itself a step toward their internal healing, a vital part of their personal management of grief. These individual panels are woven together to create the larger Quilt: the many private tales of bereavement meld together to render a statement of collective mourning. Elsley situates the Quilt in the context of Bakhtin's theory of the novel and interprets its significance as a vast, open-ended, carnivalesque text of many voices.

The final essay in the collection, Annie Dawid's "The Way We Teach Now: Three Approaches to AIDS Fiction," addresses pedagogical issues that AIDS writing raises. Dawid's essay is based on her experience of teaching three short stories that deal with AIDS—McFarland's "Nothing to Ask For," Sontag's "The Way We Live Now," and Barnett's "Philostorgy, Now Obscure"—in a class of 18 students at a small liberal arts college. The students, not surprisingly, respond most favorably to McFarland's fiction: the text allows the students to enter and exit the problematic territory of AIDS in the reassuring company of a straight, white, middle-class narrator. Indeed AIDS in the story is largely an occasion to demonstrate the resilience of friendship in the face of tragedy. Sontag's and Barnett's fictions, however, do not permit such an easy journey into the heart of darkness. In Sontag's story there is no reassuring voice the reader can comfortably connect with; her insistence that AIDS puts all of us at risk disrupts the complacency of those readers who consider themselves quite safe from the epidemic. And Barnett's story takes the reader beyond the disease itself to confront the delicately complex personal choices the characters face. It demands a response that is laden with moral risk. Dawid concludes that students, generally, respond most positively to AIDS fictions that they find safe and comfortable to negotiate. Works that force them into more threatening territories, however, leave them unsettled. As readers they resist what they fear. But it is precisely such fictions we must include when we teach now, "if we are to educate our students in a broad and caring way." Indeed, the quote with which Dawid ends her essay provides an appropriate closure to this volume: says one of Sontag's characters about the protagonist coping with AIDS, "And it was encouraging he was willing to say the name of the disease, pronounce it often and easily, as if it were just another word, like boy or gallery . . . because . . . to utter the name is a sign of health."

1

Defoe's *The Journal of the Plague Year*: A Model for Stories of Plagues

LAUREL BRODSLEY

In 1722, Daniel Defoe, a prolific journalist and novelist, published an innovative work of fiction, *The Journal of the Plague Year*. In both its content, a depiction of London life during the bubonic plague epidemic of 1665, and in its form, a first-person memoir narrated by a survivor, this novel provides a model for the way literature can provide insight into private and public responses to major epidemics. Defoe's description of the daily life of London citizens during this time of pestilence, his enumeration of governmental policies to contain the spread of disease and to care for its victims, and his evaluation of the efficacy of edicts and practices provide a paradigm for both fiction and nonfiction on devastating infectious disease.[1]

Unlike many literary works on medical themes, Defoe places individual experiences within the context of public health policies. The narrator, H. F., begins his story as a private observer, simply one of many who did not get out of the city before the plague struck. As his curiosity grows, H. F. becomes a reporter and commentator, especially on the effect of public health policies on private lives. For a while, he is assigned by the government to be an official examiner for the city's public health work, hence an active participant in plague control. In small inset stories, and then in a long section on three men who try to flee to the country, H. F. reports stories of people's behavior under

11

the terror of plague: families trapped by household quarantine in their homes; asymptomatic carriers transmitting disease to strangers and loved ones; altruistic and criminal behavior among caregivers.

Daniel Defoe's creation of this novel was part of a larger public education program developed by physicians, magistrates, and other commentators to prepare the British for the bubonic plague that swept Europe between 1720 and 1722. As a journalist, Defoe had recorded and commented on a wide range of economic, political, and medical crises in England during the early eighteenth century. His long pamphlet, *Due Preparations for the Plague* (1722),[2] systemically laid out a wide range of personal and public actions that people could use to reduce their susceptibility to infection. His advice ranged from basic health practices, including good nutrition, to household seclusion as a form of voluntary quarantine. In a long narrative depicting a fictional family, Defoe describes in detail how a group of people can isolate themselves in their home, with adequate provisions, entertainments, and forms of communication and commerce, to protect themselves from the plague.

Defoe's pamphlet and other didactic texts by his peers were full of good advice. But it was apparent to Defoe that prudent warnings and lists of proper things to do may inadequately motivate citizens to radically change their behavior or acknowledge the reality of the plague. Hence, 250 years before the AIDS epidemic, Defoe understood that public health education achieves its purpose not through logic but through passion. Educational materials, on their own, have very little effect; individual members of an audience must be touched and moved by personal experiences revealed through the vicarious power of art. Defoe's *Journal*, like television depictions of characters with HIV-related disease, touches the heart as well as the mind. As a result, London citizens might begin to assimilate for themselves information designed to help them during the plague.

Defoe published *The Journal of the Plague Year* in the same year as *Due Preparations*. In the *Journal*, the personal memoir by H. F., a London manufacturer, vividly captures the emotional as well as the practical aspects of survival during a plague. The narrator depicts the epidemic with precision of detail, compassion for its victims, and thoughtful commentary on the effect of public health policy on individuals and groups. The accuracy of H. F.'s descriptions, with their sense of immediacy and truth, have led some critics to question whether Defoe's novel should be considered a work of fiction at all.

Watson Nicolson, in his definitive study of Defoe's sources, *The Historical Sources of Defoe's* Journal of the Plague Year,[3] demonstrates that almost every statement, description, and event in Defoe's novel is based on published first-person accounts of the actual events and personal reminiscences of survivors. Defoe, however, did not simply string out these bits of historical information into a single narrative line. Instead, Watson found that Defoe deviated from the historical record. The novelist discards the high rhetoric of contemporary accounts in favor of the intimate and conversational voice of his narrator, H. F.; he adds the story of three men who wander into the countryside to illustrate the ordeal faced by plague victims in a rural setting; and he offers a narrative structure that Nicolson finds excessively digressive and repetitive, unlike the chronological descriptions of unfolding events found in the first-person sources Defoe drew upon.

Just as Defoe deliberately chose a fictional format to better educate his audience on the dangers of plague and preventive measures to combat it, he created a narrative style to best accomplish his didactic purpose. As a critic Nicolson is deeply offended by Defoe's structure, but he misses Defoe's achievement. A linear set of journal entries would, of course, capture a series of immediate moments: the discovery of the first victims, the publication of governmental edicts, the locking up of houses, and so forth.

Yet Defoe's purpose throughout the book is not to merely present events but to develop insights into the government's development of public health policy and the effect of edicts on everyday life. H. F., unlike Defoe's sources, not only describes historical facts but integrates them with commentary on governmental action. H. F. reveals the rationale behind specific policies, describes how they work in actual practice, and evaluates their success. Furthermore, H. F., who "publishes" his memoirs after the plague has passed, is able to place particular governmental actions in the context of time. To take only one example, the use of physicians and trained "searchers" to diagnose plague seemed necessary and feasible during the early stages of the epidemic when the caseload was relatively light but became almost impossible during the height of the plague.[4]

As an expression of Defoe's complex purpose for this novel, the work's structure depends on digression and repetition. Each public health action is placed within a complex web of factors. As H. F. educates his readers on a wide range of issues raised by the epidemic, the novel has an encyclopedic as well as a descriptive character. To an audience of ordinary middle-class men and women H. F. talks about the scientific and political motives for preventive and treatment strategies; personnel and materials necessary to enact a policy; financial resources required to pay for services; the willingness of citizens to accept interventions; moral issues of public good versus personal autonomy; the effect of policies among representative individuals or groups, and especially, the short- and long-term effects of policies on everyday life. H. F. ties these together through his personal voice, as his immediate observations are enhanced by his thoughtful contemplation of what it means to be a survivor. This complex analytic process, rather than a simple depiction of a series of events, is the basis for the narrative thrust of this novel.

Defoe's repetitions of policy material also reflect his fascination with the diverse meaning of continuing events within different contexts. The most crucial of these is the issue of household quarantine, or the shutting up of houses. During the first pages of the book as plague begins its spread in the city, people conceal infection in a household, to "prevent neighbors shunning and refusing to converse with them, and to prevent authority from shutting up their houses . . . and people were extremely terrified at the thoughts of it" (*JPY*, 16). Initially, fear of plague isolates families with the disease from their neighbors and friends. The reader, however, does not know why the people are even more frightened of mandatory isolation than they are of the infection itself.

Although the London citizens were terrified of quarantine, this policy ironically reflects the intuitive response of citizens: even without a government edict neighbors avoid those with disease. Suddenly, at this point in the story, H. F. abandons this topic and in a seemingly unrelated digression talks about early preparations of the London citizens for the epidemic, including their affirmation of religious values, the development of medical interventions, and voluntary flight from town. Hovering behind these descriptions of prudent behaviors are echoes of household seclusion: if these strategies are ineffective, then quarantine must be imposed. And so it will be.

However, when the Bills of Mortality showed that death rates had increased, the threat of death became more terrible than the horrors of household seclusion. To H. F., the government's enforcement of the shutting of houses seems rational, appropriate, and effective. The Justices of Peace for Middlesex, by direction of the Secretary of State, had already shut up houses in various parishes with good success. As H. F. says, "in several streets where the plague broke out, upon strict guarding the houses that were infected and taking care to bury those that died immediately after they were known to be dead, the plague ceased in those streets" (*JPY*, 44).

H. F.'s language here is bland and optimistic, reflecting a naïve belief that household quarantine is, and will be, a safe and effective form of plague prevention. H. F. reprints the Lord Mayor of London's regulations on the plague and on the specific manner in which these edicts would be enforced. (*JPY*, 45–53). The official text reveals to the reader, if not to the narrator, the draconian nature of this mode of disease control. Women "searchers" would enter homes to determine whether people had died of the plague or other disease; "examiners," after evaluating the cause of death, would mandate the shutting of houses, which were to be guarded by "watchers" night and day. This isolation was so rigorous that if a friend or relative came to help the family, any person who had "visited any man known to be infected of the plague, or entered willingly into any known infected house . . . [would] be shut up for certain days by the examiner's direction."

In clear language these edicts mandated reporting plague illness and isolating the sick in their homes behind barred doors. Hidden in the text are genuine threats not only to liberty but to life. The master of the house had no right to prevent the entrance of these officials to his home nor had he the ability to negotiate other terms of seclusion, transfer of the sick to a pest house, or flight. Instead, he was obliged to report plague found in his family and servants to the authorities and then, as we will read in H. F.'s narrative, to live immured in his house, often in anguish, until he and his family died (*JPY*, 45–48).

During this early period of the plague, H. F., as a good citizen, acknowledges that citizens felt that this policy was "at first counted a very cruel and unchristian method," and complaints were made against the Lord Mayor. But H. F. defends it, saying that it was "publick good that justified the private mischief" (*JPY*, 54–55). But the phrase, "private mischief" cuts both ways. Quarantine imposed immense "mischief" and pain on private citizens, and in return, private individuals chose to disregard the edict, and in fact became mischievous petty criminals to avoid this imprisonment, thereby spreading disease and bringing mischief back on the state.

Time again shifts. Now H. F. leaps from the present unfolding of the epidemic and governmental health care policy to his perspective as a survivor. Writing from the future, H. F. begins to recount the "great many stories" of how people responded to the shut houses by escaping from their homes. "It would fill a little volume to set down the arts used by the people of such houses" as they gulled their watchmen and devised elaborate ruses to flee.

This shift from objective data such as the published Bills of Mortality and the Lord Mayor's edicts to "stories" is a recurrent structural motif in this book. Yet, while H. F. admits that tales may be diverting, he hedges about their accuracy. "A great many of these stories . . . I met with—that is, heard of—and which are very certain to be true, or very near the truth; that is to say, true in general, for no man could at such a time learn all the particulars" (*JPY*, 58).

Some stories, as we will see, H. F. disregards as false rumors and fantasies. But these stories about escaped people, whether verifiably accurate or not, nevertheless contain truths about the human condition. Defoe, with his fundamental insight into the varieties of human behavior, allows H. F. to comment on and test what he hears. In the case of escaped people from shut houses, H. F. argues that these unfortunates were not motivated by criminal intent, no matter what harm they did; instead, their desires were intimate and personal: "The people shut up or imprisoned so were guilty of no crime, only shut up because miserable, it was really the more intolerable to them" (*JPY*, 58).

While H. F. defends these miserable unfortunates, he also admits that they were dangerous and in the long run harmed others. The imprisoned people made desperate by their isolation "would break out at all adventures" and thereby "spread the infection farther by their wanderings . . . than they would otherwise have done" (*JPY*, 60). Those who escaped made the plague worse, and the families who accepted household quarantine suffered a "misery" that was not to be expressed. From these houses "we heard the most dismal shrieks and out-cries of the poor people, terrified and even frightened to death by the condition of their dearest relations, and by the terror of being imprisoned" (*JPY*, 61–62).

Hence, Defoe provides a complex analysis of household quarantine from a range of literary perspectives: the present-tense narrator, publications of historical edicts, stories heard by H. F., the narrator's perception of the psychological experiences of plague as he lived through it, and his analysis of household quarantine after the event.

Meanwhile, H. F. explores the stages whereby a seemingly beneficial public health policy paradoxically results in further deaths. As we can see, the imposition of household quarantine in various parishes near London initially appears successful; the government accepts this model and imposes it on the whole city through legal edicts; the language of the law disregards the community's need for social support; the resulting isolation of families in their homes becomes psychologically and spiritually onerous; the people placed under these restrictions lie and cheat to avoid their imprisonment; both the healthy and the sick, driven by despair, escape from their locked homes; and those who leave transmit the disease to others, thereby increasing the rate of death, in a reversal of the intended result of this policy.

Furthermore, those men and women who were obedient to the law not only suffered from disease and death from the plague but also were driven to madness so horrible they committed suicide or suffered from conditions exacerbated by their anguish. Hence, the shutting of houses failed to retard the spread of plague, while it raised the death rates both from the pestilence and other conditions.

That this seemingly prudent public health policy can kill is particularly troublesome, H. F. indicates, because two options that would reduce transmission and death were not sufficiently supported by the government. People could voluntarily seclude themselves, as H. F. himself does during the height of the plague. And the government could have provided sufficient pest houses to isolate and care for the sick. For Defoe, a health care policy that ignores the medical needs of the sick, fails to protect healthy members of the household, disregards the power of spiritual and social support, and violates the will of the people can be more lethal than no policy at all.

But as readers we do not fully comprehend the failure of household quarantine until we have returned over and over to this theme. H. F. leaves us with the cries of anguished imprisoned families ringing in our ears, and he again takes off on a new story, the adventures of three men who leave London for the countryside, where, if anything, they fare even worse than if they had stayed in the city (*JPY*, 65ff). Throughout the rest of the novel, H. F. returns to the quarantine theme, especially treating the immense psychological, medical, and, eventually, financial burden the community suffered as a result of isolating houses. By the end of the book, the reader can only be convinced that this policy led people to madness, increased the spread of disease, and was, in the long run, a form of murder.

Through Defoe's intermixture of digressions and time frames within a personal narrative, he suggests a structure for plague literature that has been revived in contemporary works on plague and on AIDS. Camus's *The Plague*,[5] Paul Monette's *Borrowed Time*,[6] and Randy Shilts's *And the Band Played On*[7] are also retrospective memoirs by witnesses of epidemic disease. They are narrated by reasonably objective and decent men: Camus's physician, Dr. Roux; Monette's autobiographical persona, Paul Monette; and Shilts, a historical journalist of the AIDS epidemic. Like H. F., these men not only narrate the events that occur during the time frame of their texts, but also they embellish their personal narrative with stories, digressions, and retrospective commentary. Within these texts, as in Defoe's *Journal*, are compilations of medical and public health data; stories of friends, public figures, and strangers; personal observations based on private experience; and evaluations and assessments of past practices based on present knowledge.

Each author pursues sets of special themes. A poignant example from *Borrowed Time* is Paul Monette's faith in Suramin, as he narrates each dose so hopefully taken by friends and by Roger, while the narrator interjects warnings about how the medication will hasten his friend's demise. Intertwined with themes of hope and survival are themes of lost time, both in Roger's life, and in spaces of months that even Paul cannot adequately recollect. Camus, in the *Plague*, also deals with failed interventions, but in his case, the interventions are medical and public health attempts to prevent and contain the plague. He too laments the loss of time, especially in his poignant chapter on memory and hope suspended by the disease.

Shilts, as a journalist, uses a method closest to that of Defoe. He presents a month-by-month progression of HIV disease and medical and public health attempts to understand and contain the unfolding epidemic. Like H. F., he begins with the initial intimations of a pattern; the discovery and description of HIV-related disease; the first attempts at medical and public health response; the discovery of modes of transmission; the individual experiences of both patients and health care providers; and the rapid escalation of numbers revealed by the modern Centers for Disease Control version of the "Bills of Mortality." At every juncture, Shilts, like H. F., imposes the perspective of time on his material, warning the reader of the terrible consequences and loss of life that would occur because citizens and policy makers ignored early patterns of the disease. Through a combination of stories, news reports, biographies, medical data, and personal observations, Shilts gradually unfolds the history of the discovery of AIDS, the rejection of discoveries about aspects of HIV transmission, and the eventual implementation of research and knowledge. Unlike H. F.'s narrative, however, the time frame in Shilts's narrative is extended: his story is not the journal of a plague year but of the first five years of a pandemic that will wreak havoc on this planet for years.

Underlying these authors' warnings of the dire consequences of both action and inaction is the problem of uncertainty. All four authors are faced with a disease that cannot be fully grasped by contemporary science. Plague was not fully understood in the eighteenth century; AIDS is not fully understood now. A description of objective or scientific data does not fully account for the actual observations of these narrators, nor does a focus on external facts convey the intense subjective experience of those who live during these epidemics. To reveal the tragic interrelationship between the scientific and the subjective realities, both of which are fragmentary, inadequate, and half-understood, all four authors shift from the public health concerns brought up by the disease to the most intimate personal world of those who live through it.

When Daniel Defoe was writing *The Journal of the Plague Year*, the experimental philosophy of the Royal Society was responsible for a series of major medical advancements that would lead to our modern conception of illness and health care practice, especially in the fields of anatomy and physiology. By 1665, Harvey had discovered the circulation of the blood, Leeuwenhoek and Hooke had observed in their microscopes tiny creatures in saliva and blood that were thought to be related to disease, and John Gault began publishing the Bills of Mortality, weekly records of morbidity and mortality that allowed officials and citizens to track the progress of endemic and epidemic disease.

Defoe, by 1722, almost 50 years after the plague epidemic, was also influenced by the theoretical science of Sir Isaac Newton. Newton demonstrated that underlying observable phenomena are fundamental principles that can explain the motions of the universe. Defoe, fascinated with both the practice and principles of science, was as interested in the fundamental causes of disease as he was in evaluating the efficacy of preventive and treatment measures. Although he was a writer, not a physician, Defoe was a close observer of medical phenomena: he was one of the first commentators to recognize that the introduction of gin to the urban poor caused the lethal epidemic of alcoholism in eighteenth-century London. Gin, not poverty or immorality, led to miscarriages, fetal abnormalities, and early childhood death.[8]

When discussing the plague in the *Journal*, Defoe's narrator H. F. is continually frustrated by his inability to make sense of the actual causes of plague and the value of preventive strategies against it. According to H. F., plague cases were often identified by untrained women; the Bills of Mortality were fudged by doctors to exclude plague cases; death lists included cases unrelated to plague; none of the preventive measures or treatments were firmly based on proven efficacy; and, most frustratingly, the actual cause of plague was unknown.

In this state of uncertainty, H. F. repeatedly queries theories of plague's cause, treatment, and outcome. But all he has to work with, as a London citizen, are his own observations, the stories he hears about experiences outside his immediate view, and his own speculative thoughts. In this, H. F. is very much like Randy Shilts in his journalistic account of early information on AIDS, and Paul Monette, in his memoir of his personal experience of HIV disease. In all three works the narrators find that their main task is to separate truth from fiction, facts from hopes, and stories from reality. The current moment, with all its intensity, may have no basis in reality except in one's mind. Given the speculative nature of such evidence, time becomes the test for ephemeral experience; thus the narratives leap forward to bring explanatory data back from the future to give reality to a present event.

As we have seen with H. F.'s "stories" about victims of quarantine, he also uses an analytic technique from the humanities to complement scientific observation: H. F. becomes a literary critic. When he hears accounts of events, especially those that conflict with his own observations or common sense, he explores the narrative style of the accounts as well as their content. For example, H. F. comments on descriptions of atrocious behavior among London citizens during the plague. Nurses are murdering their patients and plague victims deliberately run through the streets to infect other people. H. F. presents the alleged atrocities then voices his "suspicion" of the veracity of the tellers. In his skeptical manner, he suggests that rumors and gossip are a form of literature, not science. They are "mere stories," marked by events that are "always the same." He concludes that "there was more of tale than truth in these things" (*JPY*, 89).

Hence, H. F. tries to separate what we would call "media hype" from the actual daily experience of people under the terrible stress of this disease. He acknowledges that there were nurses who might have caused the death of their patients and that infected people did run through the streets. But H. F. rejects most of the stories because they lack the verisimilitude of everyday experience and the particularity of individual cases. These stories, he argues, are too much alike. Instead, relying on his own firsthand knowledge, he observes that the impoverished women hired as nurses were "rash, fearless, and desperate creatures" even before they were hired to care for dying patients, and it could be expected that such wretched women might make money off their clients by committing "petty thieveries in the houses where they were employed." But he doubts they committed murder, and if they had, the parish records would show it (*JPY*, 89).

Whereas H. F. in Defoe's *Journal* repeatedly attempts to separate fiction from reality, ironically, during the early years of the AIDS epidemic, "real" medical facts were disregarded as unreliable anecdotal tales. Larry Kramer, in *The Normal Heart*,[9] portrays gay men whose self-interest led them to believe that recent medical findings on the sexual transmission of HIV were stories irrelevant to their personal lives. Paul Monette, in *Borrowed Time*, describes his networking between experimental science, the media, and his friends, as they shared stories about possible treatments that promised miraculous cures but that, tragically, later were found to precipitate the disease. Randy Shilts, in *And the Band Played On*, devotes pages to educating his readers and the government about unpalatable scientifically proven facts: HIV is transmitted through sexual activity, the blood supply, and from mothers to unborn children. Yet repeatedly, physicians and policy makers have refused to accept the truth behind these findings. Afraid of panic among patients, the financial consequences of tests and procedures, and the medical consequences of new data, doctors and officials have acted as if major medical discoveries could be disregarded and as if the findings were merely unreliable rumors.

Defoe, like Monette and Shilts, not only separates stories that contain aspects of truth from those of unreliable rumor, but he also explores the complex motives and underlying political and financial implications of plague stories. He is especially sensitive to the social, psychological, and economic factors that lead to an eruption of negative stories, especially those stories that portray plague victims as dangerous to the community beyond the ordinary infectivity of this terrible disease. During the time of plague, as during the time of AIDS, people were terrified of infection from an asymptomatic carrier, whether the person were a tradesman, a casual bystander, or a spouse. Even more horrible was the possibility that some plague victims were deliberately going out to infect "innocent victims."

H. F. does not deny the observations that the disease was transmitted from asymptomatic servants to masters, tradesmen to shoppers, or husbands to wives. But he does not believe in stories of wicked people who deliberately set out to infect others. To understand the basis for such rumors, H. F. analyzes both the disease itself and aspects of human nature that could lead people to accuse victims of the disease of intentionally spreading it.

H. F. tells us that physicians have found that some plague patients, during the height of their disease-induced delirium, become like rabid dogs and are seized with irrational rage and hatred toward others. In their confusion, some manage to escape their caretakers and run mad in the streets, thereby inadvertently infecting others. Hence, the plague victims are not deliberately wicked; their acts are irrational manifestations of their medical condition.

On a psychological and moral level, H. F. also describes the "corruption in human nature" that students of human nature have found among some of the diseased. These unfortunates have an involuntary wish that all men were in as bad condition as they are. Although they know they are infected, they nevertheless deny their danger to others and thereby infect them. Other people, made desperate and hopeless by their disease, become so unconcerned about danger that they abandon themselves to imprudent activities, thereby endangering themselves and infecting others. Plague victims are so overwhelmed by their personal anguish that they can no longer care about the effect they have on others.

Even though H. F. can understand how people might harm others, owing to irrational drives, selfishness, or moral turpitude, he believes such acts are quite rare, and most accounts of such behavior are probably completely untrue. "I do not grant the fact . . . I say that the thing is not really so" (*JPY*, 153–54). Instead, H. F. finds the source of these stories not in the murderous acts of the sick but in the self-protective, ungenerous behavior of people who are still well. According to H. F., these tales are primarily spread by country folk fearful that Londoners will leave town and bring the plague to them. Like townspeople who burn the houses of HIV-infected families, these English citizens deny all charity and comfort to their fellow human beings, and rationalize their acts by believing fables that infected people will deliberately hurl death upon them. Defoe, like modern medical writers, needs to repeatedly remind his audience that most infected patients and their loved ones are decent people who do their best to care for themselves and others. Only the rare person who is physiologically, psychologically, or morally deranged would deliberately expose another person to the plague.

Thus, within both the structure and content of this journal, Defoe reveals the personal anguish and communal frustration felt by a society under siege by an uncontrollable disease. Central to this torment is the narrator's realization that there are no rational answers. The best medical science of his time is inadequate to deal with the challenges of plague. Physicians and policy makers lack the data and insight into the fundamental nature of the disease that would allow prudent policies to work efficiently to save the lives of the people.

Defoe, through his narrative, suggests that a crucial aspect of the horror of a "plague" is its impregnability to rational thought. The source of the disease, its causes, transmission, preventive strategies, are all beyond the reach of current intellectual activity. When Camus writes about bubonic plague in the town of Oran, it is interesting that he invents an unusual strain of the disease that neither follows conventional patterns nor responds to available strategies. Shilts, in *And the Band Played On* and Monette in *Borrowed Time* deal at length with the frustration, confusion, and impossibility of making prudent choices while the identity, attributes, transmission, and prognosis of HIV infection are not fully known.

Hence, literary works on plague, in both their structure and content, reflect the authors' evocation of a world where rational systems have failed in the face of pestilence. Defoe, Camus, Monette, and Shilts repeatedly show that the prescriptions of medical science, the policies put forth by the government, and the day-to-day decisions people make about their own lives are made in a state of potentially lethal uncertainty.

Throughout these works, the authors not only explicitly lament the lack of reliable facts; they question our capacity to use our reason in the face of disaster. In Camus and Monette, people faced with terminal disease turn to personal interrelationships as a way to bring meaning into their lives. Defoe and Shilts, as journalists, confront the opacity of their worlds by persisting in their search for the truth about the disease. Their use of observation and critical analysis, combined with a skepticism for facile solutions, marks one perspective in the search for meaning during a plague. But equally important, as revealed by Camus and Monette, is the affirmation of the spirit, imagination, and the capacity for love. H. F. turns popularly accepted "facts" into stories to expose their inaccuracy while he acknowledges how these stories reflect the truth of the human condition. Shilts collects evidence that "proves" that facts are not mere stories but reflect the unimaginable aspects of a terrible disease. And Camus and Monette turn away from the purely rational to affirm the complexity of the human condition. For them, spirit, imagination, and the power of love can best help us cope with disastrous plagues.

With AIDS, as with H. F.'s plague, the story itself becomes as important as any "objective" truth. Defoe, through his reliance on journals, reports, and essays written in 1665, succeeds in conveying the complex texture of personal and public life during that plague. It is through this subjective experience that he hopes to move his audience to act in the face of an expected pestilence in 1722. Similarly, in our current confrontation with AIDS we have come to realize that personal stories and recitations of daily events are vitally important to an understanding of this disease. At international conferences on AIDS activists believe that the stories of HIV sufferers are as relevant as are papers by research scientists and discussions on experimental clinical techniques. Living with AIDS, like living under a plague, is an experience embodied in the imagination, personal interactions, reflections, and moral values of people. The truth of plague and of AIDS is both subjective and objective. For patients and their loved ones, the stories must be told. The major works on AIDS, like Defoe's *Journal*, are first-person narratives, whereby scientific data are filtered through the sensibilities of caring individuals.

2

Music for a Closing: Responses to AIDS in Three American Novels

JOSEPH DEWEY

Romance in the 1990s: you—and you.
                              —*Comedian Robin Williams*

Piglet sidled up to Pooh from behind. "Pooh," he whispered.
"Yes, Piglet?"
"Nothing," said Piglet, taking Pooh's paw. "I just wanted to be
sure of you."
                              —*Winnie the Pooh*

The American experience has produced remarkably few journals of plague years. After all, our most direct confrontations with the realities of epidemic infection occurred early in our nation's history, long before a tradition in fiction had begun; encouraged by loosely monitored sanitary conditions, chronic food shortages, impure water supplies, and hordes of insects, "epidemic disorders [regular outbreaks of malaria, smallpox, typhoid, and scarlet fever] visited death and destruction upon the American colonies with relentless regularity."[1] Yet with the exception of Charles Brockden Brown's *Arthur Mervyn* (1799) with its dark vision of a Philadelphia ravaged by the yellow fever epidemic of 1793 the early colonial experience with pestilence found little voice in our national literature. Plagues in our literature have been neither bacterial nor viral but rather moral and, hence, metaphoric: our plagues have been rapacity, complacency, racism, political fanaticism, sexual excesses, drug and alcohol abuse. These have been our sicknesses, simpler to diagnose than to treat; and writers as diverse as Jack London and Thomas Pynchon, William Dean Howells and James Baldwin, Henry James and Kurt Vonnegut have created our journals of these plagues. Indeed, despite *Arthur Mervyn*'s unblinking record of the horrific realities of Philadelphia's crowded hospitals and stinking streets, Brown uses the epidemic metaphorically to suggest the moral malignancy his young hero must ultimately come to glimpse as a necessary moment in his maturation.

In America, the record of our confrontations with epidemics has been recorded not in our fiction but in medical treatises. There, in its largely inaccessible language, the medical community has first defined, then isolated, and (with reassuring regularity) vanquished one after another of a score of once terrifying diseases: encephalitis, influenza, smallpox, yellow fever, cholera, tuberculosis, and, most recently, polio. Never in America's history has plague commanded the terror or immediacy that has been recorded in other national literatures. Indeed, from Cotton Mather's courageous campaign to inoculate a decidedly hostile Boston against smallpox to Noah Webster's encyclopedic *A Brief History of Epidemic and Pestilential Diseases* (1799) to the heroics of Walter Reed and Jonas Salk, the American experience with pestilence has been a defiant record of success. A scant decade ago the notion that we might confront a plague—more, a strain of virus never tracked—would have seemed the alarmist premise of bargain-bin science fiction. Yet the devastating potency of the HIV virus, with its dubious distinction as the first plague of the Television Age, has created within a half-decade after its outbreak not only a global awareness of a radically new sort of infection but also for the first time in the American literary experience a substantial body of what must be defined as plague literature.

An artistic response was, perhaps, inevitable given that the HIV virus has struck with particular virulence within the arts community, generating responses in virtually every media. The literary response, largely ignored by the reading public and the established critics in the popular press, chronicles our attempt to come to terms with difficult conditions that have carried us back to a decidedly medieval sort of mind-set. After all, at the decade's start, we sat securely within the smooth walls of our biomedical wonderland only to turn, like Poe's haughty Prince Prospero, to confront an untreatable retrovirus, with a terrifying sort of memory, that slumbers until, after stretches of years, it begins the steady work of destroying the body's fragile defenses against illness, and is so potent that divine wrath becomes a possible explanation for those struggling to answer why.

As a genre, this body of plague literature, of course, has little promise— there is no aesthetic beauty in the caved-in, yellowed faces and skeletal figures in AIDS hospices; a viral infection of this scale creates not the elegant individuality of heroes but rather an overwhelming anonymity of victims, interred within statistics; the plot must operate without the drive of suspense, propelled only by the grind of inevitability; there can be no moral—save that a virus blindly, stupidly destroys what gives it life. And because the epidemic stays immediate and vivid in the oppressive tonnage of newspaper articles, magazine photostories, and television documentaries, it resists the graceful transmutation into metaphor that has long been the aesthetic privilege of those writers who dare to work within the dark sphere of illnesses that destroy the young.

More distressing, plague literature is a body of fiction that must recognize as its first premise its own helplessness. For those who are afflicted, the written word cannot heal, cannot answer why, cannot even concoct an afterlife sufficiently believable to overcome the agony of losing this life. Where, then, can an AIDS fiction begin?[2] Given the alarming novelty of the virus itself, traditional models of plague literature—namely, Boccaccio's *Decameron*, Defoe's *The Journal of the Plague Year*, and Camus's *The Plague*—offer few relevant strategies. The bawdy insouciance of Boccaccio's storytelling with its strategic withdrawal from the plague city to refuge deep within the Italian countryside would seem glaringly insensitive—AIDS is too much with us to permit our indulging in, even with yearning innocence, the casual comedy of whiling away the darkest hours in such pleasant nullity. We cannot *not* write about it. And Defoe's unshakeable conviction that Providence alone could withstand the plague's cold illogic seems at best shopworn in the Secular City where God casts a thin shadow and at worst bald hypocrisy in the face of a disease many can accept as an instrument of divine punishment. And Camus's use of contagion as an undeniable occasion of mortality that tests whether those quarantined in the Algerian port can find significance in life within an infected geography seems too metaphoric, a luxury when compared to what AIDS victims must confront: the indignities of a slow and grinding premature death.

If the genre of plague literature seems inappropriate, so also does the genre of doomed youth. Predominantly war fiction, the literature of doomed youth is a genre of extremes. In its more elegant expression, the genre articulates a heady sort of idealism that defines the sacrifice of young life using a community vocabulary of heightened patriotism. It is a fiction that sustains a community at war and endows the war dead with significance. In this century, however, the fiction more often deals head-on with war's horrific experience to devastate inflated notions of heroism. In either case, war fiction searches for ways to teach the community, to awaken it to awareness. Although the parallel between the at-risk group confronting the HIV virus and doomed, frontline troops has been elaborated by writers (most prominently by Emmanel Dreuilhe in *Mortal Embrace*), the fiction of the AIDS epidemic cannot find its way to either extreme of the genre, to exaggerated idealism or to unsettling anger. The sick die for no ideal; anger here cannot teach. AIDS fiction, like war fiction, is left only the cold business of measuring the attrition, counting the dead.

There are few other genres into which the literature of AIDS could fall. There is the slender group of works that treats the death of the young, characters confronting mortality precisely at the moment of their fullest potential, confronting, as it were, the lie of youth's own assumptions. Such fiction—James's *The Wings of a Dove*, for example—often converts the illness into a dramatic metaphor, making the physical trauma of the disease vague, allowing the young sufferer to leap effortlessly into infinity, leaving behind the weightless advice to live fully. It is a literature that counsels with passionate seriousness to love the fragment of time we are given; in such literature the illness is awkwardly irrelevant—the fact of death is central, not the circumstances of dying. Such characters often die of plot necessity. But AIDS is far too immediate, far too available; from the thick rhetoric of government reports to the shrill white noise of supermarket tabloids, the devastation of AIDS is far too immediate to permit such elegant transmutations.

The magnitude of the illness, the steadily escalating statistical projection of the number of infected people, threatens to turn fiction finally into irrelevancy—leaving AIDS fiction to spin with linguistic opulence the elegies or flowery saintly-buddy pieces; with hope impossible to locate, the only available strategy for AIDS fiction, then, would be adjusting to the illogical intervention of the AIDS virus. Or perhaps, as Andrew Holleran argues, the only writing sufficient to the surreal horrors of the epidemic would be a simple list of the names of those who have died,[3] a list that stretches to disheartening lengths as each month 3,000 new cases of AIDS are diagnosed in the United States alone. Ironically, that necessary realism has moved the literature away from death, or more particularly away from recounting the raw experience of preparing for death's interrupting stroke. The fictional response to the fact of AIDS has turned toward the very face of the epidemic and there it has found a strategy, an approach. Although it is surely possible, given the medical community's unprecedented interest in the AIDS virus, that within a generation the infection may go the way of other pestilent horrors, the irruption of the virus has nevertheless generated a substantial body of human and humane fiction, journals of our plague years, the first generation of such novels in the American experience.

I

Doesn't it seem as if autumn were the real creator, more creative
than spring, which all at once is; more creative, when it comes
with its will to change and destroys the much-too-finished,
much-too-satisfied picture of summer?
                                        —*Rainer Maria Rilke*

Because of its radical failure of nerve, Alice Hoffman's *At Risk* (1988) is a most instructive starting point in assessing the novel's response to the AIDS epidemic. In Hoffman's novel the settled calm of an affluent family in a small New England town is upended when the 11-year-old daughter, Amanda, is diagnosed with AIDS five years after she has been contaminated by a blood transfusion during an emergency appendectomy. As the family struggles to understand the implications of the diagnosis, Amanda herself adjusts both on a public level (to the casual cruelties of friends and neighbors who, in their ignorance, initially recoil from her) and on a private level (to the reality of her denied future). As she moves uncertainly between planning for a gymnastics competition scheduled for an all-too-distant springtime and imagining what sound her death will make and what color it will be, she strikes poignant responses within the reader. With Dickensian sensibility, Hoffman stage-manages Amanda's narrative. Unlike the mainstream victims of the disease, Amanda, by virtue of her age and the method by which she contracted the virus, can be accepted unambiguously by the reader as a victim. Thus Hoffman manages to elicit sentiment while neatly avoiding the tangling complexity of questions AIDS raises about love, sexuality, and death.[4]

With Hoffman's book, however, we can enter easily into an emotional melodrama in which AIDS serves as well as any contagious, terminal infection. We are free to feel the anger and the sorrow of such an illogical stroke—Amanda is innocence intolerably violated. As such the book succeeds in recording the raw and immediate moments of Amanda's adjustment: weeks after her diagnosis, for example, Amanda, her braces newly removed, peeks into the dentist's mirror and concedes with tears that, indeed, she "would have been beautiful."[5] She is a victim, "murdered," according to her father's passionate anger (*AR*, 58). The domestic security of Amanda's family is breached much like when the wasp (pregnant, full of eggs) invades the kitchen in the opening scene or when the destructive voles rummage beneath the neat perimeter of the family vegetable garden. AIDS here is an invasion. Instead of confronting AIDS, Hoffman manipulates its impact as a hot buzzword. Forsaking the tensions caused by AIDS on the margins of society to register the impact within the settled middle, Hoffman sanitizes the epidemic, makes its reader-friendly. Not surprisingly, her book received enormous critical attention and significant sales, including movie rights.

But without exploring the effects the virus registers in those whose very identities—sexual, social, political—have been threatened, the book reads as an uncomplicated exercise in the literature of doomed youth. As in such fiction, Hoffman's characters define a natural world irredeemably infected, moving irresistibly toward exhaustion or extinction. At every turn, virtually with every character, we find a death-soaked natural world. Amanda is herself a school champion gymnast, whose stunning routines are the very embodiment of the physical world elevated to grace and near perfection. Amanda's father, an astronomer, specializes in tracking exploding stars, in "looking at dead stars" (*AR*, 54). Her brother is enthralled by dinosaurs. Once his sister is diagnosed, he is trapped within terrifying nightmares in which he imagines extinction creeping over a newborn dinosaur caught in the inexorable slide toward the Ice Age. Amanda's mother, a free-lance photographer, has just completed work on a book about coping with dying and is now covering the séances of a local medium. That medium, who comes to befriend Amanda, is herself haunted by dreams of death because many of her clients are mourning the loss of a loved one and hunger to touch a realm beyond the reach of death.

Yet, Hoffman concedes that the attempt to make contact with the dead is little more than a brave gesture, much like Amanda's brother's naïve campaign to capture on film a prehistoric giant turtle he is certain he has glimpsed in a neighborhood pond. Confirming the prehistoric turtle's existence would, of course, counter the physical world's apparent rush toward extinction. However, since the novel is locked within the iron logic of the literature of doomed youth, death claims Amanda, in this instance, melodramatically: before leaving for the hospital, she dictates her "will," consigning her few possessions to her family, struggling to give even as the illness takes everything; then her father carries her to the hospital amid a swirl of dead leaves on Halloween night. It is an uneasy moment of unearned sentimentality, as emotionally draining as it is effortlessly cinematic. When the novel closes with Amanda's brother patiently waiting pondside for the emergence of the prehistoric turtle, after he has received news that his sister is dead, the reader recognizes it as a bravura gesture and, in its own way, an act of denial. Hoffman's novel is, then, an exercise in relearning the terrifying brevity of life, whether it is measured in the handful of summers Amanda has had or in the unnerving stretches of astral years her father measures in his planetarium.

At Risk is, finally, not about Amanda or about AIDS at all. The virus seems less the subject than an occasion to test a family's resilience. Amanda's family first splinters (after the diagnosis, each family member retreats into separate rooms on different levels in the house) and then slowly, gradually repairs. The mother overcomes her awkward relationship with Amanda by watching the friendship that develops between her daughter and the local medium; the father struggles to forgive the random virulence of the natural world through the calming voice of Brian, an AIDS patient who answers questions at an emergency hotline; and the brother overcomes his all too normal sibling grudges against his older sister and affirms in the closing pages that he will never not have a sister. Stricken, the family struggles to heal in the limited time it has before Amanda's generous presence becomes sheerest absence. Hoffman's chosen vehicle for recovery—the family—is, oddly, the very unit of social support that often is inaccessible to the homosexual community. For gays creating a family, of course, is barred by biology; establishing a family is severely restricted by social webbing; and even retaining the family into which they were born is often jeopardized by the revelation of their sexual orientation and then by the devastating revelation of the infection. Hoffman's resolution of the crisis caused by AIDS that is dramatized in her novel does not ring altogether false—Amanda's hesitant movement toward death is all too immediate—but Hoffman cannot find her way to a satisfying examination of AIDS because she deliberately does not focus on the isolation and anxieties the disease has prompted within the gay community. Amanda's death is unbearably poignant but finally reductive. And because Hoffman steers clear of exploring the contrapuntal urges of love and death that a complete literary treatment of AIDS demands, her narrative can offer not hope but only adjustment. Hoffman's narrative is, finally, unpleasantly exploitative as it summons the images of the epidemic without grappling with its essential definition. As such, Hoffman's work remains at best a powerful reassertion of that leaden feeling (typical in the literature of doomed youth) that a young character has been robbed of the opportunity to experience what life has to offer.

II

Unlike Hoffman's elaborate dodge, Robert Ferro's *Second Son* (1988) directly confronts mortality as well as the more complicated questions of love and sexuality raised by the AIDS epidemic. And, offering characters compelled by such urgencies, Ferro is able to create a very dramatic journal of this plague, offering in his work what Hoffman cannot—a model for those who seek in literature not a cure but rather a strategy for coexisting with a virus of compelling potency.

Ferro centers his argument on the striking comparisons between the traditional family and the gay relationship, or more exactly between the social unit applicable to measuring the stability of presumably healthy heterosexual arrangements and the less conventional partnerships struck when sexual orientation excludes expression within such conventional lines. Against the fashionable stereotype of the homosexual life-style of the 1970s when the gay community found in limitless promiscuity a defiant assertion of identity, Ferro here traces a nurturing relationship that develops between Mark Valerian and Bill Mackey, both stricken with the virus. That construction, so apparently defined by the AIDS epidemic as infected, offers within Ferro's book the possibility of healing against the family, which here is so completely dysfunctional, so totally bankrupt of reassuring support and compassion that it, rather than the relationship defined as diseased, is ailing and terminally infected.

The novel opens with Ferro's devastating portrait of Mark Valerian's family. Although Mark often jokingly refers to the "Filial Wars" that have long wrenched his family, such posturing conceals what is indeed a family deeply divided, a busy family involved in exacting professions (one sister is named Vita). Given the fury of their upscale life-styles, they express familial affection in frictionless holiday gestures and in quick long-distance telephone calls. Mark cannot find his place within this family. Unlike two of his siblings, one a psychologist, the other a lawyer, Mark follows an aesthetic impulse— his eye for "form, decoration"[6]—and has become an interior decorator. His other sister expounds on the wisdom of abandoning the fast track to raise a family, a life-style even further removed from Mark. Mark's diagnosis only reinforces his sense of estrangement, his feeling of being (as the title underscores) one son too many. The family initially recoils from Mark's illness, finding the diagnosis distasteful, dangerous. His father, trying to define the illness within a fundamentalist Christian vocabulary, waffles between repugnance over the "sin" of homosexuality and the lamest clichés of his faith in miracles. But he cannot conceal that he finds the illness and, by extension, his second son, offensive.

Isolated, Mark takes up residence for the summer in the cavernous run-down summer cottage that the family has maintained for nearly 30 years by Cape May, New Jersey. When the family, encouraged by the reptilian older brother, moves to sell the summer cottage to help cover enormous losses incurred by the father's failing business, it is a practical decision uncomplicated by compassion. The inevitable showdown between father and second son over the sale of the house is an ugly recitation not merely of deep-seated homophobia but the far more distressing feelings in the son that his father is waiting for him to die, to be rid of the cumbersome problem of the second son. It is an "annihilating moment" that leaves nothing but "ash" (SS, 203). The family with its occasional gestures toward connection (in a tender moment, Mark is allowed to hold his niece) is a decaying construction, like the summer cottage itself. Itself more dead than alive, it cannot minister to the dying second son.

The radical failure of the Valerian family to accommodate the life of the second son defines what has emerged as the dominant theme of the literary response to AIDS—the terrifyingly simple sundering of hearts, the ease with which distance is created. In many ways, the virus and its attendant paranoias have legitimized disconnection. In the government's sobering pronouncements for safe sex, in the hysterical calls for quarantining or tattooing the sick, in the necessities of barrier nursing, in the designation of the sick as pariah, we are shaped by a logic of withdrawal. Apart from the pragmatics of health care, disconnection is part of a larger conspiracy of apathy, a determination by the largest share of the population currently enjoying the illusion of being not at risk to turn away from the flat, dead eyes of the already stricken. It is "their" disease—and unlike other diseases that emerged into prominence during the decade (Alzheimer's, for example) AIDS is perceived to be an affliction that will not cross the threshold if it is not given access. Far more terrifying than the grinding physical erosion of the disease on its victims, Ferro argues, is the fear of being abandoned. Twice marginalized, once by their sexual identity and then again by their infection, surrounded in their community by those who have learned hard lessons of repugnance, estranged from family, even from lovers, and left often with only the cold touch of sympathetic strangers in hospices, AIDS patients too often are left to play at desperate illusions of self-sufficiency. When Mark visits Bill in the hospital, he visits an AIDS patient very much alone, a boy of 23 whose only company, he groans, is death: "I feel it come into the room." Left so finally alone, he confesses to Mark that death would be better than the insufferable days of isolation. His only consolation, his heart so thoroughly destroyed, is that death will finally claim everyone. He lashes out at Mark, "Your lover will die, then you will; then all of them, one after another" (SS, 167).

Second Son cites just this irrevocable error of withdrawing into the self and counsels rather a courageous commitment to emotion—the fragile, private, man-made constructions of passion and compassion, that can serve as a heroic counterforce to the sort of poisonous webbing suggested by the insidious spread of the disease. Against the very public campaigns encouraging discipline, celibacy, and abstinence, against the withering away of the urgent, creative combustion of sexual spontaneity, against the acceptance in the gay community to live like Shakers—against, in short, a decade-long drift away from each other, Ferro asserts a most unconventional response—the relationship. Against the collapse of Mark's family, we witness the emergence in graceful counterpoint of his relationship with Bill Mackey, a set designer and theatrical lighting specialist whom he meets while on a working vacation in Rome. Like Mark, Bill has tested positive and begins even as the relationship develops to feel the first symptoms. Yet this relationship defies the grinding inevitability of the virus. When they first make love in Rome under the fabulous vermilion sunsets spoked into color by the poisonous radiation cloud from Chernobyl as it passes over southern Europe, Mark and Bill construct a marvelously fragile bond that revives for both of them emotional responses denied in the two years since their diagnoses, two years of living on the rich details of their memories.

As Mark and Bill make love—the "collected, considerate reserve of elderly lovers who worry for each other's hearts or brittle bones" (SS, 90)—it is a potent sort of magic. During the slow, late summer days when Mark and Bill return from Rome to the Berkshires to disperse the ashes of Bill's longtime companion, Mark rows to the middle of a lake one evening on Bill's instructions. He turns toward the distant haze of the shore and in the fading twilight sees flickering against the descending dusk on shore a fabulous "necklace of lights" "bleeding into the darkness," complemented by 60-foot jet streams of water arching into the simple grace of a rainbow. It is a gift from Bill. Mark is enthralled by such a lambent moment of magic that speaks a "language of brightness," all produced by Bill's creative impulse, aided by a noiseless generator, a pump, and miles of extension cords (SS, 146). Like the fragile connection forged between Bill and Mark, the display is not permanent; rather it can be maintained for only a gorgeous moment. But Bill's gesture suggests the magic of the artificial, the man-made, that is powerful precisely because it must flicker, because it must certainly give way to the darkness. Their emotional bond is an assertion against the natural world— that world is represented by the Roman sunsets infected by radiation or by the shoreline hushing into night or by the AIDS infection. The natural, here as in other fictional responses to AIDS, is decidedly limited; the retrovirus strikes, as Susan Sontag has observed, through the blood and semen, the most sacramental networks of biological life.[7] Against the autumn shoreline that moves with its natural determination toward the silences of winter, the fragile string of lights enchants Mark; indeed, it glows stronger, brighter as night descends. And under the tonic of their commitment to each other, Mark and Bill register defiant remission in their illness—lesions fade, headaches dim, appetites return. Theirs becomes a marvelous parable of restoration and reclamation, as Mark's profession might suggest.

But AIDS cannot permit magic. Despite Mark's emotional description of Bill as some fantastic being "lowered from the sky on piano wire" (*SS*, 92) and his heady pronouncements that he simply will not concede to the disease, he cannot shake dreams of boarding a train bound for a "cathedrallike, cavernous nineteenth-century railway station of steel and glass" (*SS*, 150), a haunting suggestion of approaching death. The fiction of AIDS cannot depend on recovery—the disease demands closure. Ferro will not abrogate the imperative of realism. Against a subplot that involves an exchange of letters in which a friend of Mark's (who is likewise infected as the reader gathers from remarks in the letters) writes about the money he is investing in a ludicrous plan to launch a rocketful of homosexuals to a distant planet there to recover and live in peace, Mark shoulders his way toward what must be. Toward the end of the book, the relapse for both Mark and Bill signals that indeed they are poised to acknowledge the end of any new possibilities even as Mark returns to close up Cape May for the winter. There is no cure—simply the steady assurances they offer each other that neither will go it alone.

Ferro argues that such an assurance is the sole gesture against the plague. In a poignant moment, Mark, in the hospital for tests, must deliver a sperm sample and finds himself unable to achieve sufficient erection. He begins to cry, and only in tears does he find himself aroused. That is the lesson of *Second Son*—only the steady pressure of absolute absence engenders absolute emotion. Much as Mark watches a handsome man walk slowly along the beach weaving tight circles above the wastes of the sand with a metal detector to find something of value, Ferro finds within the claustrophobic binding of the disease something of value—the overwhelming magnitude of a disease that defies connection demands connection, not in the heady excesses of cruising but in the gentler gesture of finding another heart. As Mark watches the man on the beach find something, the metal scoop he carries proves "inadequate. Only the human hand will do" (*SS*, 4). Unlike Hoffman's sentimental drama, resolution cannot be found within the constricting webbing of the family. As Mark and Bill prepare, as AIDS patients must, for inevitable closure, they wait with each other. That commitment offers them a healing of a sort, a summer that is in its brevity the very mother of beauty. The disease itself creates the occasion of their passion, for only the knowledge of their mutual infection creates the courage to love. Unable to place sufficient faith in the interminable experiments with blood tests and new drugs, unable to believe as an Italian clairvoyant assures them that the passing radiation cloud will cure them, Mark and Bill define a fragile community, an achievement of man-made magic as artificial, as momentary, as incandescent as the string of lights along an autumnal shoreline.

III

The Sunrise—Sir—compelleth Me—
Because He's Sunrise—and I see
—*Emily Dickinson, Poem 480*

George Whitmore's *Nebraska* (1987) would seem to be an odd choice as the most significant journal of our plague years. Whitmore's narrative does not directly treat the virus. Moving from the Eisenhower fifties to the summer of 1969, the very threshold of the sexual liberation of the 1970s, Whitmore's novel traces the difficult maturation of Craig McMullen, a fatherless, one-legged boy who must come to terms with his homosexuality even as his family is devastated by similar revelations about his Uncle Wayne, whom Craig fiercely admires as a surrogate father. Well within the conventions of gay literature, Whitmore centers his coming-of-age story on the difficulty of the double life, or more accurately, the fractured life necessitated by a social network unable to accept sexuality that cannot be contained within the simplest perception of "normal."

One such fractured life is surely Uncle Wayne's. Following his discharge from the navy, he returns to Nebraska to await word from Vernon, a friend from the navy, about opening a garage in California. Wayne is a man of the world, too big, too full of life to be trapped within the iron frame of Nebraska. The engagement ring he wears on his pinkie, he brags, is a token of affection from any one of a number of women who waited for him at any number of ports. Yet, he stays in Nebraska. Each letter he receives from Vernon delays his plans, he says, because of financial inconveniences. Reluctantly, Wayne accepts work, temporarily, he insists.

But Wayne is leading a fiercely destructive secret life. Because Whitmore relates events through the limited perception of a young Craig, we do not learn until much later the actual contents of the letters from Vernon to Wayne. In them, Vernon must tell Wayne that their love cannot be realized and that separation is the only response. Driven by the oppressive confines of a Nebraska home he suddenly cannot leave and by the realization that the simplest expression of his love would not be tolerated, Wayne makes uncertain gestures toward his impressionable nephew; for example, one evening he strokes Craig's penis, checking, he says, for hair. Wayne conceals his sexual identity from his family until he is arrested in a vice sweep of a men's room in a bus depot in nearby Omaha. Then, in quick succession, he loses his job, his family, his home. Without explanation to the young Craig, his Uncle Wayne is simply "gone."

What triggers the sequence of devastating events, not surprisingly, is a lie. Craig concocts an innocent lie about his Uncle Wayne during a sleepover. That night, a sultry Indian summer night, Craig feels good, close to Wesley in ways he does not possess sufficient vocabulary to explain. As they lie together in an improvised tent, a blanket pitched above Craig's bed, Wesley nervously asks to touch the stump of Craig's leg. Finding himself aroused, Craig intrigues to convince his friend to masturbate him by telling him that his Uncle Wayne had bragged that such practices were routine in the navy and that Uncle Wayne had even shown him how to do it "lots and lots of times."[8] It is a devastatingly obvious lie, told without thought during the onset of a hurricane of emotions that the boy at 13 cannot begin to understand. All he wants, he thinks, is to feel his friend's hand warm on his penis, a gesture of the simplest connection that echoes, ironically, the imperative wailed out to him when he watches a television evangelist, who wheezes enthusiastically, "SEIZE LIFE! TAKE LIFE IN THY HANDS! SMELL OF ITS FRAGRANCE" (*Nebraska*, 32). Here, the opportunity is frustrated—Wesley, a practicing Baptist, fears such acts are too sinful.

The chain reaction caused by this lie, however, culminates in Craig's testifying after his uncle's arrest. When Wesley's father informs local authorities after Wayne's arrest of what Craig revealed to Wesley, Craig must answer delicately phrased questions about whether his uncle "interfered" with him. When asked if his uncle ever touched him, Craig must admit, of course, that he had—even in the caring gesture of sponge bathing him after the accident that claims his leg. Whitmore offers pages of court testimony that deliver with cold objectivity the devastating judgment against Uncle Wayne. Cornered into testifying against his uncle, the boy, however, only completes the destruction of his uncle begun long before by the systematic refusal of the social webbing to allow him the expression of a normal life, lived as he wanted, as he had to. Destroyed by his trial, ostracized by his family, driven through a series of dead-end jobs, long separated from the companionship of his lover in California, Wayne ends up in a state medical facility where, we find out years later, he is surgically altered against his will, neutralizing what most distresses him but what most defines him—his sexual identity.

When Craig, 10 years later, finally reunites with his uncle in California, he finds a most disturbing creature. Craig first sees Wayne sprawled in four inches of water in a child's wading pool. His uncle does not seem to recognize him. Indeed, now surgically separated from his own sexuality, Wayne lives with Vernon like a child in undisturbed prepuberty. He lives in the room of a "normal" American boy—model airplanes suspended from the ceiling, sports equipment scattered about, pictures of dinosaurs, spaceman wallpaper, sheets and pillow cases with planets. But the normal assumes surreal shadings as Whitmore delivers in a spare and unemotional line of prose the horror of Craig's growing sexual realization. Lost now within the pleasant routines of going to the zoo or to the mall, now giddy in a shrill prepubescent way about sex (he giggles hysterically as he rummages through Vernon's hidden collection of male muscle magazines), Wayne is a shadow of his earlier, tormented self (indeed, in the navy his nickname had been Shadow). Distanced now from the difficult, destructive confrontation with growing up, he lives in a haunting parody of normality, in an eerie sort of suspended animation; he has become a disturbing cross between Peter Pan and Sleeping Beauty. But peace has come at a high cost. Craig observes as Wayne and Vernon watch television each night, Wayne cuddled in asexual security in the crook of Vernon's arm. They are unable now to break through to the genuine expression of passion they had shared in the navy. Vernon, feeling enormously responsible for Wayne's condition because of his hasty letters releasing Wayne from their commitment, understands that now they are each other's life sentences . . . the authentic expression of their passion has been replaced by the colder routine of careful watching. Wayne has vanished into a secret and safe world, like his miniature railroad town in the basement that he shows his nephew, with its miles of tracks, its detailed landscaping, its houses and farms, precise down to stray sheep, streetlights, and picket fences—so compellingly normal, so unnervingly surreal.

Whitmore's narrative, then, would seem a most disturbing variation on the doomed-queen genre, a revelation of the agonies experienced within the closet and the perilous experiences outside its protective darkness. But it is the destructive splintering within the boy that more concerns Whitmore. Uncertain of his sexuality, uncertain of its potency, its acceptability, even its implications, Craig moves through a difficult adolescence unloved. There are no happy couples within Craig's immediate experience. Craig's father, a reformed alcoholic, returns to his son's life quite abruptly after school one afternoon, years after abandoning his family. Despite his fervent declamations about being a born-again Christian, he is, nevertheless, capable of kidnapping his son during the height of a Nebraska snowstorm. When it is apparent the boy is more fearful than forgiving, the father douses the child with gasoline and contemplates sacrificing him to God, Isaac-style, to make up for his past mistakes. And Craig's long-suffering mother is bloated by a life of servility, first to the raging abuses of her husband and then to the petty slavery of her 15 years waiting tables at a Montgomery Ward's coffee shop. She recalls with imperfect emotions the unanticipated pregnancy that led her, years earlier, to begin the elaborate charade as mother. Other marriages in Craig's family are drawn by financial considerations or are brokered after similar unexpected pregnancies; they are sustained by the merest gestures of interest; siblings are horribly distant and casually cruel, grandparents inexplicably hostile and obscure.

It is struggling, finally, against that dead weight of oppression, corroded passion, and deception that marks the emergence of Craig McMullen. Crippled at 12 (on the very threshold of puberty) by a vicious truck accident that forces the amputation of his leg, Craig is forever isolated, marked, denied access to the normal expression of boyhood—Red Cross swimming lessons and scouting, for example. Indeed, normality seems a condition far removed from Craig's experience. He is marked—by an aberrant father, an infamous uncle, a missing leg. He hungers to be happy, a condition he defines early on as being normal; yet he struggles against the distance, the sheer inaccessibility of such a condition. He dreams of the heartbreakingly simple, of having "his own blue notebook back with the three-hole paper with the ship flags on it and inside the right number of pencils, a little sharpener for the one you lost, your three-color ballpoint and the pink eraser that works on ink too" (*Nebraska*, 52). He cannot, however, seem to make it all work. He admits to an intolerable, inexplicable weight of unhappiness, comparing himself to a young girl in the hospital who had lived her entire, short life in terrible pain assuming all the time, "This is just life" (*Nebraska*, 4). She dies, Craig overhears, from a tumor no doctor had even suspected she had.

Marked by his accident, confused by the uncertain expression of urges he cannot dismiss, Craig cannot find his niche within his corroded family in Nebraska. After his uncle's trial, his mother remarries (to a lugubrious lawyer with colorless eyes who maneuvers an out-of-court settlement after Craig's accident). No offer is extended to Craig to live with them. He goes, rather, to live with his grandparents in their run-down home. There he feels like another piece of the family junk furniture that crowds the house. When, finally, he heads to California to reestablish ties with Wayne, he goes as much in search of himself as his uncle. As his accident suggests, a piece of him is missing—he is incomplete, splintered. Departing Nebraska marks Craig's first significant gesture toward restoring his splintered interior, toward authentic feeling. Indeed, in the months after the accident, Craig's mother had been accused by concerned doctors of overdosing the boy with painkillers, which leave him like jelly, rather than working him through the first rehabilitation exercises.

The reunion with the shattered remnant of his Uncle Wayne signals Craig's movement toward wholeness, toward emotion, toward his significant split with the charade of being "normal." The undeniable evidence of his uncle's condition at first drives him to run away wildly (like a "poor cartoon creature with his tail on fire" [*Nebraska*, 124]). He ends up in the night world of a Tijuana topless bar where he loses his virginity in an unspectacular tussle with a badly scarred whore (named, ironically, Candy), whom he imagines likes him. To his astonishment in the morning he is asked to pay for her services. His traumatic introduction into the world of heterosexuality is on par with his experiences of the world of his childhood—love defined by the carnal, compelled by the mercenary. Yet against such exploitation and corruption of passion, Craig offers a loving gentler expression—he kisses Candy's heavy network of white scars, the mole she fears is cancerous, the lacerations on her feet from stepping on a nail, the lines on her forehead from a car accident, the jagged line from her appendectomy. Such gentleness, of course, is lost on the prostitute, who scolds him harshly, contemptuously dismisses his efforts at making love, and punches him fiercely.

Finding that expression comes only in the closing sequence when Craig accepts finally that he must love whom he must. Returning to Wayne's house, he stretches out next to his uncle, who is sleeping on the living room couch. At first, Craig wonders if masturbating Uncle Wayne might break the spell his uncle seems to wander in, much as the kiss returned Sleeping Beauty. But, even as Craig places Uncle Wayne's open hand on his stomach, the reader realizes that what may be a gesture too late for the uncle promises awakening for the young Craig. For Craig is the Sleeping Beauty who must be awakened. And as Craig cradles Wayne's hand, he wonders, "God what if this makes me one too? . . . but what if I am after all" (*Nebraska*, 149). It is a moment of interior confrontation, of measuring the schism within. He pulls closer to the slumbering Wayne, and "for long moments, there is no line between [them]" (*Nebraska*, 147). Craig moves gently to place Wayne's hand "down there" (*Nebraska*, 153), on his penis that begins to harden even as the morning sun spokes through the blinds. The action completes the struggle toward identity that had begun long ago with his attempt at a similar gesture with his friend Wesley during the sleep over. That gesture had proven as destructive as this gesture promises to be constructive. Craig, finally, takes life into his own hands. The sky lightens, and Craig affirms that "it is going to be a beautiful day." And in the same breath, he further notes, it is "the day they are going to try landing on the moon" (*Nebraska*, 149)—a day, Whitmore asserts, for Craig himself to begin the successful exploration of a radically new terrain, a terribly beautiful interior geography. It is a haunting moment of closing, finally, the schism within Craig, of restoring what had so long been missing, of rejecting the limiting definition of "normal." The puzzle, at last, is solved, and the reader recalls that as a boy Craig, so socially awkward, had earned his sole moment of local fame (a picture story in the local newspaper) for his amazing agility at assembling puzzles.

What, then, makes *Nebraska* the affirming testament for the AIDS decade although its action concludes in the summer of 1969? After the energetic rush from the closet in the 1970s introduced homosexuals as a rambunctious ethnic group hungry for expression, the AIDS realities introduced an entirely new rationale for suppression and denial. It is to that threat that Whitmore addresses his appeal. Denial would extinguish what Ferro had defined as the magic of the fragile constructions of emotional commitment. Denial puts all gays at risk. Like the child who dies from an unsuspected tumor, only the secret kills. Whitmore leaves Craig, restored and healed, at the very brink of the explosive energy of the 1970s when so much of the damage later defined by the AIDS virus would be accomplished. Without regret, without apology, without anger, without pity, Whitmore launches Craig, his sexual identity now powerfully asserted, into the breaking dawn of a day that would within a scant decade unleash a most absolute night. Even as he completed work on *Nebraska*, Whitmore revealed that he had been diagnosed with AIDS.

IV

Our journals of these plague years, then, are compelled not by Boccacio's supreme escapism, Defoe's religious conviction, or Camus's stern existentialism. They are not compelled simply by the awareness of death or by pity but rather (much as the disease itself) by the contrapuntal pressures of love, sex, and death. Without that countermovement of eros, the literature, as with Hoffman's work, bottoms out in graceful pathos and struggles merely to engage death humanely. Refusing the posturings of anger or frustration against the endgame of the infection, the literature accepts a poisoned universe and offers the slenderest premise of synchronicity. Forsaking the conventional coming-out-of-the-closet novel, these novels (as well as Paul Monette's *After Life*, Edmund White's "Palace Days," Andrew Harvey's *Burning Houses*, David Leavitt's "Gravity") find virtue not merely in identity but in confluence.

It is inevitable, long before the virus is decoded by the medical community, that the intensity of interest generated in the latter half of the 1980s will diminish even as the infection grows exponentially. Inevitably the rhetoric over the AIDS crisis will be lost among other threats perceived significant enough to be cased within the apocalyptic rhetoric that will only increase as the century as well as the millennium close—crises over the steady depletion of the environment, the periodic shaking of significant geopolitical entities in strategic spots, the tectonic shifts in global economic conditions, the silent oppression of nuclear weaponry. And yet AIDS has generated a significant response—novels that are finally not journals of the plague years but rather defiantly journals against the plague years, novels that argue against a disease that escalates with a surreal insistency, against the emerging definition of ourselves as biohazards, against the emerging ideology of protection, against the difficult struggle to understand that sex can kill. These novels remind us, despite the simplest impulse to withdraw from each other, how bound we are each to the other. And they argue, finally, that we are to seize not the day, but rather each other.

3

Suburban AIDS: Alice Hoffman's *At Risk*

JUDITH LAURENCE PASTORE

> It would not be too much to suggest that much of a person's
> reaction to the subject of AIDS is directly related to his chances
> of getting it himself.
>
> —*Andrew Holleran*, Ground Zero[1]

Alice Hoffman's *At Risk* (1988),[2] about an 11-year-old, middle-class girl who contracts AIDS from a blood transfusion, has been the most heavily publicized AIDS novel to date, the only one to make the best-seller list—a fact that has angered many gay writers who have also written about AIDS, but whose works have never reached the wide audience that Hoffman's novel has. Novelist David Leavitt describes the dismay gay writers felt at the 1988 American Booksellers Association (ABA) Convention when *At Risk* was the number one book that year:

> I was just one of many gay men at the A.B.A. that year, and looking back, I think we were all a little frightened by the brouhaha about "At Risk"—the huge pyramids of glossy readers' copies, the enormous advertising budget, the "six-figure paperback floor."
>
> It was not that we doubted the author's sincerity, or begrudged her the right to tell whatever story she chose. Rather we sensed, in some deep way, that this was going to be bad for us. After all, "At Risk" was

the story of a child, one of the so-called innocent victims of AIDS whose stories—because they escape our society's prejudices against gay men and drug users—are deemed more palatable to a "general" audience. What made me nervous was the implication, inherent in the phrase "innocent victim," that the majority of people with AIDS are "guilty" victims who had brought the disease on themselves by engaging in homosexual sex or shooting drugs.[3]

When I discussed David Leavitt's reaction with a colleague Charles Bazerman, he disagreed that *At Risk* would create more resentment for gays. Rather, he felt that Hoffman's novel "serves more to 'humanize' the disease for audiences and the victims that might be otherwise ostracized."[4] Many AIDS novels by gay writers are either autobiographical memorials to loved ones—Christopher Bram's *In Memory of Angel Clare*—or follow a before/after AIDS format—Paul Monette's *Afterlife*, David B. Feinberg's *Eighty-Sixed*. Or, like Max Exander's (a.k.a. Paul Reed) *Safestud* and *Lovesex*, some use gay pornography to preach safe sex. A few like Jed A. Bryan's *A Cry in the Desert* predict wholesale genocide against gays. And many, such as Paul Reed's *Facing It* (1984), the first novel to explore AIDS in depth, and Randy Shilts's brilliant journalistic account *And the Band Played On*, seethe with anger at a neglectful establishment that has ignored AIDS as long as it only seemed to threaten marginalized populations—gays, IV drug users, Haitians. By focusing on someone who belongs to the hegemonic culture—someone like Ryan White, sanitized by "innocence"—does *At Risk* distort and betray the realities of AIDS? Or by creating sympathy for a so-called "innocent victim" and showing that such "victims" experience the same prejudice as marginalized persons with AIDS (PWAs), does *At Risk* create the possibility of increased compassion for every AIDS victim regardless of how he or she contracted the virus?

Because AIDS literature treats a very serious subject, critics of the genre face a dilemma when they comment on it. No matter how inferior a work on AIDS may be, if it helps alleviate suffering and prejudice, it still has intrinsic value. One feels petty pointing out aesthetic weaknesses given that the work may help those who live with the disease. Also, as Andrew Holleran rightly points out in the epigraph at the beginning of this essay, the further one is from the danger of infection and/or caring for people with AIDS (PWAs), the less one can genuinely relate to its problems. This raises serious questions about who can write fiction about AIDS. As with a man writing about the life of a woman, or a white about the black experience, heterosexuals who have not lost a loved one to AIDS and/or do not risk getting the disease themselves have a lot more trouble proving their credentials to those— Sontag, forgive me—on the front lines. In this context, one has to ask if it was not better for Hoffman to write about the kind of suburban life her novels always depict than to attempt to write about urban gay AIDS or about IV-drug abuse AIDS?

Another question *At Risk* raises is whether Hoffman unduly sentimentalizes, thereby exploiting what is intrinsically tragic. As Bazerman asked me, does the novel merely exercise "traditional sentimental melodramatic emotions" over "today's troubles?" Any lapse into the quotidian sanitizes the horror of AIDS; thus it is difficult to write a traditional novel about AIDS that remains true to the realities of the disease. Using "innocent" children to create pity and anger at social injustice, of course, is a traditional technique that harks back to the eighteenth century's sentimental novel and that is frequently exploited in popular nineteenth-century fiction by Dickens, Dostoyevski, Harriet Beecher Stowe and many others. Although out of favor in academia today, the good tear jerker has remained popular with the public—witness the success of Erich Segal's *Love Story* and the film *Terms of Endearment.* Killing off the central female character, moreover, be she child or woman—Stowe's little Eva, Hemingway's Catherine Barkley, or Richardson's Clarissa—is a time-honored tradition, whether the death is used as a ploy to create sympathy for a cause or as punishment because the character has violated social codes. Seen in this context, fiction depicting the deaths of gay PWAs treats them as the sentimental novel long treated "fallen" women, as people who deserve their death because they have violated "accepted" sexual mores. By substituting a young girl for the young men who were usually the early PWAs, Hoffman tries to make the literary treatment of the disease conform to the conventional middle-class novel with its emphasis on marriage and family.

But attempting to place AIDS fiction within the framework of the traditional novel belies the reality of AIDS. AIDS is tragedy pure and simple. To date, in spite of speeded up research, drug development still lags far behind the needs of AIDS patients. No cure has yet been found, and any vaccine safe for humans is still years away. Consequently, learning that someone has AIDS is tragic because we know the outcome, and there is nothing we can do about it. AIDS is as relentless as the curse upon Oedipus. In this sense, the public and private medical establishment, along with federal, state, and local government, become omnipotent Olympian deities meting out an arbitrary fate against which Promethean entities such as Robert Mapplethorpe, ACT-UP, and David Wojnarowicz[5] rail at their peril.

Finally, by bringing AIDS into the midst of a typical white suburban family, does Hoffman play on illegitimate fears about the epidemic? Masters and Johnson, in *CRISIS: Sex in the Age of AIDS* (1988), insist that AIDS is rapidly spreading to the suburbs. But most experts quickly dismissed their findings as not only largely invalid but dangerously misleading. Michael Fumento, in *The Myth of Heterosexual AIDS* (1989), soundly rejects the conclusions of Masters and Johnson, arguing that gays and those doing AIDS research exaggerate the danger of heterosexual AIDS to generate more funding and to create greater compassion. Does Hoffman's *At Risk* play into these unfounded fears? I do not think it does, but before I return to these questions, let me first run through the plot of the novel.

The story of *At Risk* briefly concerns not just Amanda but her entire family, the Farrells, who are so typically middle-class that they are only saved from becoming stereotypes by Hoffman's sensitive handling. Ivan, the astronomer father, is too typically absentminded; the mother, Polly the photographer, is one of the new feminist heroines, the woman trying to establish a "meaningful" career while still maintaining a satisfying family life; eight-year-old Charlie collects everything revolting—frogs, insects, newts—and is something of a latter-day Tom Sawyer; while 11-year-old Amanda, a promising gymnast, reminds me of the many doomed spunky children in nineteenth-century novels—for example, the Captain's dying son in *The Brothers Karamazov*, who hurls rocks at his father's youthful detractors. The Farrells learn in August that Amanda had been infected with the HIV virus through a blood transfusion during an appendectomy five years earlier. Her disease is iatrogenic, or caused inadvertently by a physician.

Between August and November, when Amanda dies, the family experiences much of the prejudice and emotional trauma that traditionally accompany AIDS. Each major character, including the family doctor, Ed Reardon, who ordered the blood transfusion, goes through the stages of grief outlined by Elisabeth Kubler-Ross in a number of her works and specifically her book about AIDS, *AIDS: The Ultimate Challenge*. Each character finally becomes reconciled to Amanda's imminent death. At school, the principal must battle the myths, held by both angry parents and seventh graders, about how AIDS is transmitted: little girls are afraid to use the toilet; no one will sit next to Charlie, Amanda's brother. At home, neighbors shun the family. Polly knows that if Amanda were suffering from some other illness, the same neighbors would be bringing over casseroles and offering consolation, but because Amanda has AIDS, the family is shunned as though they were lepers. Betsy Stafford, Polly's former employer, forbids Sevrin, Charlie's best friend, from seeing Charlie. Charlie spends his days alone keeping an eye on the street, hoping Sevrin will come over. When Betsy later tries to apologize to Polly, by saying "This breaks my heart," Polly replies, "No! It makes you uncomfortable. It breaks my heart" (*Risk*, 183). Thus Polly refuses to let Betsy, the writer supposedly skilled with language, to manipulate her reaction to Amanda's condition.

Amanda's symptoms follow the frequent AIDS pattern: constant diarrhea, night sweats, weight loss, increasing fatigue and nausea; when Amanda contracts *Pneumocystis carinii pneumonia* (PCP), Ed Reardon rushes her to Boston's Children's Hospital where he manages to get her a private room. Although by law in Massachusetts AIDS must be kept confidential, the sign on Amanda's door reads "Blood and Body Fluid Precautions." Amanda pulls through the first bout of PCP but dies after the second bout.

Two major characters outside the immediate family provide much needed support. The bisexual musician Brian, dying of AIDS himself, comforts Ivan over an AIDS hotline in Boston. The divorced child-woman, Laurel Smith, has special psychic powers that she uses to help Amanda and that lead her to befriend the girl. Laurel provides a source of relief for Amanda who, in order to reconcile herself to death, must distance herself from her mother, whose intense struggles to keep her daughter alive make it harder for Amanda to reach the acceptance stage where she can let go. Barbara Peabody's poignant early AIDS memoir *The Screaming Room: A Mother's Journal of Her Son's Struggle with AIDS, Longtime Companion,* the only mainstream film about AIDS to date, and the first segment of PBS's "AIDS Quarterly" showing a son reconciling with his Mormon father and the son's subsequent death, all show a loved one finally urging the dying PWA to "let go." Laurel's friendship enables Amanda to escape from the powerful mother/daughter bond holding Amanda to life.

Brian and Laurel thus act as a foil to the conventional family depicted; their presence also introduces other levels of meaning. Laurel functions as a hinge to the "realities" of the unscientific and the mysterious. She represents what Freud labels the "uncanny," that class of experience that is old and familiar because it is primordial, suggesting laws more fundamental than those of modern science. Laurel's extrasensory powers recall nineteenth-century America's fascination with spiritualism at a time when science and technology seemed to be promising modern miracles but were also making the general public increasingly uneasy. The need for her presence signals the longing for spiritual solace in times of tragedy—a longing one reads of frequently in accounts of PWAs. The absence from the text of any figure from organized religion reminds us of the controversy in religious circles about how to respond to AIDS and the failure of established religious figures to provide leadership in fighting the myths and prejudice surrounding the disease and to aid in the struggle to educate the public about the need to use condoms.[6] Finally, the crucial role Laurel and Brian play by providing comfort and coming to the family's assistance underscores the irony that in an age that inordinately privileges science and technology, it has been the nonscientific artistic community that has come forward much sooner and much more unselfishly to assist PWAs and to help educate the general public.

Given Hoffman's tendency in her earlier novels to interject fantasy and the miraculous,[7] how accurately and effectively does *At Risk* portray what happens to a family when a loved one has AIDS? Both parents, Ivan and Polly, are professional observers, she as photographer, he as astronomer; yet the virus evades their surveillance. Polly's boss, Betsy Stafford, also observes through writing, but she refuses to believe in Laurel, a refusal that will obviously shape her representations of AIDS and cause her later failure to see through the myths of AIDS. Amanda's AIDS unties the family knot as each member searches elsewhere for comfort. Through Ed Reardon, Polly turns to traditional medicine—the myth of the benevolent family doctor—but that myth dissolves when all the doctor can offer against the grim presence of Amanda's imminent death is the life-enhancing, erotic warmth of his body. Brian and Laurel are the beneficent aspects of the irrational, whereas AIDS symbolizes malignant chaos. Brian and Laurel also help to reconstitute the initial family knot, with Amanda breaking free from the maternal and Ivan from the heterosexual. By choosing Brian, Ivan's behavior suggests a melding of homosexual and heterosexual concerns that does not posit an either/or position. By giving us the shifting relationships of Polly-Ed, Brian-Ivan, and Laurel-Amanda, Hoffman extends the original family unit and draws into it hitherto unacceptable members, including Polly's parents with whom she has been angry for years because her father had deserted the family and her mother forgave him. The grandparents provide the only stability in a family decentered by AIDS, and they give Charlie much needed attention in his loneliness.

Beyond depicting how AIDS affects the immediate family, how accurate is Hoffman's portrait of the suburban response to AIDS? *At Risk* is set in the Massachusetts North Shore area of Cape Ann, a peninsula much smaller than Cape Cod that stretches from affluent Beverly and Manchester out to the favorite tourist fishing "villages" of Gloucester and Rockport and then curves toward Ipswich before moving north to the New Hampshire border community of Newburyport. Inland in this area are many more affluent communities. When *At Risk* was written, this area had no AIDS hotline and Ivan could only call Boston. Since then, an AIDS hotline has been founded and directed by Jack Armitage in Topsfield, a small town of 3,600 on Route 1 on the western border of the Cape Ann area. The hotline, which operates out of Armitage's home, was the only suburban AIDS hotline in Massachusetts in 1989.

In a newspaper interview, Armitage stated that in the future AIDS will be a suburban teenage problem. The number of AIDS cases nationwide as of August 1, 1990, was 139,765, with roughly one-quarter of the victims between the ages of 20 to 26, and 2 percent below the age of 13. Given the relatively long incubation period of HIV, many of these AIDS victims could have been infected in their early to mid-teens. "In all likelihood," Armitage claims, "a 16-year-old playing football and injecting steroids shares his needle. That's a suburban concern. That's what mothers and fathers should start looking at. Up to now, we have felt exempt out here."[8] Essex County, one of the areas that Armitage's hotline, called Strongest AIDS Service Link serves, saw an increase in its AIDS caseload from 105 in October 1988 to 149 in November 1989, and Armitage considers these figures very "conservative" because many suburban North Shore people go to Boston for HIV testing for fear of "being recognized at home." What kind of people does Armitage's hotline serve? All kinds: gays, heterosexuals, men, women, IV-drug users. Increasingly, he is getting calls about "IV-user mothers and newborn offspring." Fifty percent of his clients have IV-drug related problems, and of these, half are women ("Topsfield," 22).

Many suburbanites attempt to conceal their infection. A September 17, 1990, article in the *Boston Globe* drew on interviews with many AIDS victims in the Cape Ann area through various support groups and found that most were afraid to let anyone know:

> Instead, they lie to their neighbors. Cancer, a Beverly woman says of her husband. Leukemia, a Salisbury woman says of her brother. In some of the small towns that dot Cape Ann, they slip into the side doors of treatment clinics or travel far beyond town borders in search of care rather than risk being identified. They shrink low in hospital waiting rooms, hoping not to run into curious high school classmates or relatives. They stay home.[9]

The increase of suburban AIDS cases came home to a Salisbury woman who took in her dying brother. Terrified about how her neighbors would react, she told no one he had AIDS. After he died, the undertaker told the Salisbury woman that embalming her brother would cost an extra $500 because of the precautions that would have to be taken. When she asked the undertaker in astonishment how he knew, the undertaker replied, "Oh, yes, we get quite a few" (Jacobs, 13).

When MIT exhibited the NAMES Project/AIDS Quilt in September 1990, several suburban mothers who had lost sons were interviewed. One woman from Medford who had lived in her community for 30 years remarked, "I expected the people I've known all my life to be here. They weren't." And in words that echo Polly's in the novel, another mother who had also lived 30 years in suburban Winthrop said, "If my son had been hit by a car or died in a plane crash, the love and sympathy would have been there. Because he died of AIDS, the reaction was different, uncaring."[10]

Beyond educating the general public about the severe strains AIDS puts on family relationships, Hoffman further depicts the psychic damage prejudice inflicts when the community designates an afflicted family as the "Other." Michael Foucault in *Birth of the Modern Clinic* details how medical scientists at the beginning of the nineteenth century shifted the language they used to describe what they "saw" and how that language controls our perception of disease. Donna Haraway, in her article "The Biopolitics of Postmodern Bodies: Determinations of Self in Immune System Discourse," observes that recent research in immunology challenges the very meaning of "inner" and "outer" and our understanding of what it means to be an "individual"—that the sense of self so valued in our culture may have to be totally revised as we learn to understand the actual workings of our immune system and its connection to the world "out there."[11] It is in this area that I think Hoffman as a writer generally and in this work specifically challenges the Enlightenment concept of the individual as rational and distinct. Hoffman's attempts to merge levels of perception and break down barriers between conventional realism and fantasy help us to reconstitute our vision of the self and its relationship to "Other." For this reason, I believe her work makes an important literary contribution over and beyond its aim to educate the general public about AIDS.

As for Bazerman's specific question about whether or not Hoffman avoids sentimentalizing her characters, particularly the two children, I would say that Amanda's death and Charlie's loneliness are genuinely tragic rather than sentimental and that their suffering is legitimate, not gratuitous. Tragedy is created when we have knowledge about cause and effect and realize that human intervention could have altered an outcome. Amanda's death could have been prevented if the nation's blood supply had been tested earlier, and Charlie's loneliness could have been avoided if people were not so ignorant about what causes AIDS. I believe, therefore, that they earn whatever pity we feel for them.

As for the criticism that *At Risk* ignores the concerns of gays, if we compare Hoffman's novel with the novels gay men have written about AIDS, we find that both reflect the same two qualities noted by Shawn O'Connor in his essay "The Big One: Literature Discovers AIDS": a strong concern for family and very negative images of those in power.[12] Indeed, much gay literature deals with troubled family relations. In some works, a longed for reconciliation takes place, which is what Hoffman dramatizes. In *At Risk*, Amanda's AIDS threatens to destroy her family, but her death ultimately not only restores the initial nuclear unit but also dissolves Polly's anger for her parents, thus forcing us to reconsider what the meaning and functions of a family actually are.

The second similarity between *At Risk* and gay AIDS novels—negative images of the relevant power system—is illustrated when parents of Amanda's classmates attempt not only to prevent Amanda from attending school but also to have the principal fired for letting her continue to attend school. There is also a negative characterization of the dental profession: finding a sympathetic orthodondist to grant Amanda's last wish—to have her braces removed—takes a tremendous effort. How true this observation of the dental community is generally I cannot say, but I have heard that next to surgeons, dentists feel the most threatened by AIDS and consequently are frequently reluctant to treat persons infected with the HIV virus.

In light of these similarities between what Hoffman depicts in *At Risk* and what many gay authors show in their fiction, the criticism that Hoffman is playing it safe by writing about a white, middle-class child—an "innocent victim" who is bound to elicit more sympathy than gays or drug addicts—to some extent misses the value of the novel as a tool for educating the general public. Moreover, the hostility that David Leavitt claims most gays felt who were made "nervous" by the popular reception of *At Risk* because it presented what the public views as an "innocent victim" may be caused by his overlooking other aspects of public fear. Susan Sontag suggests that "innocent" AIDS victims may be even more threatening to society at large than are gays or IV drug users with AIDS. In *AIDS and Its Metaphors* (1989) she writes, "Those like hemophiliacs and blood-transfusion recipients, who cannot by any stretch of the blaming faculty be considered responsible for their illness, may be as ruthlessly ostracized by frightened people, and potentially represent a greater threat because, unlike the already stigmatized, they are not as easy to identify."[13]

Beyond this, Jan Zita Grover, curator of the exhibit "AIDS: The Artists' Response," in a review of several books on AIDS points out, "The AIDS saint is as much a part of gay fable as is his *doppelganger*, the AIDS villain,"[14] Even Randy Shilts, according to Grover, follows a conventional saint-sinner literary pattern in *And the Band Played On* when he contrasts the nobility of Gary Walsh, Cleve Jones, and others with the evilness of Gaetan Dugas— Patient Zero. Both Amanda and Brian in *At Risk* are characterized as "good" people. Amanda learns to accept her approaching death with touching nobility—she makes a will and distributes her earthly valuables. By only showing Brian performing much needed community service and then dying, without showing us either his early life or the really gruesome details of exactly how AIDS destroys the body—vicious, relentless diarrhea, for example—Hoffmann "sanitizes" Brian. The closest glimpse we get of Brian "before" comes in the brief explanation of how he was infected—he shot cocaine "all through a tour of the South without ever thinking twice when he shared someone's needle" (*Risk*, 138). Now Brian works for an AIDS hotline, where he is the only one who can comfort the grieving Ivan. Brian locates the orthodondist who is willing to remove Amanda's braces. Both Amanda and Brian as PWAs can elicit general sympathy without unduly disturbing conventional attitudes. In other words, Hoffman's work follows the Ryan White syndrome: it creates enough compassion to make people angry about AIDS prejudice generally, angry enough to allocate more funds to fight it. But as to whether *At Risk* does much to combat the mounting homophobia in our society, I would have to say it does little.

Nevertheless, by giving more direct "healing" powers to Laurel and Brian than to Ed Reardon, and by omitting any reference to established religion, Hoffman raises important questions about how well the hegemonic culture has responded to the crisis. Her characterizations of Ivan the scientist and Ed Reardon the doctor conform to public stereotypes; the general media image of scientists is that they are either obsessed, ruthless Frankensteins or dedicated, caring Albert Schweitzers. As scientists both Ivan and Ed Reardon are unable to save Amanda; thus Hoffman suggests that modern science is limited. In fact, Ed Reardon's human qualities are more comforting than his healing skills. He is the family doctor we all dream of having—someone who rushes to our home every time we call. Of course, he blames himself for

Amanda's illness because he ordered her blood transfusion. The powerful sexual attraction that emerges between Reardon and Polly saves him from being unbelievable. Again Hoffman is able to dramatize in a credible way the power of the unconscious longing for life in the face of death. As a doctor, Reardon also represents to Polly power she does not possess; as a woman, her only way of gaining it is by attaching herself to a man who has it.

Over and above questions of sentimental or stereotypical characterizations, AIDS poses another problem: how does one write accurately about an epidemic whose nature changes every day because of new research and developments? For example, the major drug the novel mentions for recurring bouts of PCP is pentamidine, the first medication used to combat the virulent strain of pneumonia that was administered early in the epidemic through painful injections. PCP kills 60 percent of AIDS patients; 10 to 50 percent die the first time they get it. Recently a much less painful form of aerosolized pentamidine has been introduced. Hoffman does not mention the drug zidovudine, or AZT, long available on the black market and previously administered on a test basis, but only approved for general distribution in August 1989. Obviously questions of topicality will always be troubling in traditional realism, which is one argument the postmodernists use for jettisoning any attempt at coherent time. Those works that attempt to educate readers about AIDS using specific current research will become quickly dated, but people can get current information elsewhere.[15] What literature can do that will not become quickly dated is to try to unmask the myths and prejudices surrounding AIDS. Hoffman tries to do this.

Finally, if we deconstruct Hoffman's novel, we find that AIDS among the poor is not addressed; instead we learn about AIDS in the poor population by seeing the treatment available to affluent victims. Amanda's family can afford a new Brookline orthodondist to remove the braces no local dentist will touch. Ed Reardon provides Amanda every attention at his disposal including getting her a private hospital room. Brian can afford to remain ill in his Boston Marlborough Street apartment. Yet today approximately 50 percent of the homeless in Massachusetts are PWAs. George Whitmore, in his journalistic account *Someone Was Here* (1988), describes the mainly poor IV-drug PWAs at the Lincoln Hospital in the South Bronx. Dr. Judith Lieberman keeps an account of these patients and reveals that: "fourteen patients on the list are homeless or about to become homeless."[16] AIDS babies, born to addicted mothers or women who have been infected by their addicted partners, have to remain in the hospital either because no relative is alive to care for them or no one wants them.

Since then, costs have escalated to the point that critics such as Daniel Callahan, in *What Kind of Life: The Limits of Medical Progress* (1989), predict a wholesale collapse of our health care delivery system unless we start practicing some form of triage. Blaming AIDS for threatening to overthrow our already overburdened health care system begs the question of the system's inequitable nature to begin with. Already AIDS has highlighted the two-tiered nature of our health care system. Over 35 million Americans have no means of paying their medical bills and over 60 million have only partial coverage.[17] Around the country, there is a dramatic increase in the number of PWAs on Medicaid rather than private health insurance. Jesse Green, of New York University, and Peter S. Arno of Montefiore Medical Center, studying hospitalization for AIDS in New York City, San Francisco, and Los Angeles, found an increasing shift of the medical costs related to AIDS to the public sector. Between 1983 and 1988, Medicaid's share of AIDS costs in New York City went up by 38 percent. Lack of private coverage means inferior treatment. In New York, private insurers pay $84 for a routine visit to a doctor, while Medicaid only pays $11. "Though it is an important safety net," Green and Arno believe, "Medicaid often fails to provide access to the private physicians who are the gatekeepers to much of the US health care system."[18] *At Risk* then is very realistic to the extent that it reveals the superior AIDS health care received by upper middle-class Americans.

By introducing Brian, Hoffman briefly opens her text to the perspective of gay AIDS and IV-drug AIDS, but poverty AIDS is present only in a deconstructive sense—only in the fears and prejudices of the affluent white world that convert one of their own—a white, middle-class child—into the fearful "Other": marginalized gays, IV-drug users, and Haitians. Whether comparable realistic fiction depicting this aspect of AIDS will appear in time to stem the crisis is highly doubtful. Most probably, television and music will be the major popular forms of educating the audiences that the middle-class novel has traditionally not reached. Because the dominant middle class will still control funding, it is essential that they know the realities of AIDS so that they can cultivate empathy and compassion instead of fear of the leprous "Other." *At Risk* opens up the possibility for greater compassion by first showing AIDS in the known and then shifting briefly to the "Other" who even in an attenuated, sanitized version still has the potential of enabling people to make the necessary imaginative leap. This novel may not be the quantum leap needed, but it takes us a little closer to responding to the desperate need for understanding and caring for the "Other" during the time of this tragic epidemic.

4

Gay Genocide as Literary Trope

LES WRIGHT

"Ivan Ilyich saw that he was dying, and he was in a constant state of despair," Tolstoy wrote in *The Death of Ivan Ilyich*.[1] Ilyich grasped the logical syllogism of death—Caius is a man, men are mortal, therefore Caius is mortal—but could not grasp how this abstraction applied to him. Every experience of death is individual, unique to its time and place in history. Yet death is the one inevitable universal. As Ivan Ilyich's health declined and death approached, only Ilyich himself could grasp this great "evil," the profound disaster of his death. Because we in the modern Western world still view death as an ineffable and sublime catastrophe that inexplicably befalls us, we remain, by and large, as ill-equipped to look death in the eye when it arrives as Ivan Ilyich is.

Among urban gay men AIDS has come to represent collectively just such a catastrophe. What is most monstrous about the epistemological subterfuge in AIDS discourses, that is, the reified and morally qualified single "disease model" of AIDS, has been their refusal to recognize this communal fear of death. Both homophiles and homophobes alike "see the AIDS epidemic as threatening the social structures through which they have constituted their identities for themselves."[2] Their thinking has been infected by what Lee Edelman expresses as "Disease = Discourse," meaning "there is no available discourse on AIDS that is not itself diseased" (Edelman, 301–7). There is, of course, no discourse that does not contain the seed of its own absence, of annihilation, of death. The dilemma within gay pro-active thinking has been how to overcome the hegemony of heterosexualizing dominant discourse. As Edelman phrases it, "[I]n the case of AIDS, infection endlessly breeds sentences—sentences whose implication in a poisonous history of homopho-bic constructions assures us that no matter what explicit ideology they serve, they will carry within them the virulent germ of the dominant cultural discourse" (Edelman, 315).

The language of political paranoia is literalized in the tropological config-uration of "gay genocide," reified in the "leathersexualized antifascism" of the literary fantasies examined below. The figural concentration camp chiasmi-cally crosses the cancer metaphor of military invasion with the polemics of "pathognomic pollution," casting gay men as wrongfully victimized and under attack by the allied enemies of illness and society. These fantasies give shape to the underlying discourses behind "Silence = Death," symbolized by the superimposed pink triangle of Hitler's death camps. Gay resistance equates American homophobes (literal Christian fundamentalists) with Nazis (figural evil) and post-Stonewall American gays with homosexual, and by extension Jewish, victims of the concentration camps.

Historiography of the Pink Triangle

This conflation of fantasy and reality has caused serious confusion in the gay history of the pink triangle. After World War II a profound silence fell over the fates and even the existence of homosexual concentration camp victims. In Germany, the antihomosexual Paragraph 175, ratified in 1871 and sharpened under Hitler, remains on the books to this day. In the United States no mention was made of homosexual prisoners in the concentration camps.

The first reports began to surface a generation later. In the 1970s James Steakley located the first published report in the German homophile publication *Humanitas* in 1954. In West Germany Harthauser's "Der Mas-senmord an Homosexuellen im Dritten Reich" (The mass murder of homosexuals in the Third Reich) was published (In *Das große Tabu* [The great taboo]) in 1967. Harry Wilde's book-length study, *Das Schicksal der Verfemten: Die Verfolgung der Homosexuellen im "Dritten Reich" und ihre Stellung in der heutigen Gesellschaft* (The fate of the banished: the persecution of homosexuals in the Third Reich and their position in contemporary society), appeared two years later. In 1972, the pseudonymous Heinz Heger published his autobiographical *Die Männer mit dem rosa Winkel (The Men with the Pink Triangles)*, a source of much vaunted and decidedly inaccurate fantasy of homosexuals surviving the camps by offering pederastic services.

The social position of the homosexual in the Nazi order of things has been seriously misunderstood, and the victim stereotype (homosexual as Jew) has been translated into gay counter-memory and subsequently propagated as given historical fact. It is vital to grasp two points of misconception here. First, homosexuals under Hitler were not rounded up and sent to the camps en masse in a campaign of mass extermination, like the "race" of Jews.

Rüdiger Lautmann reports that homosexuals (pink), political prisoners (red), and Jehovah's Witnesses (violet), generally were sent to the camps "for purposes of *re-education*. They were supposed merely to renounce their particular orientation, and to prevent their ideological comrades outside from becoming active. Otherwise they were useful for national-racial purposes and were in fact so used."[3]

The social hierarchy within the camps reflected the social hierarchy of German society at large. In the popular mind Jews and homosexuals were associated with each other as similar sorts of people. "The homosexual movement led by Magnus Hirschfeld for more than three decades, and the scientific sexual research which was strongly determined by Jewish doctors, served as a kind of mental bridge between the two categories" (Lautmann, 83). Lautmann concludes that wearers of the pink triangle were, and have continued to be, associated with the habitual criminal category (green). To this day homosexuals have not been considered victims of the Holocaust by German courts of law and hence no reparation payments have ever been paid to them.

The second misconception concerns persecution of homosexuals as part of some uniquely Nazi-generated homophobia. Such persecution has, in fact, had an uninterrupted history in twentieth-century German society, as Hans-Georg Stümke points out in *Homosexuelle in Deutschland: Eine politische Geschichte* (Homosexuals in Germany: a political history). Under the Hitler regime homosexuals fell under the categories of "sick" and "criminal"; hence they were persecuted for reasons of "racial hygiene."[4] Indeed, Manfred Herzer has found that the Nazis did not have a unified policy, nor were they even in agreement as to whether homosexuality was biologically or environmentally caused.

News of the rediscovery of the first homosexual emancipation movement in Germany received wider dissemination in the English-speaking world through the publication of John Lauritsen and David Thorstad's *The Early Homosexual Rights Movement: 1864–1935* (1974), James Steakley's *The Homosexual Emancipation Movement in Germany* (1975), and Arno Press's series of ten reprinted *Documents of the Homosexual Rights Movement in Germany, 1836–1927* (also begun in 1975). The term "homosexual genocide" is employed in English for the first time in Steakley's *The Homosexual Emancipation Movement*.[5] Steakley's ground-breaking work garnered roughly estimated information. He found a Protestant Church of Austria estimate, for example, that "220,000 homosexuals were killed during the Third Reich." And elsewhere, "ten, perhaps hundreds of thousands of homosexuals were interred in Nazi concentration camps" (Steakley, 106). Homosexual survivors remained silent after the war. A certain Neudegg, author of the 1954 *Humanitas* article, articulated this widespread reluctance when he concluded, "I must be silent about the effects of this series of experiments, which proceeded with unspeakable pain, fear, blood, and tears, for it is impossible to put the misery into words" (Steakley, 115). At times, Steakley's observation on Hitler's private view of homosexuality has been assumed, erroneously, to represent official National Socialist policy. "With its mingled elements of condemnation, dread, and admiration," Steakley wrote in 1975, "Hitler's view appears to be a concatenation of eugenics, fear of conspiracy (similar to the "Elders of Zion" legend), and the theory of homosexual superiority advanced by Hans Blüher" (Steakley, 109–10).

We need to remember that by the mid-1970s gay liberation was well under way in the United States. The rediscovery of an earlier homophile movement in pre–Nazi Germany was an important step in the development in the American ethnic minority model of homosexuality. On a parallel track, political reverberations of the Paris 1968 student uprisings were transforming social theory into gay emancipatory practice in West Germany. Rosa von Praunheim's 1972 film *"Nicht der Homosexuelle ist pervers, sondern die Situation in der er lebt"* (It is not the homosexual who is perverse, but rather the situation in which he lives), a Stonewall-inspired undertaking, raised *schwul* (queer) consciousness.

In Germany the elevation of the pink triangle as a political symbol of gay resistance followed a somewhat different track from its American counterpart. Let us remember that Americans read Nazi Germany pornographically, a phenomenon that is impossible and plainly incomprehensible in contemporary Germany. In 1976, three Bielefeld University sociology students, Peter Recht, Christiane Schmerl, and Detlef Stoffel, produced the film *"Rosa Winkel? Das ist doch schon lange vorbei . . ."* (Pink triangle? but that's long since over . . ."). In the same year, the Oedipus collective of Hamburg toured West Germany with their *"schwuler Jahrmarkt"* (gay fleamarket) Brühwarm stage performance, playing to gay male audiences. In 1977, Rüdiger Lautmann's anthology *Seminar: Gesellschaft und Homosexualität* (Seminar: society and homosexuality) was published by Suhrkamp. In the 1980s research into the fate of homosexual men in Nazi Germany came into its own in German letters. Wilfried Eißler's 1980 *Arbeiterparteien und Homosexuellenfrage: Zur Sexualpolitik von SPD und KPD in der Weimarer Republik* (Workers' parties and the homosexual question: and the sexual politics of the SPD and the KPD in the Weimar Republic). examined left-wing homophobia. And Georg Stümke and Rudolph Finkler's *Rosa Winkel, rosa Listen: Homosexuelle und 'gesundes Volksempfinden' von Auschwitz bis heute* (Pink triangle, pink lists: homosexuals and the popular sentiment from Auschwitz to today) appeared in 1981.

In the United States, by comparison, we were treated to a translation of Heger's *The Men with the Pink Triangle* in 1980. The following year journalist Frank Rector's *The Nazi Extermination of Homosexuals* was published by Stein and Day. Both texts offer stereotypically pornographic readings of gay internment. The most highly respected autobiographical account of internment, Richard Plant's *The Pink Triangle*, did not appear in

English until 1986. Plant's extremely painful, personal account and careful compilation of relevant sources go far in countering the notions perpetrated in the first two books, which nevertheless contributed to perpetuating misconceptions prevalent in the American gay community. Lautmann refutes the most damaging notions outright, noting that "the claim that homosexuals were able to save their lives by offering pederastic services proves to be superficial imputation. It is a further example of that stigmatization which was not only imported from society into the camp but [which] has now also crept even into historical writing on the camps. The stigma controls and distorts our knowledge even forty years on" (Lautmann, 86–87). Lautmann also stresses the source of some of the misconception that homosexuals were able to escape death by wile. "The especial character of the destiny of the homosexuals in the camps can be linked to their social upward mobility and therefore *over-cultured social background*. . . . Prisoners with such a professional background, even if they wore the pink triangle, would have had better chances of survival" (Lautmann, 85).

Reading Nazis as Pornography

In American culture the mythologization of the Nazis has replaced its historic significance with its marketability. "The Nazi has become the quintessential element of pornography and sells more books, films, magazines, and related paraphernalia than any other subject," Susan Sontag has noted. "[E]specially in the United States, England, France, Japan, Scandinavia, Holland, and Germany, the SS has become a referent of sexual adventurism."[6] The literary leathersex appropriation of gay genocide, translated into American fundamentalist-as-Nazi, collapses two purposes into one: the sexual outlaw imagery is evoked instantaneously, while the outside observer is put on notice that he or she is excluded. It works an SS shorthand, translating the fundamentalist into a Nazi, ascribing real and potential evil at its mythologically most inflated exponential power, while waiving all need for any further gay-internal examination. This leathersex fantasy plays on the pornographic elements of the Nazi mythology, usurping the erotically pleasurable portions and discarding the broader political implications. Both fascism and sadomasochism are theater, as Sontag observes. Leathersexual fantasy theatricalizes politics. Is there no greater story told than the drama of history?

Perhaps the greatest disservice done to understanding the sociopolitical situation of homosexuals in the shadow of Nazi concentration camps is the automatic, assumed status of "me too" victimization. Gay men fall unconsciously into the "me too" victim mentality. Contemporary gay counter-memory automatically assumes that all the horrible things that happened to the Jews happened to gay men too, without reflecting on the historical truth or on the viability of simply appropriating the counter-strategies of "Never forget." "The Nazi" becomes the singular icon of evil in the modern world. There is only one light in which to see "the Nazi," namely as the last social taboo. The Nazi-as-boogeyman mythology often serves another agenda altogether in the United States. "Evil Nazis *versus* good Allies, good Americans, good War Department, good military-industrial complex, good American wars in Vietnam, Nicaragua, Saudi Arabia" asserts an unassailable social taboo with politically useful ends. Even to raise the question of examining the sources of this taboo comes perilously close to committing secular heresy. So it goes unquestioned.

Gay Leathersex Heroes

The greater catastrophe of the AIDS epidemic lies in our unwillingness to face death, individually or collectively, and in our desire to find someone or something to blame, to take the responsibility for this massive "evil," to give meaning to death. Ivan Ilyich was not able to distinguish between his victimization by illness and the inevitability of death until he was drawing his final breaths. A similar gap in consciousness separates the sick from the healthy, in general, and in the gay community a new distinction has emerged that distinguishes gay PWAs from their "healthy" compatriots. The sense of being victimized by AIDS runs deep in the gay community; the reaction has often been to express a deep-seated rage, based on protracted oppression and compounded by the further impossible frustrations of the AIDS epidemic, and a desire to avenge this further injustice to an oppressed minority.

Although the 1969 Stonewall riots mark the beginning of gay liberation, and a broadened collective resistance to our social oppression, many of us have been unable or unwilling to escape completely the role of homosexual victim. Our collective experience has been one of victimization and we have created a social identity, in part, out of this shared experience of oppression. It follows that this victim mentality permeates our collective counter-memory in subtle and insidious ways. The myth of gay genocide has roots in the historical past, but it has become a hyperrational talisman. It is the battle cry urging us to resist the incipient fascism of everyday life in contemporary American society. It has assumed greater rhetorical power in its challenge to the conceptualization of AIDS as a "gay" disease. It evokes a range of gay political agendas that presume a historically universal homosexuality.

Fantasies of victimization and revenge have been given free play in a number of small-press gay novels published between 1978 and 1988. This literary trope of "gay genocide" typically formulates a particular type of post-Stonewall gay hero. In the three small-press novels examined below, *Project Lambda* (1979) by Paul O'M. Welles, *The Boiled Frog Syndrome* (1987) by Marty Rubin, and *Gentle Warriors* (1989) by Geoff Mains,[7] we encounter an Americanized version of the Nazi myth that demonologizes Christian fundamentalism. The collective gay counter-memory being encoded in these texts sifts history and appropriates mythologies to arrive at a true statement of the "gay condition," reading "Nazi" in that secular strain of puritanism that results from the discursive separation of Church and State in the U.S. Constitution. In these readings I have uncovered a rather uncomfortable subtext, which runs throughout gay writings on Holocaust. It begins with Heinz Heger's survivor's account of a death camp as a wearer of the pink triangle and culminates in the mass commercial market for "Nazi" narratives as voyeurist-exhibitionist spectacle, a pornography of hysteria.

Typically in this scenario of the post-Stonewall gay community, the gay hero has cast off his mantel of discursive illness through personal (private), then social (public) acceptance. In his community of like-minded individuals, he has grown strong and righteous. Collectively the community establishes a new center on the discursive margins of dominant society, literally creating gay pockets within urban centers. It is the dominant American society and its leaders that have become corrupt and morally ill. The new, liberated gay man inverts social values, accepting the hero's mantel, and valiantly fights for truth, justice, and the new gay social order of the 1970s and 1980s.

The leathersex gay hero, whose own life is usually cast in social terms as obscene or pornographic, usurps this power, declaring himself a sexual outlaw, morally somewhere between Jesus and Robin Hood, persecuted for his beliefs while attempting to redress social wrongs. In these novels the leathersex outlaw hero lays claim to the moral high ground of underground resistance movements, typically modeled after those of World War II resistance groups. He incorporates the gay social doubling, identifying himself simultaneously as inside and outside gay society and dominant society. While AIDS has infiltrated the gay community, prejudice and hypocrisy in the disguise of Christian piety have infiltrated mainstream society.

The gay community is under attack, being invaded both by the HIV virus and by the pathognomic counter-contagion of the social diseases of prejudice and hatred, figured or personified by the "Christian fundamentalist." In these narratives gay men respond with fantasies of military counter-attack. This new gay hero must combat the obscene society, whose depiction of homosexuals is rendered pornographic in the gay accounting. The result is a double chiasmic transference: The historically disempowered, polluted homosexual turns the tables, identifying mainstream heterosexuals as pathognomically polluted and declaring them therefore evil. The homosexual claims victim status by virtue of the fascism of heterosexualizing society and casts his moral battle in political terms. The outsider becomes hero; disease is rendered seemingly value-neutral. Fire is fought with fire, so to speak—paranoia is attacked with paranoia.

In these fantasies, the gay man's fears of being "flushed out" (through infection with tell-tale HIV) are countered by his affirming those qualities used to stigmatize him. In post-Stonewall politics there have been two broadly defined camps—activists and assimilationists. The terms and tactics in these novels pursue the activist tack, elevating "life-style" as a mark of difference. The assimilationist is seen as innocently misguided but a potentially serious threat and ridiculed for his desire to conform (an impossible task) to dominant society.

In the discussions that follow we will progress from the material to the spiritual, the transformation from covert pleasure-seeking to deeper self-awareness, as it shifts from a narcissistic selfishness to the enlightened self-interest of compassion. In what follows the political and polemical dynamics underlying this gay leathersexual politics of gay genocide will emerge. We begin by mapping the tropological bias of gay genocide as it stood just prior to the AIDS catastrophe in the post-Watergate small-press gay novel, *Project Lambda* (1979) by Paul O'M. Welles.

Project Lambda

The U.S. Marine Corps has set up detention camps in Colorado. The reactionary fundamentalist U.S. Senator Chester Markowski has begun manipulating a corrupt press to fan the flames of hysteria and win over public sentiment for his proposed legislation to outlaw homosexuals and offer them "rehabilitation," a cynical code word for death. Together they have secretly created Project Lambda, a system to incarcerate and execute America's homosexual population.

Markowski plays on the American stereotypical fears of the moral outrage of homosexuality. He is ideologically related to Joe McCarthy, Jimmy Swaggart, Lyndon LaRouche, and Jessie Helms. In private life, he is a monster; his life is a catalog of stereotypical bad environment. His wife has become a chronic alcoholic out of self-defense. His son appears to be a spoiled brat and has no respect for his father. The family is nonetheless well rehearsed for their public appearances. The hypocrisy of public moral values is revealed in the discrepancy between the hollow public image and the private moral corruption of Markowski's home life. This hypocrisy resonates with many gay men's experience of growing up gay in such morally stifling homes. The corruption of the authority figure symbolizes the corruption of puritanical authority throughout society, typically a code word for homophobia.

For the gay hero, no such corruption is possible because in gay liberationist politics, the personal is the public and rigorous moral honesty is the civic duty of every good gay man to his community. In *Project Lambda* Tip Benjamin embodies this new gay modern hero. Raised in the 1950s and 1960s in a "Democratic, Unitarian, and foursquare American" family in Salisbury, Connecticut, he was taught tolerance and "the values of self-control, integrity, and perspective." He attended Dartmouth, "lived openly as a homosexual," thereby acquiring "a self-confidence and stability unknown to many young men his age." His prowess on the football field eventually earned him his peers' respect. And Tip accomplished all this without becoming the kind of "militant homosexual" whose motives he distrusted (*PL*, 18–20). Graduating to Greenwich Village living, Tip finds work in a publishing house, falls in love first with a transvestite ("a performance" Tip regarded as a "monstrous put-on"), then with a somewhat older man, George Tailor, who owns a travel agency. Tip's life is the presumed universal fantasy of every gay man of the generation between Stonewall and the advent of AIDS. He has a good job, a good apartment, and the perfect lover, and both men are traditionally masculine.

A decade later, Tip and George are living in Boston in domestic bliss—a house with pet, comfortable friends, exquisite food and drink. Tip is starting a serious journal of gay opinion, *Oblique Angles*, "to explore the role of homosexuality in all fields of creative endeavor, from architecture to Zen, not exploitative or sexsational" (*PL*, 43). Tip's dedication to the intellectual integrity of a fair and free press as the bastion of social parity in America is matched by that of newspaper publisher Tony Abracan, heterosexual friend and colleague, who instigates the covert media sting operation to uncover the secret of the Colorado death camp.

In idle conversation at a party these friends casually link Senator Chester Markowski with Nazi Germany. With this, the Hitler allegory—the pornographic mythology of Nazi Germany—unfolds. The senator's duplicity is well known. The duplicity among the bad guys, highly placed men in the federal government and the military, is staggering: Colonel Brontor, who will oversee the death camp, is aggressive and stupid (*PL*, 87); Stuart Robin, the senator's Roy Cohn look-alike aide, is a consummate sycophant and invariably uncomfortable around others of his own ilk, such as the duplicitous Rotarian Rocco Stevens (*PL*, 113) or the driven, Uncle Tom–like Sidney Johnson, who established the processing points for Project Lambda. The lot of them, all paradigmatic variations of a duplicitous puritan intolerance, seem to deserve each other.

Gay men begin disappearing. Computer records of their existence are erased. The FBI and local police departments' offices reveal no evidence that these allegedly missing persons ever existed. George's travel agency notes, sub rosa, that gay men are purchasing one-way tickets and departing from the United States in large numbers. Gay men have a supposed intuitive "sixth sense" about the so far publicly unrecognized disappearances. (This paranoid projection parallels closely the emotional climate of the same early years of AIDS, as rumors of "gay" diseases spread through the urban gay communities in America.) Newspaper publisher Tony Abracan is tipped off. Tip is brought in as an undercover combatant/journalist to document and expose whatever they might find in Colorado, where the "finalization" process is under way (*PL*, 121).

In public, unincarcerated gay men must wear a lavender lambda button. "Tony stared at it. The obscenity of it shocked him. There was something of the Star of David yellow armband about it that the Nazis had used. It was the pink triangle Hitler had forced homosexuals to wear in Germany before their liquidation, even before the Jews suffered their own holocaust" (*PL*, 168). The buttons are distributed at the post office, following the Selective Service registration model.

The scenes alternating between the federal government's (bad guys') duplicity in action and the gay community's (good guys') free exchange of ideas are eventually subsumed by *tableaux vivants* of incarcerated homosexuals, scenes of torture and mutilation, and finally the triumphant hand-to-hand combats in which the good guys vanquish the bad guys. What carries over from the former to the latter is the typical gratuitous violence, a secret pleasure of the narrative. What is not typical is the partial reversal of values: Watergate yielded a new version of the corrupt politician cliché, but Welles presents the post-Stonewall bourgeois gay man as the classic all-American hero placed in a Hollywood script of American liberators at Auschwitz.

Camp doctors experiment on inmates. "One was known as an injection and application therapist. . . . One day he might use acid, another mercury, another gasoline. He would inject joints, veins, testes, even skulls. . . . A second was an excisor. . . . Not only would he remove limbs, kidneys, and unnucleate eyes, but he also removed intestines, muscles, nerves, and brain sections. . . . A third doctor dealt with exhaustion. . . . The fourth medical man concerned himself with electric shock" (*PL*, 189). Brontor and his men are sadistic torturers who specialize in Trophy Room activities, castrating gay victims for their personal amusement. Such torture scenes are described several times in the novel. The character George, for example, is taken prisoner, bears the indignities of captivity, and is miraculously assisted to escape by a sympathetic blue beret (as the elite death camp guards are known), though not before being subjected to an experiment "dealing with the effects of hyper-frigidity upon the human testes" (*PL*, 232), in which a catheter is inserted in his penis. George survives and escapes and in the end, even though he has been castrated, love keeps him and Tip together.

Underlying the Christian morality tale in which the good victims conquer the victimizers there is a self-contradicting conflict. *Project Lambda* asserts the claim that homosexuals can be wholesomely middle-class, liberal American citizens who value the separation of Church and State and who delegate sexual practices to the bedroom while asserting their homosexual social identity openly. And yet, in order for the gay good guy to emerge, a stereotypical Nazi-like bad guy has to be inscribed onto the conservative (read therefore puritanical, and therefore Nazi-like) ruling forces. There seem to be several ideological conflicts embedded in this logic. And this conflict seems to emerge most discernibly in the trope of "the pornographic Nazi." In contemporary American culture the Nazi is always morally bad and pornographically bad, and the Jew is always the good guy, victimized. Welles employs a simple substitution of Jew with homosexual to fit the script. The post-Watergate politicians and related authority figures become interchangeable with Nazis. The civilian puritan's aims are abetted by their military collaborators. Welles chooses the Marine Corps, the "butchest" branch of the American military, making them in his presentation interchangeable with the Nazi SS of popular mythology.

If, as Welles disclaims, "No resemblance to real people, dead or alive, is intended. Nor, God help us, is the plot to be taken as prescient, although the time is tomorrow," then why does he belabor the parable? It seems the pleasure of the text and the catharsis for the (ideally, gay) reader identifying with Tip finds its climax in this chiasmic transference, from morality-play-as-political-thriller to pornographic-tale-as-investigative-journalism. The reader is *shown* what horrible things are done to these gay men in detention camp; the reader is made to witness torture and mutilation and murder.

Welles employs Heger's voyeuristic seduction of the reader to take secret pleasure in the sadomasochistic stock-in-trade fantasies portrayed here. Here Welles engages in the same kind of stereotypical thinking his characters condemn in their antagonists. For example, in a gay male psychology, testicles are not mandatory for "manhood," if manhood is defined as being able to produce offspring. Testicular manipulation, or "cock and ball torture" (CBT) as it is known in sadomasochistic parlance, is an act around which extensive sexual scenes can be constructed. In Welles's text homosexual gratification for the reader can be achieved in the same way that a heterosexual reader responds to James Bond fantasies, or perhaps even more precisely in the way the ideal (heterosexual male) reader reacts to the misogyny of *film noir*. It is the titillation of the uninitiated conjuring his own idea of what sadomasochistic sex must be like. The confluence of sex and violence continues to hold the reader's attention, even when the story line fails to entertain. In this case, underneath the liberal white good-guys values, linger racist, sexist, male chauvinist undertones. We catch furtive, unreflected glimpses into an obscene world of passionate violence, where the primary voice of reason is moderate, middle-class, almost coincidentally homosexual.

Gentle Warriors

Set in San Francisco, Geoff Mains's *Gentle Warriors* is both a historical document and an elegy, documenting the presence of a particular gay life-style and gay space. It mourns the passing of the era when Folsom Street, the center of leathersex culture, was known as the Miracle Mile. "That was another important thing about this experience: people saw it not only as living but as art and the Leather Mile had throbbed with persistent people who were damn well going to write and paint and dance and play about the glories and sorrows of their living" (*GW*, 175). Mains began writing this novel as his health declined from AIDS-related illnesses. He died the day after publication.

The plot of *Gentle Warriors* is predicated on the conclusion that AIDS *was* a government plot. The unfolding events reflect San Francisco's history in the 1970s and 1980s, drawing on knowledge of Dan White, Diane Feinstein, and the JFK conspiracy theories. Moral outrage in the gay community, brought about by discovery of the AIDS conspiracy, is invoked to justify an assassination counter-conspiracy. The heroic resistance fighters are a band of leathermen, mostly middle-class and from traditionally masculine lines of work. The chief protagonist, Gregg, is a Vietnam vet, and one of the many dying from AIDS. However, an important change in the AIDS era signaled in Mains's novel is the reassertion of the homosexual as sexual outlaw, a tradition since Wilde and Genet that was Americanized by John Rechy. *Gentle Warriors* retains a quintessentially American character, articulating what it means that it is every citizen's right and duty to rise up against tyrannical government (*GW*, 210–11).

Mains's position remains appropriate to the the trope of gay hero-as-resistance-fighter. By making Gregg a Vietnam vet, Mains creates a link to the anti-war movement of the 1960s and 1970s, another important informing element in the formulation of gay liberation and resistance to the government as patriotic. Resistance fighters as leathermen plays on the element of a quasi-military camaraderie, but more significantly it emphasizes the tribal aspect of gay community, an idea explored and documented by Mains in *Urban Aboriginals*. The paranoia that brings gay men together is substantiated in the novel by the AIDS conspiracy. But the bonds of sexual affinity are also articulated as mythic. For example, Mark, who is part Anglo-Canadian and part Native American, symbolically dreams the future in forest and animal spirit symbols. All leathermen are hunters and hunted sexually. The sexual hunt is a mystical, spiritual hunt for union with the spirits of the earth. The irony of the leathermen's hypermasculine iconography may be understood in the cannibalistic desire to ingest the strength, the bravery, the prowess of one's enemies. In place of the bourgeois Freudianism of Narcissus, Mains invokes a pagan spirituality of cannibalism—by internalizing one's enemy one may overcome that enemy.

In *Gentle Warriors* Gregg, the leatherman, is on a solitary journey inward. He is a warrior who must go into the spiritual desert to battle the evil spirits and return a mature man. Declaring himself an outlaw has been the first step toward freeing himself of social constraints so that he can discover personal truth. In this frame of mind, Gregg ponders the meaning of good and evil, questioning the potential evil of the leathermen's conspiracy as he waits in a secret lair, poised for the assassination he is about to commit. Ironically, something goes wrong. The reader accompanies Gregg through hours of acute pain as he begins to have fevers and chills and HIV-related illnesses take over his body. In the end, Gregg realizes he is dying and that the real demon he is fighting is his sister's husband, a religious fanatic who has been scapegoated by the government for releasing the AIDS virus. Gregg decides against killing the President: "What is justice against the immeasurable forces with which evil has to play in this universe? Can justice, countering a single little act, ever stem the tide, ever overcome the relentless subversion of evil? . . . We can only try, but in all our efforts we must beware. When is an act good, or just, or simply evil speaking in another flame?" (*GW*, 284).

Meanwhile, Gregg's fundamentalist sister, Jo-Lyn, has found herself ostracized by the elite circle of Washington fundamentalists because they have scapegoated her husband as the culprit who released the AIDS virus into the homosexual population. Jo-Lyn is the one who avenges their betrayal and assassinates the president. For her this act is the will of God. In her medieval Christian worldview "[t]he universe can become a series of concentric spheres, each enclosing the other so that the soul lies at the very center. . . . [Actions] underlie the justice and righteousness of God's holy patterns, whether they be the actions of a congregation, a child, or a president." (*GW*, 155). Jo-Lyn is the spiritual child who attains maturity and apotheosis and who atones for the sins of the heterosexuals in her moment of martyrdom.

The second moment of change in this novel is represented in its vast grieving—an unburdening of long-endured rage, acknowledging the transience of life and the great losses through AIDS, and praising the virtues of gay San Francisco as symbolized by the passing of the Miracle Mile. The AIDS epidemic brought an end to the innocence of gay life in San Francisco, casting a long shadow over the gay communities of the Castro, Polk Gulch, and South-of-Market (Folsom Street). With the fading of South-of-Market leather establishments in the early 1980s there was a major influx of nightclubs catering to the newly affluent San Francisco suburbanites, who renamed the territory "SoMa," a term used pejoratively by the gay community in San Francisco. SoMa has come to represent the neoconservativism, and increased racism, and anti-Semitism, and fag bashing endemic to the Reagan and Bush years. SoMa also suggests the quasi-currency drug of Aldus Huxley's *Brave New World*. Nonetheless, the leathersex communities of San Francisco have continued to thrive.

Gregg's decline into AIDS-related illness and inescapable death represents the passing of an era and a dream. His passing is paralleled by that of other HIV-infected characters. Mains maintains a running roster of AIDS dead (actual people) throughout the novel, suggestive of the NAMES Project's Quilt. The Ambush, a now defunct South-of-Market bar, recalls the old leather dream of fraternity: "[T]hey were to be armies of dreamers and lovers, and once they grew through the initial, indulgent ramblings of self-discovery and its joys, they would change the world. Oh, how sweet had been that dream. An army for humanity, not one against it. An army anchored in the sea of caring, touching brotherhood, of men who would rather love one another than kill" (*GW*, 260). The novel stands as an indictment of the passing of justice in the age of AIDS.

Like Tolstoy's Ivan Ilyich, Gregg, his friends, and his community, have raged against the dying of the light, and even as it passes it remains very difficult to let go. Mains counters the rage and fear of the early 1980s with a plea for compassion—for oneself, for one's own community, and for one's enemies. *Gentle Warriors* stands as a *Trauerarbeit* (grief work), personal and collective. It is modeled on the military elite/tribal community of the gay leathersex community, a convergence of Whitman's democratic adhesiveness and his praise of fallen Civil War heroes on both sides of the battle line. The model also evokes another, earlier gay political struggle, the homophile movement of Germany's Wilhelminian and Weimer Republic years.[8]

The Boiled Frog Syndrome

Marty Rubin's *The Boiled Frog Syndrome* is set in Amsterdam, the European equivalent of San Francisco in gay iconography, a city that represents the freedom to live openly gay. Anne Frank is the metonymic ghost of this novel, conjuring up collective (counter-)memories of Dutch resistance to Nazi occupation. In this novel Amsterdam combines American fantasies of quaint northern Europe with the ideal gay holiday—gay hotels, gay callboys, gay hospitality and entertainment, even a dash of the European gay's presumed envy and admiration of the liberated gay New Yorker or San Franciscan.

American gay resistance fighters living as exiles in Europe are of the perspicacious activist type who do not succumb to the "boiled frog syndrome." Like Jews who left Germany in the early years of Hitler, they read the writing on the wall in time. Others not so alert fail to notice the pot is boiling until it is too late. By that time, their frogs are cooked. At the opening of the novel the adverse political climate has been brought to a rolling boil: any frog dropped in *this* pot would jump out again.

This is straightforward cautionary tale of gay *Endlösung* (final solution). The seething cauldron of America is again a fundamentalist qua fascist land. AIDS has been discredited as a conspiracy to justify the legal persecution of homosexuals, who are being surreptitiously rounded up and herded into death camps. The role gay resistance fighters play in the struggle to liberate this American is, alas, very murky and most reminiscent of a "Mission Impossible" plot. The primary plot revolves around two separated lovers, the politically progressive photojournalist Stephen Ashcroft (who escaped to the Netherlands early on) and the wealthy, conservative Troy Anderson, who believed it "couldn't happen here." He is being held for ransom in an American death camp, but there are fears that he may be assassinated by the CIA before the ransom is raised. This adventure plot figures predominantly as background for several gay romance stories.

Ashcroft is described as very masculine, promiscuously virile (he is keeping Kiki, a 19-year-old Dutch boy) and is the object of the other gay characters' sexual desire. Sex is portrayed as affectionate, comradely, vaguely democratic. Ashcroft's love affair with Troy Anderson has been torrid. The pair met in a gay bar in Florida, and their mutual preference for leathersex symbolizes their inherent masculinity (true leather "comes from within" [BFS, 39]). Ashcroft recalls that during their first encounter it "was I, not he, who finally had to call 'Limits!' There was no punishment or pain, no matter how intense that Troy would not have endured; he was self-disciplined beyond belief. As much as I reveled in his submission to me, there was, however, no way that I could have brought myself to actually harm him, and what I really wanted was to get this phase of the encounter behind us so that we could make love all night" (BFS, 36). Ashcroft's resistance politics becomes personal when Anderson is captured by fundamentalist forces.

Ashcroft is the gay all-American hero, a romantic idealist, a writer, an intellectual, but very much a man of action. He is the rugged individualist of the new frontier; he is the keen social observer (Mark Twain), the new leathersex-outlaw-as-hero (John Rechy, Geoff Mains). Ashcroft is the gay paradox—an antimilitaristic hero who incorporates the masculine ideals of the warrior; he also expresses a Whitmanesque democracy of gay sexual freedom yet belongs to the leathersexual elite. His patriotism is a revery half-dreamed, half-recalled in a bittersweet exile. He is admired, even worshipped, pampered, and accommodated. Ashcroft has risen from the lower classes (preserved in his poor but proud puritan work ethic) and has transformed his values into liberal and middle-class. His political and sexual values are contrasted with Anderson's—sexually compatible, yet a conservative, moneyed Republican—and the boorish hedonism of Greasy Grossberg, a repulsively overweight gay Jewish New York writer living in opulent exile in Luxembourg. Grossberg's version of the leathermaster life-style is a parody of Ashcroft's.

Ashcroft's private sorrow is at the core of the story. This fantasy is not primarily about genocidal paranoia or polemical argument. It is a post-Stonewall, middle-class American gay fairy tale. Ashcroft represents the gay heroic ideal, the responsible activist who rages against a universalized injustice, rather than the literalized gay genocide of the novel. Ashcroft draws upon support from both the self-indulgent intellectualism of Grossberg and the class and wealth of his complementary "other half," Troy ("Tory") Anderson. The larger synthesis of activism and assimilationism, their sexual and political common ground, is embodied in Doug McKittrick, the great gay white hope in the Florida gubernatorial race. The assassination of McKittrick on the eve of his political coup (echoing the death of Harvey Milk) destroys the gay dream of pluralist assimilation and triggers the fundamentalist uprising that swept freedom away in America.

True love is mirrored in two romantic subplots. One is Kiki's love for an even younger boy. The other mirror is a comparison of Ashcroft's situation with that of Aaron Ten Eyck, the wealthy Jewish member of Dutch Parliament and World War II flying ace whose story of secret anguish is redeemed in the reunion of Ashcroft and Anderson. The older Ten Eyck serves as a foil to Greasy Grossberg's Jewishness, to Troy Anderson's class consciousness, to Kiki's youthful whoredom, and to Ashcroft's American version of democratic values. The Nazi/Jew parallel is expressed in Ten Eyck's biography. Ten Eyck's lover had been the Canadian Jew, Herschel Cohen. This was a different time; the other men understood and admired these two symbols of masculinity. Their Jewishness seemed a more acceptable badge of victimized difference.

The gay solution is an adaptation of the Jewish solution: a fair and free press in America, higher educational standards, an ever alert populace will be the only answer. Grossberg serves as the tie between the Nazi Holocaust and the boiled frog syndrome. This message "never forget," is echoed explicitly by drawing Yad Vashem, the Holocaust museum in Israel, into conversation, and echoes the contemporary *Homodoc* (the Dutch name for the documentation center for homosexuality in the Netherlands). As the Jew-as-outsider serves as one kind of social model, so the Dutch historical tolerance for all (and most notably the Jews and more lately the homosexuals) serves as another. Fulfillment of political desire is momentary, and the homosexual foursome at the close of the novel transform into the tropological "wandering Jews," carrying their sense of family within them and living out their society in this portable domestic space.

Gay Genocide as Literary Trope

All three novels project a Hollywood version of Na(r)zistic fascism onto the prototypical gay American enemy, the fundamentalist branches of Christianity, which are morally hypocritical, professing Christian love but manifesting hatred and intolerance, and politically hypocritical, abridging the fundamental distinction between Church and State in American Constitutional law. In all three novels the Jewish situation in an anti-Semitic Christian world in general, and overt persecution of the Jews in eugeneic Nazi Germany, is more evocative than programmatic. The parallels are useful in certain ways, functioning as a kind of sensationalized shorthand to fill in the social injustices that both groups have experienced. Their enemies are drawn as common to both, the same wolves in different sheep's clothing.

In the gay scenario of fundamentalists as fascists, psychological "doubling" justifies the fundamentalist's hypocrisy and leads plausibility ("it *could* happen here") to the paranoid fantasy. AIDS may trigger the fantasy, but AIDS serves primarily to intensify the concept of homosexuality as disease; AIDS is more nearly a redundancy than a legitimate dilemma in its own right. The novels considered here do not examine the implications of AIDS for the gay community of the United States but rather employ AIDS as a justification to construct social identity—to project and paint an enemy in traditionally crude and dehumanizing strokes and to formulate ideals of gay social identity in rather traditionally masculine terms.

As George Lipsitz has stated, those who live in the social margins develop double and triple identities. The contemporary gay man lives consciously with a double awareness, of being excluded from dominant society on grounds that homosexuality is a disease as well as a sin, and of belonging to a community of fellows, banded together in political resistance and fighting to be included in an allegedly pluralistic society. The sense of double bind is made explicit in the choice of leathersex gay heroes, members of an outcast society (Folsom) on the margins of the quasi-mainstream gay community (Castro). It is a truism bordering on the stereotypical to say that gay men learn how to be their own worst enemies, internalizing both their male identities (master, ruler, victimizer) and gay (and thus by definition, feminizing) identities (servant, obedient subject, victim). The Nazi/Jew associations play on both sides of the slash: it is easy to identity superficially with being Jewish in a Christian society (puritanical Nazis function fascistically in ways comparable to puritans of the American fundamentalist variety), and to identify with categorically defined members of a victim class.

Perhaps more interesting is the warrior-male identification with the hypermasculinity cult of Nazism. Politically Nazis are the prototypical enemy, but they are also men who embrace a hypermasculine self-image. The homoerotic undertones of Nazi dress and protocol appeal overtly on a homosexual level, as uniform fetish, as sadomasochistic fetish, as stylized masculine behavior. This internalized love/hate dynamic can be an ironic doubling for a gay man. Following Deleuze and Guattari's argument that pre-oedipal physical desires and impulses are an integral part of the psyche, we may understand the explicit sex-and-violence language of fascism, "'the conscious coding' or the 'over-explicitness of the fascist language of symbol.' This fascist symbolization creates a particular kind of psychic economy which places sexuality in the service of destruction. Despite its sexually charged politics, fascism is anti-eros: 'the core of all fascist propaganda is a battle against everything that constitutes enjoyment and pleasure'."[9] For the leathersex gay man (as hero in the above novels), the battle *for* sexual enjoyment and pleasure is everything. It is an inversion of fascist values. The gay man's doubled identity enables him to embrace both aspects— male/female, victimizer/victim, Nazi/Jew—but the adventure into leathersex necessitates that he gain a heightened awareness of this dynamic with the goal of becoming master of those internalized social mechanisms that are intended to repress or oppress homosexuality. Initiation into the leathersex world reconstructs a transgressive boundary that is erased with the normalization of homosexuality through the gay liberationist act of coming out.

In this sense, the homoerotic impulse traditionally cast as narcissistic (self-worship) may be understood as transformed from within gay discourse into a mythic cannibalism (other-directed hero worship). In cannibalism, one internalizes the qualities of one's enemies in order to turn them to one's own advantage. In cannibalistic hero worship, one eats one's enemy as one eats one's most dearly beloved or any other suitable attractive other, metaphorizing the literalness of gay sex as men eating men. The metaphysics of digestion is merely different. If fascism is really about fear of ego disintegration, fear of union with another person, and flight from the feminine, then gay leathersex can easily be seen as antifascism—the joy of ego dissolution in sex, the joy of union with another person, and *not* a flight from the feminine, but a flight to the dynamics of personal and collective empowerment. To the extent that leathersex suspends notions of masculine and feminine, replacing them with the polarities of top/bottom, master/slave, butch/femme, or similar symbolic power relationships, it becomes meaningless to equate the biological gender of sexual partners (male/female) with their sexual roles (passive/aggressive).

Nonetheless, as becomes apparent in the trope of gay genocide, the double bind between literal and figurative renders this "fascist/antifascist" polarity as "natural." The trope of gay genocide assumes the essentialist position that homosexuality is a biological fact and refutes the biomedical paradigm that created the hetero/homosexual polarity in the first place—we can decide who is gay and who is straight; AIDS can become a rallying point for gay activism; we can claim AIDS as an ideological gay disease while denying its viral pathology. Despite the ideology of resistance, the figural terms of gay genocide subsume the homophobic discourses embedded within the dominant cultural discourse.

The gay metaphor acts out a heterophobic bias, distancing itself from everything that is perceived as "heterosexual," countering one totalizing effect with another. Lifton focuses exclusively on the compartmentalizing of the "evil" side of oneself,[10] accepting the polarized separation in a fragmented identity. This would appear to be common in any out-group dynamic that establishes a positive self-identity, wittingly or unwittingly in the dominant society's terms. The particular thrust of leathersex fantasy intensifies the sense of difference and literalizes the social power dynamics. Leathersex usurps the dominant society's power by mythologizing it, by "acting out" power dynamics sexually. It translates heterosexual power relations into their underlying sexual dynamic and inverts the destructive power impulse into a constructive sexual one.

Rather than impugning leathersexual erotics, it has seemed appropriate to raise questions regarding the appropriateness of exploiting sexual fantasy for seemingly political ends without analyzing the ramifications of doing so. This is particularly important since leathersex itself is often equated with Nazi mythology and categorically dismissed, by the dominant culture and the gay community at large, as part and parcel of the great evil of the modern world.

Leathersex is often read, incorrectly, as a parody of straight society. Of course it is not. It may be understood as an appropriation of the terms of dominant sexual discourse redefined in new relations that promote and extend leathersex self-definition, analogous to the self-definition of "gay" itself. In one sense it may offer an escape out of the dominant paradigm. But the metaphorical translation of the politics of resistance into heroic fantasy cannot succeed if it maintains an undifferentiated life/death, sadist/masochist, omnipotence/powerlessness polarity. Gay pride or gay resistance, it is to be hoped, will avoid this tendency to slide into a heterophobic attack on homophobia that simply inverts the identical paradigm.

Gay genocide generates a collective gay counter-memory, codifying the collective experience of oppression and establishing a moral yardstick by which to plot the acute degree of pain created by oppression. As a collectively experienced catastrophe, AIDS *has been* a gay disease. The gay movement's adoption of Jewish persecution at the hands of German Nazis is a specious argument and reveals dangerous epistemological slippage. And the production of discourses about AIDS by gay men has assured posterity that it will be remembered as a gay disease in spite of our every effort to resist that valorization.

Finally, it would seem that gay genocidal fantasies serve productively now in the process of grieving, a gay *Trauerarbeit* that has begun collectively in the gay communities of the United States. We have experienced grief at being shut out and pushed to the margins of society. For a decade we have dealt with AIDS using our own resources while being told we were making much ado about nothing. We have already lost an entire generation, and many more gay deaths are waiting in the wings. It is time to let the rage of this grief out. We are everyone of us, gay or straight, alone in our encounter with death.

5

When a Risk Group is Not a Risk Group: The Absence of AIDS Panic in Peter Cameron's Fiction

MYLES WEBER

In the opening scene of Peter Cameron's novel *Leap Year* (1990) a thirty-four-year-old bisexual named David tells his friend Lillian, "The nineties are going to be the decade of friendship. . . . Everyone's just going to have a lot of really good friends. The whole notion of lovers and partners and spouses will fade."[1] Nowhere else in the novel or in Cameron's twenty-odd published short stories does a character or narrator make another observation or prediction of this kind—that is, an observation or prediction that can be interpreted as having been formulated at least partly in response to the burgeoning AIDS pandemic. Although included among the main characters in *Leap Year* are David and his 26-year-old boyfriend Heath, and although at least five of Cameron's short stories address either explicitly or allegorically the contemporary gay male experience, AIDS is not an alarming concern of any of the characters in Cameron's works. Far from wanting to chide the author for this "omission" or accuse him of ignoring a fundamental reality of the past decade, I hope here to suggest that in these pieces of fiction Cameron presents an often obscured facet of that reality: that the gay population is not monolithic—that, in fact, the personal behavior, sexual and otherwise, of male homosexuals is as various as that of heterosexuals. Because the threat of AIDS to the "gay community" cannot be accurately understood and redressed if diversity among homosexuals is overlooked, it is significant that Cameron places part of that diversity on public record.

Most of the fourteen stories in Cameron's debut collection *One Way or Another* (1986) tell of a troubled or broken relationship between a man and a woman, but two stories, "Jump and Dive" and "Excerpts from Swan Lake," feature a romantic relationship between two men. In the former, the teenage narrator and his parents spend several days and nights at the narrator's uncle's house, which the uncle shares with his male lover. In the latter, a young man named Paul and his boyfriend Neal take care of Paul's 88-year-old grandmother for part of a summer. In both, parallels are drawn between a gay relationship and long-term straight relationships. In "Jump and Dive," when the narrator, his mother, and his uncle's lover Jason return from grocery shopping, the narrator observes the following mating ritual: "Jason kissed Uncle Walter on the top of his semi-bald head. My father watched and then stood up and kissed my mother. I didn't kiss anyone."[2] In "Excerpts from Swan Lake," when Paul's grandmother cannot remember how many husbands she has had (she has had only one), a new thought occurs to Paul: "Someday, I'll forget Neal, just like my grandmother has forgotten the great love of her life. And then I think: Is Neal the great love of my life? Or is that one still coming, to be forgotten, too?" (*OWOA*, 140).

AIDS is not mentioned in either of these stories. Nor is it mentioned in "The Café Hysteria" or "Slowly," stories published subsequent to *One Way or Another* that also feature gay characters. The same might even be said of "The Secret Dog," an allegorical piece in which the story's married narrator hides his clandestine pet in "a closet" because his wife Miranda is "allergic to dogs" and will not allow them in the house.[3] Every night, he sneaks the dog outside for exercise while Miranda is sleeping. During the day, he believes his wife's cooperative denial will keep the animal's existence a secret: he simply places a sign on the door to the noisy closet that reads "Miranda: Keep Out." One night when the dog cannot be found, the narrator returns to his bed crying and his wife—whatever she knows, whatever she has done—assures him that there never was a secret dog.

While perhaps best read as an allegory of homosexual longing—and behavior—in a married man, this story contains nothing analogous to a life-threatening disease arising as a consequence of taking the dog out of the closet at night. In this and other of Cameron's stories with gay characters or gay themes, AIDS does not figure prominently. In fact, it is not of great enough concern to the stories' characters even to merit mention.

In the novel *Leap Year*, which appeared first in serialized form in 1988 in *7 Days* magazine, AIDS is acknowledged in passing, but it does not interfere with any character's romantic decisions. In brief, the plot of *Leap Year* follows the lives of four young New Yorkers—David, his boyfriend Heath, David's ex-wife Loren, their friend Lillian—and the life of Loren's mother during leap year 1988. With the notable exceptions of a false murder charge brought against Heath and the kidnapping of David and Loren's daughter, the important plot elements all involve the various characters' romantic entanglements, yet AIDS is hardly an issue. Late in the novel Heath does mention that he had previously worked for the Gay Men's Health Crisis—"visiting men with AIDS, and shopping for them and stuff"—and that he was in an AIDS walk (*LY*, 176), but he does not seem to have chosen the specific nature of his volunteer work for any explicitly personal reasons: he does not mention any friends or close acquaintances with AIDS, nor does he seem deeply concerned about acquiring the syndrome himself. Perhaps the lack of urgency in regard to AIDS among Cameron's gay characters in general is best summed up in particular by David's response to his mother after he has told her about his romance with Heath, and she, flustered, asks, "You're careful, aren't you?" David's answer: "Of course" (*LY*, 200).

That "of course" might sound glib to some in the gay community who have seen numerous friends die from AIDS-related diseases several years after male homosexuals started to follow closely safer sex guidelines. And simply by suggesting that Cameron's fiction points to diversity among homosexuals I probably run the risk of implying that Cameron is guilty of what Paul Monette calls "playing *us* and *them*." In *Borrowed Time*, his memoir of the 18 months he spent helping his friend and lover Roger Horwitz battle AIDS, Monette writes that he and Horwitz played this game early in the epidemic. "We all wanted to believe the whole deepening tragedy was centered on those at the sexual frontiers who were fucking their brains out. The rest of us were fashioning our own little Puritan forts, as we struggled to convince ourselves that a clean slate would hold the nightmare at bay."[4] Left unchecked, the game of *us* and *them* as played by frightened homosexuals produces a corollary to the blame-the-victim line of reasoning that some segments of society at large bring to AIDS. The gay corollary states that it is perfectly understandable if *promiscuous* homosexuals who have engaged in *esoteric sexual experiments* are dropping dead from a sexually transmitted disease, considering the acts that they (but not "good" homosexuals) have committed against nature.

But there is no hint of this kind of panicky moral judgment anywhere in Cameron's fiction. Unlike Monette and Horwitz, neither Cameron nor any of his characters seems unnerved by the threat of AIDS—at least no more so than other educated Americans their age, male and female, straight and gay, the majority of whom do not share needles or engage in unprotected sex.

At the very worst, I suppose the characters in Cameron's fiction could be said to conform too closely to standards of "proper" gay behavior like those set by Marshall Kirk and Hunter Madsen in *After the Ball: How America Will Conquer Its Fear and Hatred of Gays in the '90s*, though Cameron's work discussed here predates the Kirk and Madsen book.[5] That stain of propriety might be enough to draw charges from some gays that the conventional aspirations and essentially monogamist life-styles of Cameron's characters qualify them as "guilt-ridden," their stories as "anti-erotic." Furthermore, those who accept Andrew Sullivan's assertion that "no gay man has lived without the risk and fear of HIV infection"[6] might accuse Cameron of creating gay characters whose lack of concern for their own health is inexplicably out of step with reality; they might accuse Cameron himself of acting irresponsibly by offering these characters as typical, well-adjusted sexually active gay men when in fact these characters' attitudes are both atypical and foolishly smug.

But assuming that our current understanding of how HIV is spread is accurate, Cameron's gay characters are not suffering from dangerous self-delusion. Rather, they have been the beneficiaries of a set of circumstances that make their lack of alarm both plausible and reasonable. Cameron's stories are set during a time in which AIDS prevention techniques have become widely understood and generally practiced in this country, at least by sober adults. More importantly, the sexual histories of Cameron's gay characters predating the widespread acceptance of sexual precautions do not put them at high risk of past exposure.[7] During that period of vulnerability when the virus was spreading undetected, each was involved in a long-term monogamous relationship, if he was sexually active at all (Heath in *Leap Year* would have been 18 in 1980, and Paul and Neal in "Excerpts from Swan Lake" seem to be of the same generation as Heath). As best we can tell from the most current information on HIV transmission, as long as Cameron's gay characters (and comparable men in real life) continue to act with care as a matter of course, none is at particularly high risk of exposure to HIV or of contracting AIDS. Cameron's fiction simply reflects this reality.

During the past decade, numerous authors—Armistead Maupin, Andrew Holleran, Edmund White, among others—have created gay characters whose reality vis-à-vis AIDS has been quite different from that of the characters in Cameron's work. A number of these characters—such as Mark in Edmund White's short story "Palace Days," to single out just one—participated during the 1970s in what they saw as self-defining acts of sexual liberation. Mark, we are told, "trusted excess" in his younger days, acquiring numerous venereal ailments, each of which he regarded as "a badge of courage in the good fight against Puritanism."[8] In turn, the middle-aged Mark of the present narrative, set in the mid-1980s, lives in fear of AIDS.

In contrast to Mark and other fictional characters who "experienced" the 1970s, most of Cameron's characters came of age in the 1980s or, if they are gay, recognized their homosexuality at this time. They are the products of circumstances radically different from those under which Mark entered adulthood; in turn, their behavior is significantly different.

AIDS is only partly accountable for this variance in behavior. Generational differences also play a role. While some in the gay community might accuse monogamous homosexuals of backtracking toward Puritanism, that catch-all bugaboo of 1970s gay liberation, younger men often dismiss such accusations as steeped in the dogma of a previous generation. These younger homosexuals were raised by parents from roughly the same generation as Edmund White's Mark, parents who were themselves,, in many cases, scornful of sexual Puritanism. (In "Jump or Dive," it is the narrator's *father* who stresses to his children how important it is that the entire family treat his gay brother "normally." "Once he hit [my sister] Jackie because she called Uncle Walter a fag," the narrator reports. "That's the only time he's ever hit either of us" [*OWOA*, 114]). If the Puritan life-style practiced by some in the gay community was no longer entirely new, anonymous gay sexual activity had already become thoroughly commercialized, and the deleterious effects on the body of prolonged drug use was beginning to be acknowledged. The glamor associated with "trusting excess," then, had already been tarnished by the time AIDS hit. The appearance of a new lethal sexually transmitted ailment accelerated the movement among male homosexuals away from the sexual voracity of the 1970s toward the less "trusting," less "excessive" behavior of today. A decade ago, gay men who embraced monogamy might have been branded "self-loathing" and their behavior condemned as "sex-negative" by the most determined foes of Puritanism in the gay community; by the end of the 1980s such words of condemnation were less often heard. Surely, AIDS in and of itself has scared some people into exclusive relationships "against their will," but for others it has done little more than usher in an era more conducive to monogamy—an era in which their chosen life-style appears less freaklishly conventional and is less subject to scorn by the most vocal of gay spokesmen. This is the era in which Cameron's works are set.

Quite simply, Cameron is not creating a Puritan literary world in the era of AIDS. David and Heath, Neal and Paul, and Cameron's other gay characters never expect or demand monogamy of other gays or straights, nor do they themselves wear it like a straitjacket. And whereas an anti-Puritan gay character in a work by Edmund White might view venereal disease as a proud token of political defiance, it is inconceivable that the gay characters in Cameron's fiction would similarly attribute undue significance to a sexually acquired disease; so the behavior of Cameron's gay characters is *post*-Puritan. Having come of age when they did—Reaganism notwithstanding—and having had the sort of parents they had, Cameron's characters (and those persons similarly reared) have had little to rebel against sexually except perhaps gratuitous rebellion itself. This upbringing has led them back to the very monogamy that the previous generation found, in Paul Monette's words, "trivial and bourgeois." None of them is unaware of the anti-Puritan option: they have witnessed it in others but are not attracted to it themselves, nor are they more attracted to something else.

Their attraction to homosexual monogamy—as they see it anyway, and I would agree—is not necessarily or primarily the result of repressive societal expectations (mainstream society, after all, expects them to be straight, and gay society expects them to eschew monogamy). Their behavior is less a sign of unthinking conformity than it is the exercising of free individual choice, to the extent that free choice is ever possible for individuals buffeted by outside influences. Significantly, in this case those outside influences include a new lethal sexually transmitted disease.

I do not mean to suggest, however, that all gay men who seek sexually exclusive long-term relationships have been scared into their monogamy by AIDS, or that characters who do so are mere reflections of this big scare. In many cases, AIDS has had less impact as a direct panic-inducer than it has had more generally as an indirect influence on the prevailing zeitgeist among homosexuals. At the time that AIDS was first diagnosed in America, it was called the anti-ailment and, conversely, condemned, puritanically, as the wages of sin. This kind of metaphorical adornment of physical suffering would seem entirely inappropriate for many reasons, most importantly because their contracting a serious venereal ailment, and particularly AIDS, would seem to be in defiance of great odds. In their own eyes, and in the eyes of the author, it would be indicative of nothing but sheer chance, of randomness.

Of course, it is entirely possible that their understanding—our under-standing—of how HIV is spread is not fully accurate. Perhaps the mysteries of the virus (its prevalence, its resilience, the length of its incubation period, its mutability) have escaped the understanding of medical scientists in some fundamental way; perhaps the Davids and Heaths, both in Cameron's future fiction and in the gay community at large, will one day be helping each other battle AIDS in large numbers, perhaps within this decade. But, for now, Cameron has done us the service of helping to define the parameters of HIV risk as best we understand them and at the same time has avoided the trap of assigning metaphorical weight to AIDS.

Susan Sontag has argued quite effectively against ever using illness, and more specifically AIDS, as a metaphor, mainly because plagues, both in real life and in literature, tend to be regarded as judgments on the sufferers.[9] An implicit association of evil and sinfulness with AIDS patients would be inevitable if the syndrome were used as a grand metaphor in literature. That would be particularly unwelcome in this case since several spokesmen for the political right have already made that suggestion explicitly in regard to certain "risk groups": gay men and IV-drug users. In fact, the widespread "meta-phorical" emphasis on risk groups, rather than risky behavior, has encouraged discrimination all along towards persons believed, rightly or wrongly, to be at risk. By citing hemophiliacs (rather than the use of Factor VIII, which not all hemophiliacs require), IV-drugs users (not all of whom share needles), and gay men (whether celibate, monogamous, or highly active sexually) as being at risk, the medical community and the government early on established broad and inaccurate targets for public fear and scorn. Even worse, they generated confusion and disbelief among the people truly at risk, which made it more difficult to convince them that they should alter their behavior, and probably resulted in some AIDS deaths among gay men.

It happened this way: in the early 1980s, when doctors first detected a pattern among the newly diagnosed cases of *Pneumocystis carinii* pneumonia and Kaposi's sarcoma in California and New York, the common denominator they cited was sexual orientation. Though in truth all persons who participate in unprotected sex with numerous partners are at risk, it was widely announced that gay men were at risk. That categorization stuck, and gay men were singled out and told to alter their behavior or risk contracting a fatal disease. According to accounts by Randy Shilts and Francis Fitzgerald, many of the gay men whose behavior placed them most at risk ignored the warning and were even angered by it. There was a tendency to dismiss the warning as merely more homophobic rhetoric from hostile establishment institutions. The notion that a disease could single out gay men sounded illogical, and was. Many gay men interpreted the official statements not as a caution against high-risk sex but as a command to stop being homosexual. Ignoring the warning, many men continued to participate in unprotected anal and oral sex with multiple partners, and HIV continued to spread as a result.

Such is the outcome of inexact categorization, which results from the tendency to view all members of a certain group—particularly a group with which one is unfamiliar—as uniform. In his fiction, Peter Cameron familiarizes his reader with one segment of one generation of that larger category known as gay men, thereby helping to provide a more accurate and complete picture of contemporary gay life and, in turn, drawing a clearer distinction between the officially recognized AIDS risk group and those persons actually at great risk. Though he himself risks appearing complacent—or at best detached—in the face of global catastrophe, Cameron, by not forcing exaggerated concerns about HIV infection into his stories, helps to round out the larger body of works in which contemporary gay characters appear. Taken together with works by other authors who have written often of gay characters—White, Maupin, Holleran, David Leavitt, the late Robert Ferro—and authors whose works have featured gay characters, but rarely—Tobias Wolff, Ann Beattie, Alice Adams—Cameron's fiction helps to elucidate a more precise understanding of how extensive the threat of AIDS is to gay men—as diverse as that category is—and to all sexually active people.

6

Babaluaiyé: Searching for the Text of a Pandemic

BARBARA BROWNING

Because what follows is a reading, because it involves a fiction, I want to ground it at the outset in the literal reality of the AIDS pandemic. I wish I could ground it further, because I find myself resorting to statistics—figures— and the figures provided us by the World Health Organization (WHO) and the Centers for Disease Control (CDC) have an uncanny way of sliding into figuration. I mean that these numbers begin to lift off the page, signifying to us something other than literal, living, dying men, women, and children. But here they are: of the 20 countries worldwide with the highest per capita incidence of AIDS, 18 are in Africa and the Caribbean.[1] In the United States, 45 percent of AIDS cases are among blacks and Hispanics.[2] In New York State, 723 of the 807 children diagnosed with AIDS are or were black or Hispanic;[3] that is nine out of ten. In New York City, over 85 percent of women diagnosed with AIDS are or were black or Hispanic: 3,294 out of 3,843.[4] What do these numbers mean? Too many people are dying; many too many people of color are dying.

The Epidemic and the Missing Text

> So Jes Grew is seeking its words. Its text. For what good is a liturgy without a text?[5]

I said what follows is a reading, but it is not actually a reading of a text about AIDS. In fact, it is a reading, one might say, of an absence of a text. But I

76

want to begin in a text that seems to me all the more present and meaningful if we place it within the context of the AIDS crisis. Ishmael Reed's *Mumbo Jumbo* was published in 1972, several years before the Human Immunodeficiency Virus (HIV) was identified or even hypothesized.[6] My desire here is not to read *Mumbo Jumbo* as a parodic prophecy of the AIDS pandemic but as a possible clue to the absence of a text.

Mumbo Jumbo is not an easy book to summarize. Its plot resists reduction, as it itself subverts the idea of a time line, either historical or narrative. But for the sake of argument I will try. The novel recounts the outbreak in the 1920s of a fictional epidemic called Jes Grew. The origin of the epidemic is not exactly given, but its spread is particularly virulent in an area of profound Haitian cultural influence: New Orleans. Epidemiologists trace its course and suggest it will "settle" in New York and then progress to a pandemic. *Mumbo Jumbo* does not give an explicit explanation of the significance, past, or, as I said, origin of the epidemic, but the novel suggests that a text does, or did, exist that contained these secrets. Various groups attempt to secure the ancient text of Jes Grew, but finally it is destroyed by Abdul Sufi Hamid, who was translating it into the language of "the Brother on the Street" until he determined that "black people could never have been involved in such a lewd, nasty, decadent thing as is depicted" in the book (Reed, 202).

The ancient text is destroyed, so a number of questions go unanswered. Thus, in a sense, *Mumbo Jumbo* is a mystery novel without a conclusion. Henry Louis Gates, Jr., has described the novel as having two "basic mysteries . . . [that] remain unsolved"[7]: These are the mystery of the epidemic itself and the absence of its text. What is Jes Grew? It is not AIDS: "Actually, Jes Grew was an anti-plague. Some plagues caused the body to waste away; Jes Grew enlivened the host" (Reed, 6). The epidemic of *Mumbo Jumbo* is an inversion of our notion of disease: It breeds life and animates those that it attacks. A simplified reading might say that Jes Grew represents pan-African culture. It bears some resemblance in particular to animist or "possessional" pan-African religious practices. It is gorgeous and pleasurable, and it is not life threatening.

Another sense in which Jes Grew clearly opposes itself to AIDS is by its age. While *Mumbo Jumbo* seems to depict an "outbreak" of Jes Grew at a certain historical moment, there is every indication that the disease is a traditional, in fact ancient, condition. In contrast, certain hypotheses exist surrounding the historical existence of HIV, but none of them seem particularly convincing. We consider AIDS an essentially new phenomenon.[8]

The place of tradition, and specifically pan-African cultural tradition, in *Mumbo Jumbo* is extremely complex. Reed seems to be making ironic a notion of atextual, nonliterate African cultural tradition by suggesting that the tradition has always been textual, yet the text of the tradition has been suppressed and ultimately destroyed. Pan-African textuality, however, might be recuperated by the book itself. Reed's insistence on demonstrating to the reader his or her own insufficiencies in reading the pan-African text—*Mumbo Jumbo*—is perhaps part of the point. But rigorous study of the novel does bear fruit. The reader who looks at the book in the context of the cultures it represents may actually make a step toward solving its mysteries.

In a more restricted sense, *Mumbo Jumbo* critiques another tradition, the specifically African-American literary tradition. Gates has argued very persuasively that the book creates a postmodern discourse that parodies the African-American textual modes of the preceding decades. But again, I find the question of irony here a very delicate one. It strikes me that there may in fact be an unironic quite serious cry for pan-African textual identification within the novel, for a coalition of writers of color to address the specific experiences of their communities in crisis. I do not want so much to attribute the plaintiveness of that cry to Reed in 1972; rather, it seems I hear a voice emerging from *Mumbo Jumbo* as I read it today, in the midst of a literal pandemic.

I should note a final difference between Jes Grew and AIDS, in relation to notions of textuality I have just discussed. Jes Grew, we are told, would be spread through its own inscription. It would be too simple to suggest here a direct inversion of the theory, to say that establishing a literal text of AIDS in the pan-African community would halt its spread. Certain silences are themselves meaningful and need to be read.

If I have been marking the differences between Jes Grew and AIDS, I should pause to mention their similarities. I said it was a simplification to call Jes Grew the pan-African cultural tradition. The meaning of Jes Grew must remain somewhat suspended, since the only explanation of the disease is absent in the book. Our understanding of HIV is similarly confounded. The logic of the retrovirus seems strangely backwards, because the retrovirus marks its presence, symptomatically, through causing an absence, that is, through the diminution of T–4 fighter cells. Although it is possible to culture the virus itself, our primary mode of identifying its presence in human beings is through the antibodies produced in a futile effort to eradicate it. That is, we read it through its negative image.

Another similarity is the sense of uncontrollability of the two epidemics. In *Mumbo Jumbo*, the lack of control over Jes Grew is underscored by an apparent lack of narrative control. The book slops out of its own boundaries, spills into alternative genres, and the very title warns us of impending confusion. "Mumbo jumbo" means, in American usage, language that is impenetrable—meaningless. Specifically, the title relates to an American perception of the impenetrability of pan-African cultural difference, although one might want to rephrase that as a racist disinclination to attempt to understand that difference. Reed gives the *American Heritage* etymology within the text: "Mandingo *ma-ma-gyo-mbo*, 'magician who makes the troubled spirits of ancestors go away': *ma-ma*, grandmother + *gyo*, trouble + *mbo*, to leave." (Reed, 7). "Mambo," a related term, refers not only to an

Afro-Latin musical style but also to the high priestess in the pan-African religious system of Haiti, vodun. The mambo is hardly a figure of meaning-lessness; in fact, she is an arbiter of meaning, a maker and interpreter of signs. The logic exerted by the mambo is not causal, not linear, but operates on a figural level. Thus it is ironic that she should be construed as lacking linguistic control. She is always reading for deeper meaning.

The interpretive structures within pan-African cultural systems have been consistently perceived by white cultures as unintelligible, spooky, and even dangerous. Various animist religions in West Africa, vodun in Haiti, *santería* in Cuba, *candomblé* in Brazil, and hoodoo in the black United States[9] have been not only dismissed but also persecuted by colonial powers. The reader who would recuperate the wisdom embodied in these belief systems in trying to understand the meaning of AIDS in these communities must not try to isolate the interpretive systems from the political histories of the people.

Babaluaiyé: The Meaning of Epidemia

> You see, its not 1 of those germs that break bleed suck gnaw or devour. It's nothing we can bring into focus or categorize; once we call it 1 thing it forms into something else. No man. This is a *psychic epidemic*, not a lesser germ like typhoid yellow fever or syphilis. We can handle those. This belongs under some ancient Demonic Theory of Disease.
>
> —*(Reed, 4–5)*

Mumbo Jumbo incorporates figures from the constellation of belief systems mentioned above, which might be loosely termed Yoruba/Dahomean–derived religions. The deities vary slightly from one ex-colony to another, and in all they have undergone some Christian modification. But whether called the *loa* of Haiti or the *orishás* of Cuba, they are essentially principles of nature. These principles exist whether you worship them or not: *Yemoja* (salt waters, productivity, maternity, generosity); *Shango* (thunder, divine justice, reason); *Oshosi* (verdure, the hunt, dexterity); *Oya* (wind storms, menstruation, feminism). These are some of the most revered gods, here called by their Yoruba (Nigerian) names. But there is a deity who gets less press, one who is not in fact named in *Mumbo Jumbo*, but who might be the clue to its mysteries: *Babaluaiyé*.

Babaluaiyé is the Yoruba god of epidemics. Reed is not alone in not articulating his name. Pronouncing the god's name is extremely dangerous. Babaluaiyé, in fact, is not his "true" name but a praise name (Father, Lord of the World) meant to appease him. His first name, Shopona, means smallpox. But it would be a misreading to suggest that the avoidance of his name is based on a naïve belief that saying the word provokes the thing. The logic of Yoruba/Dahomean belief is not, as I have said before, simplistically causal, but it does acknowledge the power of signs, and specifically the power of language.

Words are dangerous. This is not naïve but proven true by experience. And this is painfully clear in the present AIDS epidemic. Articulating one's HIV status is profoundly dangerous, because it may result in loss of medical coverage, housing, employment, and acceptance in one's community. Articulating the prevalence of HIV infection in a given community can result in widespread social discrimination against that group. This is obvious to all members of so-called risk groups, regardless of their individual HIV status.

What does it mean to worship a god of epidemics? As I have said above, these principles of nature addressed in Yoruba/Dahomean belief exist whether you worship them or not. Worship is an acknowledgment of power, and of meaning. The colonial authorities in Nigeria completely misunderstood: in 1917, they legally banned the worship of Babaluaiyé, charging that his devotees were attempting to spread smallpox by pricking victims and exposing them to infected bodily fluids. The charge was unfounded, but subsequent to the ban, Babaluaiyé's worshipers were understandably disinclined to speak of their real practices (Bascom, 91–92; Thompson, 61–68). William Bascom suggests that the Yoruba can exhort the god to provoke disease by a figural act (involving naming an enemy while presenting an offensive article on Babaluaiyé's altar). But "[worshipers] regard this practice as evil . . . and contrary to the very purposes of their cult, which are to prevent the spread of smallpox and to aid in the recovery of those who are suffering from it" (Bascom, 91). I would add just one more clause to this description of the purposes of worshiping the god of epidemics: to try to understand the significance of the spread of disease in the community. Babaluaiyé is powerful, but not because he is an evil spirit or a divine executioner. He is the principle by which we understand what is healthy and what is diseased not only in an individual but in a society.

My insistence that an epidemic can be read as meaningful is clearly a complicated position. Susan Sontag has urged us not to read too much into illness.[10] A reading of AIDS might seem abhorrent—particularly the literal-minded kind of reading that would see the physical illness as causally related to a moral or sexual "illness." That was the kind of literal-minded reading offered by colonial authorities who saw Babaluaiyé as both evil spirit and divine executioner. But if we bring Babaluaiyé's principle back into political and historical perspective, we might be able to find a deeper meaning.

Disease might be read as a literalizing or making manifest of the social atrocities practiced against the afflicted—in the case of AIDS, the atrocities practiced against gays, the urban poor, women of color, and pandemically, Pan Africa. Rather than reading AIDS as a punishment, I am suggesting we might read the pandemic as a superficial lesion, the sore on American society that evidences deeper sicknesses: we do not concentrate our medical energies on the marginalized; urban poverty leads to substance abuse; and people of color in particular are denied adequate health care, education, and access to barrier-method birth control. Babaluaiyé is not the arbiter of these violences; he merely makes evident, readable, the violences that are not articulated in a society. If we praise him here, it is our manner of expressing a commitment to understanding the manifestations of disease in our community. And we believe that understanding could literally help to relieve illness and prevent its spread.

Haiti: The Site of an Outbreak of Significance

Holy Wars have been launched against Haiti under the cover of "bringing stability to the Caribbean." 1 such war lasted longer than Vietnam. But you don't hear much about it because it was against niggers. From 1914 to 1934 Southern Marines "because they knew how to handle niggers" destroyed the government and ruined the economy in their attempt to kill Jes Grew's effluvia by fumigating its miasmatic source.

(Reed, 213–14)

Babaluaiyé resides in *Mumbo Jumbo* unnamed. But he is evoked throughout the book by the incorporation of other Yoruba/Dahomean divine figures. They are drawn from across the diaspora, but if a particular diasporic site can be located as a source for the novel's figures, and their meanings, it is probably Haiti. Within all Yoruba/Dahomean–derived belief systems, divine principles are not merely represented but make themselves present in the bodies of their worshipers.[11] But despite their belief in the literal presence of divinity in the body of the possessed, these religions redouble that presence in an extraordinarily elaborate system of representations, mirrorings between the human and the divine. The phenomenon of spirit possession has been misapprehended by white cultures for hundreds of years. In this country, gross misreading of the significance of spirit possession has resulted in especially horrific media representations of Haiti, in particular, as a land rampant with evil spirits and superstitions, both dangerous and naïve. *Mumbo Jumbo* reappropriates Haiti and renders problematic the representations of that island and its culture in white discourses. Haiti in the novel seems to be the terrain in which textuality is opened out from a causal logic to a figural logic. That, of course, is the logic of the book itself, although in both Haiti and in *Mumbo Jumbo* historical, political causality does not drop out; it gives the figures their deeper significance.

Political history is, of course, also what gives significance to the gruesome American representation of "voodoo." Haiti was the first independant black republic; in fact, it was the only such republic for nearly a century. Its defeat of French colonial forces in 1791 was the only successful slave revolt ever. That improbable war lasted 12 years, pitting barely armed peasants against some of the most sophisticated military forces of Europe. African divine principles were called upon in formulating a successful revolutionary strategy against political oppression. This history of resistance has inscribed itself into the Haitian belief system.[12] Vodun modified Dahomean belief by doubling the divine figures, such that each has not only a "cool" aspect but also a hot, violent one. The *loa* were invoked constantly by revolutionary leaders (and the *loa* continue to play a role in political rhetoric—unfortunately in an all too often manipulative way). Thus belief can be used not only to unify and protect a community, but also to resist an oppressive one.

Haiti, in 1791, was an American nightmare—and an embarrassment, because the Haitians also tended to invoke American revolutionary rhetoric in their struggle. But a black revolution was never what the United States had in mind. This country has, ever since, held a threatening posture toward Haiti, and from 1915 to 1934 the United States maintained a military occupation. It was during this occupation that the sensational literature on Haitian rites and "superstitions" began to appear, later spawning even more fantastic cinematic representations.

If America has failed to comprehend Haitian belief, Haiti has understood very clearly the political consequences of racism and cultural imperialism. That understanding has become inscribed in the hot, resistant aspect of the *loa,* known as the *petro* side. But vodun also has a conciliatory, nurturing, cool side—*rada*—that is invoked to bring health and cohesiveness to the community. If vodun can accommodate political violence, how does it accommodate the ravaging of disease? Most practitioners of vodun—in Haiti as well as in the United States—do not discount Western explanations of disease, but vodun accepts that not only germs or viruses cause illness.

In a fairly pulpy account of his investigations of the Haitian phenomenon of zombification, *The Serpent and the Rainbow,* Wade Davis makes some redeeming observations on the political context of certain vodun beliefs, and on the complexity of the Haitian understanding of disease. Zombification is a psychomedical procedure involving deathlike symptoms, live interment and disinterment—a trick called "the Human Seed" in *Mumbo Jumbo.* After doubting the authenticity of the practice, Wade Davis comes to concede, "A society can generate physical ailments and conditions that have meaning only in the minds of the people."[13] But that does not mean that zombification does not happen—it does. The social psyche can have physical effect, but the physical manifestation will only have *meaning* within that society. What I have suggested above regarding the meaning of AIDS in our community, as well as in the world community, is in a sense an inversion, or perhaps just a different articulation, of the same formulation. Physical manifestations of social ills such as racism and cultural repression need to be read as meaningful. My reading of AIDS as a manifestation of racism, sexism, classism and xeno- and homophobia is not just figural; it is given significance by political causality. If a poor black adolescent woman does not have access to condoms or information regarding their use, she will likely risk infection.

But the white medical establishment must recognize that its responsibility is not simply to educate other cultural communities; it also has much to learn. Davis's book began, ostensibly, as an ethnobotanical doctoral dissertation, funded by pharmaceutical interests. Western scientists are just beginning to acknowledge the sophisticated herbologies of some traditional religions. Herbology constitutes only a part of vodun's understanding of healing. Chemically active preparations vary in efficacy according to the social context in which they are applied. The Western medical establishment is increasingly accepting of this fact and has documented the profound effects of community and family emotional support on the T-cell counts of AIDS patients. In terms of research, as well, the AIDS crisis has put pressures on the medical profession to rethink its strategies. Clinical testing of medical treatments resembles, more and more, the process that Lévi-Strauss called *"la pensée sauvage"*—"primitive" science (Lévi-Strauss himself used the term ironically), haphazard, far-ranging *bricolage*, a willingness to try anything, until something works.[14]

The pharmaceutical speculators in Davis's book are cast in a dim light. Their motivations are evidently *not* to help the Haitian community cohere and heal its ills. Could Western science investigate vodun's herbalism without corrupting its meaning? *Mumbo Jumbo* tells us that the Western healer is always a charlatan, a Faust: "Can't you imagine this man traveling about with his bad herbs, love philters, physicks and potions, charms, overcharging the peasants but dazzling them with his badly constructed Greek and sometimes labeling his 'wonder cures' with gibberish titles like 'Polyunsaturated 99 ½% pure'" (Reed, 90). Faust's magic is deceptive, individualistic, power hungry. Vodun calls the ill-meaning sorceror a *bokor*—a figure that stands in opposition to the priest who seeks to heal his people through his knowledge, the *houngan*. "Western man," Reed writes, "doesn't know the difference between a *houngan* and a *bokor*" (Reed, 91).

It is a *bokor* who would overcharge the peasants for bad herbs. AZT costs $8,000 a year—an unconscionable amount for the uninsured. It is the best we have to offer, yet it destroys bone marrow, sometimes further debilitating weakened immune systems. But in fairness, even vodun recognizes that all medicines are poisons. Our badly constructed Greek should remind us that *"pharmakon,"* in the Western tradition, as in vodun, always meant three things: magic charm, medicine, and poison. All healing takes place on three levels, which is why placebos are used in clinical trials (the *cipher* of the pill is magical), and why our best available treatment is toxic.

All this is of course not to suggest that Western medicine cannot be used toward socially responsible, humane ends. Haitian herbalism is also by no means without its hurtful potential. Zombification is a medical and magical procedure performed on socially unacceptable individuals, on the intractable imaginations. It renders them tractable—as do Western psychotropic medications, or "rehabilitating" therapies. A society's notion of its own health always involves violences against what it considers uncontrollable or excessive. On extremely unusual occasions, the Haitians may figuratively kill, and resurrect, their undesirables. But there is nothing figurative about the AIDS deaths we are seeing; except that we read them now as a violence against the intractable imaginations of homosexuality, black and underclass politicization, and feminism. Does that sound excessive as a reading? I am merely taking my argument a step further, a logical step it seems to me: repressing an articulation of political causality is tantamount to repressing political conscientization.

I am not the first person to draw together zombification and AIDS deaths. But the Western press has made the connection in a causal, not figural sense. Believe it or not, the *Journal of the American Medical Association* published an article by Dr. William R. Greenfield entitled "Night of the Living Dead II: Slow Virus Encephalopathies and AIDS: Do Necromantic Zombiists Transmit HTLV III/LAV During Voodooistic Rituals?" Hypotheses regarding HIV transmission and certain pan-African cultural practices, including scarification and circumcision, resurge periodically, but they seem consistently to be unfounded.[15] Such traditional practices are usually limited to rural communities, where rates of infection are very much lower than in urban communities where transmission is attributed to the familiar means: unprotected anal or vaginal sex, reuse of hypodermic needles, or transfusion from an infected blood supply.

"Voodooistic rituals" do not cause AIDS. But some have wondered if invoking the vodun religion might aid in educating the Haitian community about HIV transmission. A social worker in Belle Glade, Florida, has said:

> Many of the Haitian immigrants I talk to are not only illiterate, but living in a situation where they are deprived of accurate information about a lot of things which affect their daily lives. In some ways this results in them having a very simple world view. I ask them what they know about AIDS, and if they relate sickness to evil spirits, I talk to them about AIDS as an extremely mean spirit that tries to trick them, to make them feel well, so that they go out and spread the evil spell among the people they love. And then I follow the voodoo principle by telling them that they can trick the spirit by practicing safer sex (Panos, 66).

The problem with this educational strategy is obvious. It is insufficient to simply appropriate the articulations of a culture without understanding its logic. This use of spiritual figures attributes an extremely naïve, causal logic to the Haitians. I doubt very much that this misuse of "the voodoo principle" is very successful. Illiteracy and lack of information *are* problems, but so is the cultural illiteracy of the translator.

Back to Africa: Figures of Origin

. . . the essential Pan-Africanism is artists relating across
continents their craft, drumbeats from the aeons, sounds that are
still with us. (Reed, 83)

Haitians figuratively link mortality to Africa by saying that when a member of the vodun community dies, his or her spirit goes "back to Guinée." Brazilians similarly speak of death as a passage "back to Luanda." Such statements are not merely poignant or nostalgic; they mark a political, historical affiliation that transcends the life of the individual.

The West has made quite another kind of figural link between death and Africa—a much more insidious link, which found its most famous articulation in Conrad's *Heart of Darkness*. Readers find varying degrees of irony in Conrad's use of the Congo as a field of psychic disease and deterioration. But more recently, Alex Shoumatoff has published a decidedly despicable and racist account of what he calls *African Madness*. The title is an unironic turn on Reed's "mumbo jumbo." It refers to a very general notion of the state of politics, culture, and health on the African continent. Is "African Madness" another name for Jes Grew? It is figured as infectious. In the introduction to the book, Shoumatoff explains that after years of traveling through the Central and South American tropics, he went to Zaire: "and there, as a Belgian friend who has lived in Kinshasa for twenty years describes the process, I caught *la microbe:* Africa got into my blood. (This was before the AIDS virus was identified and spoiled his metaphor)."[16] AIDS may have spoiled the metaphor, but Shoumatoff is still happy to retain Africa as a figure—not as the site of political affiliation to which one returns, of course, but on the contrary as the very origin of death.

The final chapter of Shoumatoff's book is an essay, first published in *Vanity Fair*, called "In Search of the Source of AIDS." Like a detective, Shoumatoff hops from one decimated town to another, on the track of the original carrier. He acknowledges that epidemiologists are not convinced by the theory of an African origin of AIDS. Researchers feel the project of locating an origin of a virus is futile, and furthermore infinitely less important than predicting— and controlling—its future course. But Shoumatoff argues, "To the Western man in the street, however, the question of the African origin of AIDS is important because he has been told that it's only a matter of time until the pattern of AIDS in the U.S. and Europe becomes 'African'" (Shoumatoff, 200). Current epidemiological trends do not surprise us particularly. The only segments of the U.S. population that are "becoming African" are those that share the African community's problems of inadequate nutrition, health care, and HIV information and protection. These are the urban underclass communities, and they are disproportionately black and latino.

Shoumatoff and other journalists have justified their search for an origin as epidemiologically important. But the marking of Africa as "source" seems far more loaded when Shoumatoff articulates the eery, seemingly oblivious wish "Wouldn't it be marvelous if AIDS . . . just went away, mutated out of existence, *went back wherever it came from?*" (Shoumatoff, 188; my emphasis). And as Harlon Dalton has observed from within the African-American community, when arguments of origins have arisen, "We understood in our bones that with origin comes blame. The singling out of Haitians as a so-called risk group confirmed our worst fears."[17] Dalton has written an extremely sensitive and powerful analysis of African-Americans' understanding of the meaning of the epidemic. Despite the disproportionate toll being taken on this community by AIDS, blacks and latinos are not forming the kind of political alliance in the face of the crisis that has formed in the gay community. Dalton argues: "many African-Americans are reluctant to acknowledge our association with AIDS so long as the larger society seems bent on blaming us as a race for its origin and spread" (Dalton, 243). Not acknowledging, or in Dalton's words, "owning," AIDS is a self-silencing of people of color that may seem disempowering. But it is not naïve. It is dangerous to speak the name of Babaluaiyé. It is dangerous to own AIDS, as an individual or as a community.

Dalton ends his essay by expressing the hope that African-Americans will work through their silence and begin to speak for themselves on the problems they are encountering in the crisis. I, too, am hoping in earnest for the pan-African text of the epidemic. The drama and poetry now proliferating from the politicized gay community includes pan-African voices.[18] But we continue to search for the text generated by a collective, politicized pan-African community, including women.[19] If the text is missing, the first question to ask is not necessarily why wasn't it written? but if it has been written, will it be published, and will it be read? Current conditions certainly do not make us believe that available funding will be used to encourage literary or artistic productions from marginalized communities, particularly those dealing with AIDS. *Mumbo Jumbo's* fictional publishers advertise "NEGRO VIEWPOINT WANTED" (Reed, 76), but the "real" text of Jes Grew gets rejected. Before he destroyed the text, Abdul submitted it for publication and received this response:*"A Negro editor here said it lacked 'soul' and wasn't 'Nation' enough. He suggested you read Claude McKay's* If We Must Die *and perhaps pick up a few pointers"* (Reed, 98).

Reading means looking for meaning, and perhaps looking for texts. AIDS as a pan-African pandemic, both literally and figuratively, needs to be given a voice by writers. But as we have seen, saying the word itself is dangerous. Babaluaiyé must be called by his praise names. That is not superstition; it is a manner of recognizing the power of a meaningful reading of epidemia. As readers, we bear the responsibility of recognizing that power, even in our reading of absent texts, or those that predate and seemingly prefigure the AIDS crisis. This recognition may enable the text to come into being. Harlon Dalton writes, "The black community's impulses to distance itself from the epidemic is less a response to AIDS, the medical phenomenon, than a reaction to the myriad social issues that surround the disease and *give it its meaning*" (Dalton, 237; my emphasis). When white society begins to understand Pan Africa's difficulties in its own terms, perhaps a genuine exchange of information will be possible.

Reed concludes *Mumbo Jumbo* with an image of the "neon Manhattan skyline. Skyscrapers gleam like magic trees" (Reed, 218). America has attempted to imagine Africa and Haiti as the distant bush—a sequestered world where uncontrollable imagination rules. But I am writing these words from the urban bush, a terrain overgrown with political significance. In Harlem, possibly 15 percent of the adult population—men and women in the prime of life, some barely teenagers—are infected with HIV and are highly unlikely to receive adequate treatment. And we are not responding.[20] Babaluaiyé, I write this in full recognition of your power, I call on you by your praise names: Make some sense of this.

7

The Mystical Body: Frans Kellendonk and the Dutch Literary Response to AIDS

GERT HEKMA

AIDS has attracted only minor attention in Dutch literature. There is a collection of short stories *Dit verval* (This decay), half of them written originally in Dutch, the other half translated,[1] and there is Frans Kellendonk's novel *Mystiek lichaam* (1986; *The Mystical Body*). Some (auto)biographies of AIDS victims had been published,[2] and several AIDS-plays, some translated and some written in Dutch, have been staged but not commercially printed.

The major gay writers in the Netherlands, Gerard Reve and Gerrit Komrij, have not mentioned or even alluded to AIDS in their work up to now. Other gay or bisexual writers and poets such as Jaap Harten, A. Moonen, Boudewijn Büch, and Hans Warren remain largely silent on the topic. An explanation for the relative silence of Dutch gay authors on the topic of AIDS could be that the authors mentioned belong to an older generation that has been only marginally influenced by the gay movement of our days or by AIDS itself. Their involvement with the homosexual movement can in most cases be traced back to the sixties when the aim of emancipation was integration into straight society, rather than the development of autonomous gay cultures. This preference for integration above separation is probably the main reason why the older gay writers have not been affected by the blossoming of gay and lesbian cultures in the eighties and have not taken up the major contemporary gay issues. But the younger gay generation has not yet produced writers of significant literary merit. These appear to be the main reasons why AIDS has not attracted much attention in Dutch literature until now.

The only exception is Frans Kellendonk's *Mystiek lichaam*, a superb novel that caused a major literary debate in the Netherlands. The discussion did not focus on homosexuality or AIDS but on the supposed anti-Semitism of the book. A comparable debate was waged when R. W. Fassbinder's play *Der Müll, die Stadt und der Tod* (1981; The dirt, the city and the death) was to be staged at the end of 1987. After public protests and reluctance of the actors, the play was cancelled at last because of its alleged anti-Semitism. The controversy in Germany, as in the Netherlands, focused on the same issue. Whereas the stereotypical and prejudiced portrayal of a Jew in a work of art was considered discriminatory, a similar portrayal of a gay man did not raise any objection. Both in Germany and in the Netherlands the anti-Fassbinder lobby won the struggle and the play was not staged in either country. The suggestion that Fassbinder's metaphorical figures did not necessarily represent the view of the writer, or could actually be intended to uncover the latent racism and homophobia of Germans (or Dutch people), did not gain any credence.[3]

In his novel, *Mystiek lichaam*, Kellendonk also provides negative portrayals of both a Jew and a gay, and indeed a discussion started on his supposed anti-Semitism. Again, no one cared about the apparently homophobic content of the book: Kellendonk was generally known to be a gay man. By the time of these discussions Fassbinder had died, so he never had an opportunity to rebut the criticisms brought against his play, but Kellendonk was still alive. (He died in 1990 of AIDS.) He reacted angrily to the accusation of anti-Semitism. In his view, the critics were more interested in scandals than in the content or literary merit of his book, which could certainly not be read as anti-Semitic.[4] And indeed, the reviewers did create a scandal, repeating each other's opinions several times, yet they never brought forward any factual proof of their allegations. The scandal died slowly. In the end, most readers were left with the strong impression that Kellendonk was indeed a dangerous writer.

Kellendonk was born in 1951, in a Catholic family, in the city of Nijmegen, where he also studied English. He translated English and American literature into Dutch.[5] He started a literary career of his own in 1977 with a collection of short stories *Bouwval* (*Ruins*). He belonged to a group of writers organized around the literary journal *De Revisor* and described as "academic" because of their reaction against and opposition to the dominant trend of realism in Dutch literature in the sixties and seventies.

In Kellendonk's works the theme of homosexuality becomes gradually more important, culminating with *Mystiek lichaam*. This novel is not only the major work in his oeuvre but also one of the best Dutch novels of the eighties. Dominant themes in all of Kellendonk's works are truth and illusion. Most of the characters in his novels and stories live in a fantasy world, and they lose control of reality. In his first novel, *De nietsnut* (1979; The good-for-nothing), the storyteller, recapitulating his father's life, transforms more and more into his father. In the last story of *Ruins*, "The Truth and Miss Kazinczy," Kellendonk writes about a student who is doing research in London and discovers that the papers he is studying are falsified. In order not to be left without a topic, he decides to falsify the papers that prove the falsification, but without success. At the same time Miss Kazinczy, his landlady, is telling him stories that he does not believe, but that are much more truthful to her than are his true stories of falsifications. In the end, he leaves England, disillusioned, sure of neither truth nor illusion.

The second novel of Kellendonk is *Letter en geest: Een spookverhaal* (1982; *Letter and Spirit: A Ghost Story*). In accordance with the title the novel is completely devoted to the theme of illusion and reality. A young man decides to start working in an archive to gain a greater sense of reality. But after many adventures, life at his workplace seems to be more illusive than his life of languor at home. Kellendonk's second collection of short stories is *Namen en gezichten* (1983; *Names and Faces*) In one of the stories, "Other Destinations," a young man prostitutes himself for his beloved male friend who wants to visit India for "spiritual enlightenment." Again, the end is disillusion, the prostituted boy leaving for another destination.

Mystiek lichaam is Kellendonk's major and last literary work. Irony permeates the novel from beginning to end. It is the saga of the Dutch family Gijselhart (meaning, more or less, "heart in hostage"). The father, living near a city resembling Nijmegen, resides by himself in a large house. This mansion and its garden are described as icy, revolting, dark, barren and inhospitable until Gijselhart's pregnant daughter Magda returns home. In the book, she is mostly called "Prul" (trash, dud), a name symbolizing her stupidity. Her return to the family home changes the house and its garden completely: The house becomes alive, bright, warm, and hospitable, and the garden bears fruits and vegetables again, because a child will be born. Prul has become pregnant out of wedlock by the Swiss-Jewish Dr. Pechman (man of bad luck). Subsequent to her return and the birth of her child Victor, her gay brother Leendert also comes back to the family home. He had been an art critic in New York, successful in creating and destroying reputations and making a lot of money in doing so. In the novel, New York stands for homosexuality, and for culture and artificiality, in short for the unnatural and death. In New York, "brother" had a lover, "the riper boy," who died of a terrible disease, clearly AIDS, but the name of this deadly disease is not mentioned at all in the book. Also the names of the characters are rarely used in the novel; instead, the characters are referred to by their familial relationships. This is probably a conscious strategy on the part of the novelist to make the narrative less particular and more universal.

The centerpiece of the novel is a flashback to the times when the brother met his lover. The brother had traveled to Brussels together with his sister to celebrate the marriage of a girlfriend who had betrothed herself to a rich American pedophile. After the party the brother and sister stay in Brussels and join the newlywed couple in bed, together with a friend of the husband, the riper boy, whom the brother has already met at the reception. The boy is a male prostitute, a pedophile, and also a procurer of boys for the American husband. Straight sex does not succeed in the marriage bed, and the meeting is a rather embarrassing end to the party.

The only one who does not bother about the difficult situation is sister Prul: she is depicted as a gosling, rather stupid, but also very direct. She comments on the impotence of the males and of (male) culture: "Male delusions, thin male delusions. Their history of fights, their culture of dead things, only envy of the womb. Which male has ever been able to create something so absolute and so irrefutable and so beyond criticism as a child out of himself?"[6] Her language may be sloppy, but she represents the female voice of truth. Earlier in the novel, Leendert states about his sister, "The truth came from the womb . . . hysteria was a form of clairvoyance" (*ML*, 77).

The meeting in the bed of wedlock leads to intimacy between the brother and the boy, while the sister is observing them. She criticizes their rapprochement: "The fools, they waste their love on each other, see them. They said goodbye to mother earth, they have gone on a sexual space race. Fancied and stupid they are and lonely they will die, that is where their male delusion will bring them. That I have to see my bloody own brother behave so unnaturally" (*ML*, 97). The brother does not feel content with his situation, and he remembers the first kiss he exchanged with the boy in this bed as follows: "Brother realized that this kiss which was incredibly earnest, from the inside, and should be the kiss of his life, was considered from the outside as a droll counterfeit kiss. . . . For the first time brother knew that they were a parody, the riper boy and he, if they liked it or not, an antiphony in the biological tragedy" (*ML*, 97–98). It is noteworthy that the crucial message on homosexuality in this novel is delivered by the sister, this unintelligent girl. As Diotima is the mouthpiece on male eros in the all-male society of Plato's *Symposium*, the female in this novel takes the position of truth, from which males are excluded, according to Kellendonk.

But there is also the story of the brother's attitude toward his homosexuality. He had not consciously defined his sexuality before meeting the riper boy. He shied away from marriage in order to avoid the messiness of domestic life. He liked sex for the pleasure, not for the costs. Kellendonk seems to suggest that the brother paid dearly for his pleasures in the end, contracting AIDS instead of producing children. He continues, "Their love had never had a future. It could not procreate anything. It had to be turned inward, maintained in an atmosphere of sublime folly. Therefore, it had to become an obsession. In bed they managed best to conjure the lack of prospect" (*ML*, 123). Brother explained to the riper boy "that there should exist in a supernatural world beyond time an eternal vase, fallen from a celestial balustrade into the here and now, and they were two temporary potsherds of that vase. Most human beings had no idea of that vase, but both of them had sharp edges which fitted exactly in each other, partaking in it together. They lived down here already a little bit in heaven, so to say" (*ML*, 107). The riper boy did not like the metaphor of the vase, and suggested, "A vase . . . You have to be a precious queen to invent such a story. When we should live in heaven, why not call us two angels? There have been fallen angels, isn't it?" (*ML*, 107). The boy seems to reverse the story of the brother, substituting the temporary exclusion of the fallen potsherds for the eternally excluded fallen angels. The boy, like the sister, is not very clever, yet he seems to be nearer to the truth than the brother.

Homosexual love is sterile, and heterosexual love is creative. Because it is primarily women who continue nature and history by bearing children, for Kellendonk, the male is rather irrelevant to procreation. Men will never know whether they are really the biological fathers of their children. In *Bouwval* he states his idea thus: "It was the woman who continued the human race. The daughters of women and their daughters. Man is only a paltry being in comparison to them."[7] And gays, such as the brother, stand primarily for artificial and sterile culture. Thus Kellendonk reverses the classical defense of homosexuality. Whereas gays formerly boasted of their contribution to culture to counter the argument of their sexual sterility, Kellendonk trivializes this creativity in cultural matters. For him it is completely irrelevant.

Kellendonk even goes further in his criticism. In his novel gays not only fail to procreate, but also when the boy induces the brother to drink his lymphatic fluids, he impregnates him with "that new disease" (*ML*, 100). And after the brother's return to the paternal home, there is the one and only idyllic gay scene depicted in the novel, the seduction of a young, innocent boy, which results in another transmission of the disease.

After the publication of *Mystiek lichaam* Kellendonk stated in an interview, "I discuss the dynasty of life and the dynasty of death. The homosexual has long since been oriented toward death, death is a homosexual obsession, which is only emphasized by the outbreak of this disease."[8] (AIDS, this time, is indeed mentioned.) Kellendonk asserts this dichotomy between straight and gay, and even more so the dichotomy of mother and queer.

There is an ample body of literature that discusses the relative merits of homo- and heterosexuality, and it seems that Kellendonk, himself a gay man, favors heterosexual love and female procreativity. But for how long? After the sister's child Victor is born, the father of the child joins the paternal home to look after his child. First, Dr. Pechman is considered a dangerous outsider to the family, especially by the brother, but eventually the doctor is accepted and also wins the favors of father Gijselhart. Pechman lives in the main house; whereas the gay brother is put away in one of the sheds behind it. And Pechman gains power over the child, which is acknowledged as his child. At the end, he takes Victor out of the paternal home to his relatives, renaming him Jacob. The sister again becomes childless and disappears, leaving her father and brother in a house that is again haunted by death. Father Gijselhart will die of old age, and the brother of AIDS. In a last effort, the brother sings the Song of Songs, imagining his death as a celestial marriage to the riper boy. It seems to be a barren song, or is this the victory, given by Kellendonk to gay loves in the end?

To be sure, Kellendonk leaves us with the possibility of different interpretations, but it is easy to conclude from his novel and from what he has said in interviews and debates that his view of gay love is not very favorable. He seems to have come to believe the traditional Catholic views with which he was reared, but only after a detour. He was familiar with the postmodern critique of enlightenment and clearly intended to go beyond modernist belief in reality and truth; and he was also a gay man, partaking of Amsterdam's gay subculture daily. But instead of opting for differentiation, he returned to the mysteries guarded by the Catholic Church. Although embracing Catholic beliefs is rather popular among Dutch gay artists, the extent to which Kellendonk succumbed ideologically to these beliefs is amazing to Dutch gay sensibilities. But for him, there is something very personal about Catholicism: "Brain-washing? I rather think that I, an unbeliever, yet do God's work, that I am his blind tool and through my works create myself after His image and resemblance, as He creates Himself through me."[9] God is as man-made as man is God-made.

In a remarkable article for the weekly *Haagse Post* Kellendonk reported on a famous trial in Utrecht in which gay and lesbian groups accused the Cardinal of Utrecht of homophobic statements. Although he did not support the clergy, Kellendonk strongly criticized the gay and lesbian movement's use of the judicial apparatus of the state for ethical debates. His article is in the first place an attack on the enlightened philosophy of nature that negates the existence of evil and leaves it to the state to implement the good in society. But as we know, he declares rhetorically, this belief in the state and good society has resulted time and again in terrible crimes. The philosophy of the Enlightenment, Kellendonk argues, is bankrupt, but nevertheless the gay and lesbian movement is erroneously grounded in it. In his criticism of rationalism and the ideals of progress, Kellendonk is very much a postmodern writer. But when he uses postmodern thinking to revalidate Catholicism, he is substituting one repressive system for another, and he is well aware of this. In the same article he uses the occurrence of AIDS to suggest that the promises of the sexual revolution were false and resulted in disaster.[10]

The novel *Mystiek lichaam* of Kellendonk is not at all typical of the social or political reaction to AIDS in the Netherlands. It is the work of a writer who did not feel comfortable with contemporary Catholic doctrines but who resisted even more the language of the gay and lesbian movement. His answer was a return to the sources of Catholic tradition, and a rejection of what he perceived as the self-victimization of gays and lesbians and their superficial faith in a utopian society without discrimination and other evils. How could a gay man who was a regular participant in Amsterdam's gay nightlife and knew all liberal and libertarian theories feel so negative about this world and its inhabitants? Kellendonk's views indicate that free space to live and think for gays and lesbians is more difficult to attain, even in the Netherlands, than is generally assumed. Forging and maintaining a wholesome sense of self is certainly a strenuous and lifelong battle. The often flat polemics of the gay and lesbian movement with its utopian hopes and its outright denial of evil makes this struggle more hazardous. It has been the accomplishment of Kellendonk to pose this problem, among others. Now others have to find the answers.

8

The Best of Times, the Worst of Times: The Emerging Literature of AIDS in France

DAVID WETSEL

Viewed from the perspective of 1991, a particularly chilling conversation takes place near the beginning of Hervé Guibert's new novel *A l'ami qui ne m'a pas sauvé la vie* (*To the Friend Who Did Not Save My Life*). Upon hearing the first reports of a new disease attacking homosexuals in the United States, Guibert's character Muzil—a thinly veiled portrait of philosopher Michel Foucault—falls to the floor in a fit of laughter: "Un cancer qui toucherait exclusivement les homosexuals, non, ce serait trop beau pour être vrai, c'est à mourir de rire!"[1] (A cancer afflicting only homosexuals. No, that's too perfect to be true. I could die laughing!)

The perception of AIDS as a pure invention of American puritanism, homophobia, and sexual hysteria persisted, indeed flourished, among the Parisian gay community well into the mid-1980s. The principal gay party organ, *Gai Pied Hebdo*, eventually disavowed its initial satirical attacks on the new gay plague. But the perception of AIDS as a distinctly American phenomenon persisted in the form of an entrenched psychological resistance to what was perceived as yet another import of American sexual hysteria. When first introduced into France by such nascent AIDS organizations as

95

AIDES, "le safer sex" was almost universally ridiculed or ignored by the Parisian gay community.

Factored into this perilous formula was a dangerous fatalism perhaps not unrelated to the longstanding French suspicion of American cultural hegemony. For seven or eight years, American visitors heard the same refrain: "France has experienced plagues for a thousand years. We're too culturally mature to be capable of an American-style panic. If we get it, we get it." As late as 1989, the Parisian gay scene seemed stuck in the year 1974, San Francisco time. American AIDS activists attending a giant Gay Pride party at the Cirque d'hiver were stunned by the schizophrenic spectacle of the entrance to an officially sponsored *blackroom* (backroom) standing ten feet away from a booth staffed by French AIDS organizations.

Statistics alone cannot explain the psychological time lag that complicated the French perception of the AIDS crisis during the 1980s. But statistics are revealing. In 1985, there were only 260 officially recognized AIDS cases in the whole of France. Of these, only 160 were French gay men.[2] Of the estimated 15,000 cases documented by January 1991, nearly a third (4,600) dated from from the year 1990 alone.[3] Towards 1986, the myth of AIDS as an American fantasy began to give way to another image: AIDS as a new plague brought from America. French AIDS literature is riddled with passages in which characters attempt to trace the source of their infection to someone who had visited New York or San Francisco in the early 1980s.[4] Guy Hocquenghem's *Le Gay voyage*[5] (1980), a fascinating French perspective on gay America *avant le déluge*, serves to remind us of just how popular such visits were.

Mirko D. Grmek, professor of the History of Medicine at the Ecole des Hautes Etudes Pratiques, argues that although the AIDS virus was introduced into France via several routes, the particular strain of HIV responsible for the epidemic among Parisian gays "clearly originated with the virus of the New York homosexual community."[6] Epidemiology aside, it was in some sense natural for French gays to view AIDS as something imported from America. The decade between 1975 and 1985 had seen an almost complete Americanization of the Parisian gay scene. The old club scene, so poetically evoked in Jean Noël Pancrazi's *Les Quartiers d'hiver* (Winter quarters), had been swept away into near oblivion. So, too, had the old-fashioned, and suddenly embarrassing, French gay organization ARCADIE.

In more than one of the new French AIDS novels there exists a discernable note of hostility toward the imported American gay culture that the Parisian gay community had so slavishly imitated for over a decade. The only two American characters in these novels are distinctively sinister. Both are survivors of another epidemic. Both bear its stigmata. In Guy Hocquenghem's *Eve*, we meet Boy, an Irish-American international drug trafficker from Queens. Of massive proportions and with a temper to match, he is reported to have once hurled a roommate, cocktail glass in hand, from the window of a tall apartment building. A childhood victim of the postwar polio epidemic, he is obliged to speak though an open tracheostomy in a voice broken by a perpetual death rattle. His "moon-like" face is "permanently deformed in one corner by a terrifyingly perverse smile."[7] After he is murdered by the novel's protagonists, his putrifying corpse contaminates and infects the main tourist attraction of an obscure Caribbean island (*Eve*, 161).

In Hervé Guibert's *A l'ami qui ne m'a pas sauvé la vie*, the friend in question—Bill[8]—also bears the scars of childhood polio. "One of those ultimate monsters of fate," the entire right-hand side of his face remains paralyzed in a grotesque "zone morte" (*Ami*, 179). Bill, too, is an international trafficker in drugs. The head of a worldwide pharmaceutical company specializing in the development of new vaccines, he has ingratiated himself into the confidence of Professor Melvil Mockney, the American discoverer of the first polio vaccine who is currently at work on an AIDS vaccine. Forty-five or 50, an inveterate pursuer of pretty boys, Bill has suddenly been dealt a flush by fate. He controls access to an experimental protocol in which Mockney's vaccine is being used to halt the progression of HIV disease. During the course of the novel, Bill subtly manipulates the character Hervé Guibert with the hope of a cure. If a French protocol cannot be set up in time to save Guibert, Bill promises to fly him to America to have him inoculated by Professor Mockney in person (*Ami*, 192).

Guibert's final chapters chronicle Bill's merciless betrayal. Delays and excuses occur, and Guibert's T-4 cells drop below the level required by the protocol. Fervent promises are followed by months of silence. There are dinners at fashionable Parisian restaurants during which maladroit cruelties fall from the usable half of Bill's lips: "Anyway, you could never have handled getting old" (*Ami*, 226). Exulting in his power over a circle of handsome and talented men who have never taken his advances seriously, Bill exacts his final revenge. He finds a better candidate for Mockney's protocol—the recently infected (1,000 T-4 count) brother of his new Spanish lover—and flies him to the States to receive the experimental treatment. Guibert, bent upon his own revenge, proposes to prick his finger and put infected blood into Bill's glass of red wine. But Bill, ever vigilant, never takes his eyes off his glass during the course of the meal. Guibert's ultimate revenge is purely literary. The novel's penultimate chapter mercilessly chronicles the humiliations of Bill's pathetic sexual life-style. Upon the novel's publication, Guibert told the newspaper *Libération*, "By treating me as he did, he's killing me. . . . This book is my weapon to kill him. His very existence makes me sick to my stomach."[9]

A genuine best-seller (100,000 sold copies in less than a year), Guibert's novel won the prestigious Prix Colette for 1990. The presence on the award committee of such luminaries as Bernard-Henri Levy, Jean d'Ormesson, and Philippe Sollers seemed to signal the willingness of the French literary establishment to receive the emerging literature of AIDS into the contemporary canon. But what of the novel's immense popular success? The French have always had a particular taste for *romans à clefs*. But *A l'ami qui ne m'a pas sauvé la vie* is more than that. It is a rather special genre the French call a *règlement de compte* (settling of scores). Whereas Parisian critics were virtually unanimous in their praise of Guibert's excruciatingly truthful account of his coming to terms with his illness, more than one reviewer expressed reservations concerning Guibert's revelations of details of the private life and final illness of his friend the philosopher Michel Foucault, via the character Muzil. One detail in particular seemed to rankle. After Muzil's death, "a large sack filled with whips, leather hoods, leashes . . . and handcuffs" is found hidden in the back of his closet (*Ami*, 29). Writing in *Le Monde*, critic Michel Braudeau wondered if such sensationalist "tittle-tattle" would not have been best left to a writer like Roger Peyrefitte.[10]

In an interview with *Libération* (March 1, 1990), Guibert insisted that *A l'ami qui ne m'a pas sauvé la vie* is, after all, a novel. His characters, even the character "Hervé Guibert," are not "completely what they are in reality." However, a certain fidelity to Guibert's models proved essential. "I tried to transform the characters, to give Muzil [Foucault] long black hair," he told *Libération*, "but that didn't work at all." Guibert's perspective, very much in tune with contemporary French literary theory, bears noting: "Je parle de la vérité dans ce qu'elle peut avoir de déformé par le travail de l'écriture. C'est pour cela que je tiens au mot roman" (I speak of truth in the aspect of truth as deformed by the writing process. That's why I insist on using the term novel).

In the same interview, Guibert explained that the day after Foucault's burial he wrote a homage to him in the form of a short story.[11] From that moment on, however, fear of having AIDS himself forced Guibert to "obliterate the very image" of his close friend. It was in the course of writing *A l'ami qui ne m'a pas sauvé la vie* that every memory flowed back into his consciousness. In effect, the narrative of Guibert's novel might be compared to the necessarily cruel discourse of one undergoing psychoanalysis: To leave any memory, however terrible, unspoken is to cheat. Guibert told *Libération* that his books have always exacted from his friends "une demande exorbitante . . . une demande d'amour assez abusive" (an exorbitant price . . . a rather abusive demand for love). His friends, he insists, have never censured him, have always accepted him as a writer, and have always proved capable of making the distinction between his books and themselves.

At least one of Guibert's friends was apparently not capable of making this distinction. Actress Isabelle Adjani, who once appeared on French television to deny that she had AIDS, is portrayed in Guibert's novel as the rather pathetic Martine. Among all the people portrayed in the novel, Guibert admits, only Adjani has yet to contact him.[12] But, in general, Guibert's confidence in his friends' solidarity has seemed to hold true. French reviewers of the novel noted Guibert's somewhat indelicate portraits of the first French AIDS activists. Daniel Defert, founder of AIDES, appears in caricature as Muzil's lover Stéphane. Guibert is particularly merciless in his depictions of the first gay doctors to take on the cause. "AIDS," he writes, "became the source of social aspirations [and] public visibility . . . for [certain] doctors who used the cause as a means of hoisting themselves out of the daily drudgery of their office practices" (*Ami*, 132). Yet, when I spoke with a Parisian physician and prominent AIDS activist whom I suspected served as the model for Guibert's "le docteur Nacier," he had only words of praise both for the novel and for his friend Guibert. "This is the only AIDS writing to date," the doctor told me, "which really speaks to the fears and anger of those who are positive or who have progressed to AIDS. . . . It's ridiculous to call the novel a *règlement de compte*. Hervé's use of models drawn from life is better compared to that of Proust."[13]

In the tradition of Montaigne, the novel's protagonist comes to have a kind of grudging respect for his illness. AIDS affords him a *"perspective d'intelligence"* (intellectual perspective) and serves as a paradigm in his project of *"dévoilement de soi"* (unveiling of self). Inexorable, AIDS is like a long staircase ultimately leading to death. Yet each step of the staircase represents an unparalleled *"apprentissage"* (apprenticeship). Not only is AIDS an illness that gives one "the time to die"; it gives death itself "the time to live, the time to discover time and to discover, in the last analysis, life": "Le malheur, une fois qu'on [est] plongé dedans, [est] beaucoup plus vivable que son pressentiment, beaucoup moins cruel en définitive que ce qu'on aurait cru." (*Ami*, 181–82; Unhappiness, once one has plunged into it, [is] more bearable than its anticipation, much less cruel, in the last analysis, than one would have believed).

Ultimately, it is Guibert himself who is the object of his most fierce *règlement de compte*. As a portrait of narcissism in the face of death, *A l'ami qui ne m'a pas sauvé la vie* is an artistic triumph. But what of the novel's political implications? It is scheduled for publication in the United States during the course of 1991. American readers, I suspect, will be somewhat puzzled by Guibert's lack of solidarity (or even concern) with the wider AIDS community extending beyond his immediate circle. Cultural differences in part explain the narrowness of Guibert's vision. The very notion of a "gay community," at least in the American sense of the expression, hardly exists at all in France. Moreover, as Hugo Marsan observes in *La vie blessée* (*The Wounded Life*), the French attitude toward death effectively precludes any movement of solidarity in France among those affected by AIDS. "Le Names Project," he argues, would have very great difficulty catching on in France because terminal illness is considered such a private matter (Marsan 1989, 133–34).

The first AIDS memoir published in France, Alain Emmanuel Dreuilhe's *Corps à corps: Journal du sida* (*Mortal Embrace: Living with AIDS*) serves to remind us of the extent to which Guibert's perspective on the AIDS epidemic is peculiarly Parisian. A courageous work, both personally and politically, *Corps à corps* is quintessentially French in style and sensibility. Dreuilhe's many allusions to Proust (his favorite writer) reveal his keen sense of writing within the French literary tradition.[14] Yet Dreuilhe's perspective on the AIDS crisis could not be less French. Whereas Guibert seems almost totally unconcerned with the consequences of the epidemic outside his own network of friends and lovers, Dreuilhe (who lived in New York for the 11 years prior to his death in 1988) has a passionate vision of AIDS as an assault upon an entire community and culture.

Dreuilhe's organizing metaphor—the framework in which he tells the story of his personal struggle—is that of a Third World War in which the "occupied territories" are the bodies of PWAs. The Gay Community is Troy, which welcomed the fatal horse into its city gates "à bras ouverts" (with open arms). American gays, liberated from the oppression of American puritanism, thought the Greeks had departed for good and abandoned all prudence, "but the sexual revolution . . . was only a ruse. The [enemy] soldiers were hidden in the womb of the horse, in the needle, in the phallus. No sooner had the homophobes lifted their siege than the massacre began," according to Dreuilhe:

> Mon SIDA et la guerre de Troie ont été provoqués par l'Amour, par Aphrodite, divinité tutélaire de Troie. . . . Le dérèglement des sens, dans lequel plongent Aphrodite et ses charmes, debouche sur l'aveuglement des Troyens . . . qui décident de faire entrer le fameux cheval malgré les objurgations de Cassandre. . . . Il y a six ans, les Cassandres américaines étaient accusées par la masse des Troyens, dont j'étais, de faire le jeu de l'adversaire en demandant une pause des ébats érotiques jusqu'à ce que ce cheval SIDA révèle ce qu'il avait dans le ventre.[15]

> My AIDS and the Trojan War were brought about by Love, by Aphrodite, the patron diety of Troy, goddess of sexuality and even lust. . . . The sensual abandon and derangement induced by the seductive Aphrodite led directly to the blindness of Priam and his men, who decided to bring the wooden horse within the walls of the city despite Cassandra's warnings. . . . Six years ago, the American Cassandras were accused by the majority of Trojans, myself among them, of playing into the enemy's hands by calling for a halt to all erotic revels until the AIDS horse had revealed what was concealed in its belly.[16]

Corps à corps rather sadly stands in a no-man's-land somewhere between France and America. American readers, unused to the French rhetorical tradition, perhaps have misunderstood Dreuilhe's truthfully courageous vision. French readers (particularly gay ones) have been mystified and even offended by Dreuilhe's brilliant and extended martial metaphor. Dreuilhe's narrative culminates in a call to arms and in a moving vision of the gay New Jerusalem:

> Jour après jour, il nous faut brûler notre cheval de Troie et reconstruire à sa place l'Arche Sainte de notre Alliance. Le monument aux morts de la guerre du SIDA devrait en toute logique ressembler au Mur des Lamentations. . . . Comme Job, nous devons nous refuser à maudire, et concentrer nos forces pour survivre jusqu'au moment où Dieu et le Diable se lasseront de nous accabler, où le virus aura été expulsé de notre temple profané. (*Corps*, 195)

> Day after day we must burn our Trojan Horse to ashes and in its place construct the Ark of our Covenant. The war memorial to those felled by AIDS should logically resemble the Wailing Wall. . . . Like Job, we should refuse to curse our fate, instead devoting all our strength to surviving until both God and the Devil tire of tormenting us and the virus is expelled from our desecrated temple. (*Mortal Embrace*, 155)

Writing in the January 3, 1991, issue of *Gai Pied Hebdo*, Hugo Marsan proclaimed 1990 "l'année du sida-roman" (the year of the AIDS novel).[17] Another AIDS novel, Jean-Noël Pancrazi's *Les Quartiers d'hiver*, had just won the coveted Prix Médicis. Pancrazi poignantly conjures up a world—the old-style gay club scene—that was well on its way to extinction long before the AIDS crisis ever hit Paris. This world, which had begun to fade in the mid-1970s with the Americanization of the Parisian gay milieu, is represented in Pancrazi's novel by the "Vagabond Club." A last holdout of sorts, the club is a world unto itself. Almost everyone is a regular. Rival cliques, presided over by the gentlemanly and ever vigilant manager Auguste, coexist in a quarrelsome but close-knit camaraderie. Pancrazi's cast of characters, brilliantly real to anyone one knew the gay scene in Paris before 1975, includes the blind former proprietor of a defunct rival club (now a perpetual guest of honor at the Vagabond), a fading drag artist, and a young Moroccan in perpetual quest of a protector.

Les Quartiers d'hiver, which a Parisian friend of mine described as "our version of the Quilt," is a remarkably lovely tribute to those who will never again take part in the weekly fêtes organized at the Vagabond. At the beginning of the novel, the narrator tucks Eduardo—the Vagabond's terminally-ill bartender—into a couchette of the train that will take him home to Spain to die. Feigning nonchalance, Eduardo utters an adieu that serves as the novel's title: "I'm taking up my winter quarters."[18] Over the course of a long Christmas season, the festive mood of the Vagabond is repeatedly darkened by news of the deaths of friends. The narrator receives a hauntingly evocative notebook kept by his Dutch artist friend Joep during the last few weeks of his life. The diary's last entry is followed by blank pages on which bits of indecipherable marks suggest "la recherche d'un dernier mot, un nom de couleur rêvée—celle qui lui aurait servi à peindre la fin des choses," *Quartiers*, 177; (the search for a last word, the name of a color dreamed of—the one which would have served to paint the end of things).

The news of Eduardo's death, imagined by the narrator in a passage of rare beauty, seems to coincide with the Vagabond's rapid loss of clientele. A few weeks later, the owner arrives to assess the club's financial situation. The novel's final chapter chronicles an anxious evening during which the faithful, suddenly fearing the unthinkable, watch the owner go over the accounts. As the club is closing, the announcement comes: "Le Vagabond, c'est fini." But before being ejected onto the sidewalk with the others, the narrator catches a glimpse of a final visit to the Vagabond by those who have been lost to the epidemic:

> Glissant le long des parois de glaces . . . surpris que Le Vagabond fût encore ouvert à cette heure . . . revenaient ceux qui nous avaient quittés au fil des hivers, ceux que nous avions aimés—Michel Lardeau, Paul, le décorateur de la rue de Paradis, Philippe, le postier de La Villette, André Germain, l'ingénieur de Villejuif. Chacun allait vers le garçon qu'il avait préféré ici, avec lequel il avait eu une petite aventure, une passade de quelques nuits ou une liaison de tout un été. Vers moi c'était Joep qui venait, à peine fatigué d'arriver des extrémités du monde. . . . Eduardo . . . demand[ait] à tous de danser. . . . Les vivants dansaient avec les morts. . . . Tels d'affectueux frères aînés, ils nous montraient le chemin à suivre. . . . Non, il ne fallait pas avoir peur, il suffisait, au dernier instant, de se laisser emporter comme pour une danse. (*Quartiers*, 189–90)

> Stealing along the wall of mirrors . . . surprised that the Vagabond was still open at that hour . . . those who had left us over the past few winters, those whom we had loved, were coming home—Michel Lardeau, Paul, the interior decorator from the rue Paradis, Philippe, the post office employee from La Villette, André Germain, the engineer from Villejuif. Each was making his way toward the boy whom he had especially liked here, with whom he had had a little affair of a few nights or a whole summer's romance. Joep, hardly tired at all after a trip from the end of the world, was making his way towards me. . . . Eduardo . . . called out for us all to dance. . . . The living danced with the dead. . . . Like affectionate older brothers, they showed us the path to follow. . . . No, one didn't have to be afraid; one only needed, at that last moment, to let oneself be swept away by the dance.

The French literary response to the AIDS crisis dates only from 1987. That year saw the publication of not only Dreuilhe's *Corps à corps* but also the first two AIDS novels: Dominique Fernandez's *La Gloire du paria* (The glory of the outcast) and Guy Hocquenghem's *Eve*. The same year there occurred what many in France now view as a critical juncture in the history of the epidemic there: the publication of philosopher Jean-Paul Aron's article "Mon Sida" (My AIDS) in *Le Nouvel Observateur*.[19] In that article, Aron became the first French *personnalité* to speak openly to the media about his illness.

Dominique Fernandez's *La Gloire du paria*, a rather classic gay novel about a relationship between two men separated by age and background, casts a bit of a shadow on France's reputation as the one country in which the arrival of the AIDS emergency was greeted with a minimum of hysteria and AIDS patients have always received competent medical care.[20] Elements of Fernandez's narrative seem to me to ring true to the situation as I remember it in Paris of the early and mid-1980s. Fernandez's characters reveal (now rather a taboo subject) that "*Gay Pied* a commencé par nier la gravité du sida" (*Gay Pied* began by denying the seriousness of AIDS) and make reference to the effort by the newspaper *Libération* to stifle the rumor that Michel Foucault had died of AIDS. His characters also lament that French physicians have only recently begun recommending "le Safer Sex" to their gay patients.[21]

Fernandez's novel dramatically evokes the AIDS denial rampant in the Parisian gay world of the mid-1980s. His narrator Bernard—like those of Guibert and Hocquenghem—is by profession a writer. Thinking that he might write a play about AIDS, Bernard consults his friend Xavier, a gay *mondain* (man about town) who appears to know everyone in Paris. Xavier is horrified and tells him, "The less we talk about AIDS the better. Life is already complicated enough for us without hanging out our dirty laundry" (*Paria*, 94). In order to convince Bernard that AIDS is the last subject he wants to write about, Xavier arranges for him to have a tour of an AIDS ward in a major Parisian hospital. What Bernard witnesses is a very ugly picture. The AIDS patients look like concentration camp inmates. The professor in charge of the ward, convinced that the microbes responsible for most opportunistic infections hide in human hair, has had all of his patients' heads shaved. Abandoned by their friends and lovers and neglected by a terrified nursing staff, the patients beg to be allowed to go home to die. The chief AIDS doctor, intent on beating the Americans in the race for a cure, views his patients as human guinea pigs and reserves his most promising treatments for the most interesting cases.

Fernandez's curtain falls at the end of the hospital tour and rises again to find Bernard himself stricken with the disease. His lover, Marc, who is caring for him at home, must shop outside the neighborhood because of the hostility of terrified local shopkeepers. The couple are abandoned by their families and by both straight and gay friends. A close woman friend, terrified of visiting Bernard, attempts to render him "innocent" by arguing that he must have been infected via a blood transfusion. Marc's ex-lover urges him to think of himself first and to leave Bernard. The novel ends in a somewhat melodramatic but not unmoving double suicide.

The ending of *La Gloire du paria* serves to recall the state of panic and hopelessness that reigned in France prior to the widespread availability of AZT. Indeed, the setting of nearly every work we are considering can be dated via pharmacological references. Guibert's novel turns on the promise of the Salk vaccine, which excited so much hope in 1989. In Guy Hocquen-ghem's *Eve*, AZT is just coming over the horizon. In Fernandez's novel, French doctors are still testing HPA 23, the treatment for which Rock Hudson went to France. In Copi's *La Visite inopportune* (The untimely visit), the drug of choice is Suramin. In the later case, however, the doctor (though a madman) offers a curiously realistic piece of advice: "Switch to herbal remedies. . . .
You're going to die anyway. When things get really bad, a cup of chicory will be more pleasant than an I.V."[22]

Une Visite inopportune was first performed in February 1988 at the Théâtre National de la Colline, two months after Copi's death. Raul Damonte, who adopted the pseudonym "Copi" upon arriving in Paris from his native Argentina in 1963, has been described by veteran actor Michel Duchaussoy (who played the protagonist of *Une Visite inopportune*) as "more Parisian than real Parisians."[23] Long famous for his cartoons in *Le Nouvel Observateur*, Copi gained official recognition as a literary genius only posthumously. His seven novels and eleven plays[24] tended to be received by Parisian critics as countercultural or cult pieces. *Une Visite inopportune*, which won the Prix de la critique dramatique for 1988, produced a flood of critical acclaim.[25]

Perhaps only Copi, writing for a Parisian audience, could have brought off a farce on the subject of AIDS. Critic Michel Cressole, noting how little *Une Visite inopportune* resembles the tradition of American AIDS plays,[26] observes the extent to which the play represents Copi's tribute to the French theater itself: "Règles classiques, coups de théâtre moliéresques . . . tournures et balancements des phrases XVIIe siècle, férocité d'humour pédé magnifié Grand Siècle." (Classical unities, Molière-like *coups de théâtre* . . . a 17th-Century phrasing and weighing of lines, ferocious gay humor magnified in the style of the *Grand Siècle*). Cressole's account of the play's opening night gives us a vivid sense the play's effect upon its audience:

> Devant . . . les atroces petits détails cliniques, les spectateurs se sentent d'abord visiteurs inopportuns. Les premiers rires sont nerveux. Aussi rapidement que l'échange des répliques, le cynisme extravagant de la pièce s'impose. . . . Entre deux spasmes de rire, le public . . . frissonne, noué. . . . Avec Copi—le vrai Copi—, le SIDA est contagieux comme le rire.[27]

Confronted with . . . [the play's] awful little clinical details, the audience at first feel like unwelcome visitors. Laughter is at first nervous. But as rapidly as the exchange of lines, the extravagant cynicism of the play takes hold. . . . Between two spasms of laughter, the audience . . . shudders, in knots. . . . With Copi—the real Copi—AIDS is as contagious as laughter.

Une Visite inopportune opens on the day that Cyrille, a famous Parisian actor, is celebrating the second anniversary of his AIDS diagnosis. His doctor, Professor Vertudeau—a genial lunatic whose hobbies include performing lobotomies on Sundays and making love to his nurse while perched on a tricycle—calls in to check on his patient's condition.

"Nothing grave in the last few days?" he asks.
    "Only two heart attacks and a coma," replies Cyrille.
    "Very good indeed, indeed much too good," the professor observes. "You should have been dead six months ago."
    "Realistically," Cyrille asks, "when am I going to die?"
    "You'll live," replies the professor, "as long as your AIDS does."
(*Visite*, 28)

Une Visite inopportune is, of course, complicated by an autobiographical element. Copi's earlier hospitalizations were reputed to have often turned into considerable *événements mondains* (social events). Cyrille's nurse calls him "the Sarah Bernhardt of the Public Assistance" (*Visite*, 11). Professor Vertudeau requests that Cyrille follow Sade's example and use psychiatric patients to put on performances in the hospital. Jorge Lavelli, who had directed many of Copi's other plays,[28] later admitted that he was at first shocked by the idea of beginning to rehearse *Une Visite inopportune* as Copi himself lay dying at the Hôpital Claude-Bernard. Recalling that Copi himself was "enormously amused" by his new text, Lavelli qualifies the play as "une pièce tonique"[29] (a tonic piece).
    Attending Cyrille is his friend and longtime admirer Hubert Dubonnet, who has come to show him aerial photographs of the mausoleum (equipped with television room and giraffe-skin chairs) that he is having constructed for Cyrille at Père Lachaise Cemetery. Enter two other characters: a handsome young journalist seeking a deathbed interview, who turns out to be Cyrille's disappointingly straight (in both senses of the word) son; and a madcap diva, Regina Morti—all of whose lines are sung in Italian—who wants to marry Cyrille in order to play his mourning widow. A quarrel ensues as to who will have the rights to Cyrille's corpse. Regina Morti, having her own *pànteon* constructed in Genoa, proposes that Cyrille's remains be allowed to summer in Italy. Intractable, Hubert points out that it is "strictly illegal to send corpses on vacation, even within the Common Market" (*Visite*, 24).

Cyrille, who has been pursued for his entire career by hysterical female admirers, is horrified by the diva's proposal. "I can't possibly marry you," he tells Regina Morti. "I'm afraid I have AIDS" (*Visite*, 22). Going into a mad scene, the diva attempts suicide with a roast-beef knife but accidentally chokes on a chicken bone from a buffet catered by Fauchon. Mistaken for a lobotomy patient by the nurse, who is stoned on Cyrille's opium, the diva is wheeled away to the operating room. Several scenes later, Regina Morti returns equipped with an artificial brain of Professor Vertudeau's invention and sets into motion a final mad scene culminating in an outbreak of pistol fire. In the midst of it all, there arrives a giant sorbet covered with bees. Professor Vertudeau, dressed for the tropics, reappears on his way to found an AIDS mission in Africa.

Cyrille, dressed for the role of Hamlet, stages his own death before the enthralled assembly. But it is only acting. An Aztec poison turns out to be nose drops. After the others depart, the play modulates into a lyrical dénouement in which Cyrille and Hubert prepare to set off to read Lorca in the moonlight under a cherry orchard in Père Lachaise Cemetery. But a fatal heart attack intervenes. In a deft tribute to Lorca's *Llanto por la muerte de Ignacio Sánchez Mejías (Lament for Ignacio Sánchez Mejías)*, Copi punctuates Cyrille's peaceful and untheatrical death with three lines of elegant simplicity:

> [CYRILLE:]   Hubert, quelle heure est-il?
> [HUBERT:]   *Las cinco en punto de la tarde, señor.*
> [CYRILLE:]   C'est l'heure. (*Visite*, 73)

Recalling that Molière died on stage while playing *Le Malade imaginaire*, Copi's friend Guy Hocquenghem invokes philosopher Gilles Deleuze's distinction between "*ironistes*" and "*humoristes.*" Copi, Hocquenghem insists, is a master of the latter tradition, a tradition more Jewish or Argentinean than French. For Copi, Hocquenghem observes, no subject—not even AIDS—is taboo: "Rire de tout . . . ce n'est pas mépriser les malades mais être victorieux contre la souffrance et la peur, la haine et l'égoïsme"[30] (To laugh at everything . . . doesn't mean making fun of those who are ill; rather, it represents a victory over suffering and fear, over hatred and egoism).

Nowhere is Copi's subversion of death and triumph of the imaginary more remarkable than in those lines in which Cyrille invokes the theater itself in a metaphor for the no-man's-land separating life from death:

> Dès les dernières scènes, j'ai toujours attendu avec impatience la fin d'un spectacle. Je voulais me débarrasser au plus vite de mon personnage. Quand le rideau est tombé, avant de regagner votre loge, il y a un instant où vous n'êtes personne. C'est un plaisir inimaginable. Je vais essayer de me faufiler dans l'au-delà par l'un de ces trous noirs. (*Visite*, 62)

As soon as we used to get to the final scenes, I was always impatient for the performance to end. I always wanted to throw off my character as quickly as possible. Once the curtain's fallen, before getting back to your dressing-room, there's always an instant in which you're no one. It's an unimaginable delight. I shall attempt to sneak into the beyond via one of those black holes.

Guy Hocquenghem's name is inseparable from the history of the post-1968 gay movement in France. Because he was an early militant of FHAR ("Le Front homosexuel d'action révolutionnaire"), Hocquenghem's early writings[31] soon secured him a reputation as a leading theorist in European gay studies. A professor at the University of Paris VIII (Vincennes) and journalist at *Libération*, he began to publish novels in 1982 with *L'Amour en relief*.[32] The six years preceding his death in 1988 would see the publication of four more remarkable novels: *Les Petits garçons* (1983; The little boys), *La Colère de l'agneau* (1985; The wrath of the lamb), *Eve* (1987; Eve), and *Les Voyages et aventures extraordinaires du frère Angelo* (1988; The voyages and extraordinary adventures of brother Angelo.)[33]

Like *La Colère de l'agneau (The Wrath of the Lamb)*, his novel about the origins of Christianity, *Eve* was strongly influenced by Hocquenghem's seminar on Gnosticism and modernity at Paris VIII. That seminar would also lead to his writing (with philosopher René Schérer) the philosophical work *L'Ame atomique* (The atomic soul).[34] According to Hocquenghem's friends and students, Olivier Leclair and Bernadette Perrin, *Eve* did not begin as an AIDS novel; rather, it grew out of Hocquenghem's passionate research into the phenomenon of identical twins. The writing of *Eve*, however, coincided with Hocquenghem's own HIV diagnosis. The subject of AIDS, recall Leclair and Perrin, "seemed to invade the novel as it was being written, transforming a projected psychological study about narcissism into a philosophical meditation on the problem of suffering."[35]

Though *Eve* proved Hocquenghem's greatest popular success, Parisian critics did not generally seem to understand the extent to which he had successfully revived a long-defunct genre in French literature: the philosophical allegory. One interviewer, completely misunderstanding the function of the *invraisemblable* (improbable) in the novel, asked the writer, "Isn't it all really a bit too melodramatic . . . a story about a young woman sleeping with her homosexual uncle at the moment he learns he has AIDS, . . . genetics, Nazi war crimes, international drug trafficking?" Hocquenghem's reply is instructive: "You couldn't compliment me more than by saying I've written a melodrama. I adore this literary genre which says something essential about the human condition: that nothing of what happens to us is just. . . . The hospital is the modern equivalent of Greek tragedy."[36]

Eve opens with a commando raid on the AIDS ward of a Parisian hospital by a splinter group of the Islamic Revolution. Intent upon purifying the world of the "germ of Sodom," the militants rip IV's from the arms of the patients and proceed to a perfunctory "trial." Taunting the narrator that he has never "known" a woman, they prepare to execute their mission. Machine-gun fire breaks out. A telephone rings. An answering machine picks up. It has only been someone's nightmare. Or is the nightmare just beginning? Adam Kadmon, 40-year-old-novelist and expatriate Argentinean, comes to consciousness to find his bedsheets drenched by the onset of inexplicable nightsweats.

Hocquenghem adores manipulating the improbable. The plot of *Eve* begins to unfold when Adam catches a glimpse in the metro of a young woman who appears to be his double. Is she the daughter of his sister Anne, who left Paris after the events of 1968 to found a feminist commune in the depths of the provinces? Or is she his daughter, conceived the single time he was maneuvered into making love with Judith, another feminist who has relentlessly pursued him for years? Introduced to Eve by the sinister Boy, Adam falls under her spell when he takes her to the gay ball held on the Quai de Tournelle on Bastille Day.

Urged by his publisher to write (for once) a novel with a female character, Adam stages a visit to his sister's feminist commune in the Berry, where he finds the clock has stopped at the year 1968. Adam and Eve, fleeing from the spectacle of the feminist furies ("exalting in the death of this enormous male") eviscerating a hog, steal away to make love for the first time in the dovecote. But the exquisitely erotic episode is interrupted just at the moment of penetration. Judith, her bloody mallet still in her hand, appears on the scene to denounce the act as incestuous. At this very moment, Adam is summoned to take an emergency phone call from Paris. His doctor, just returned from the Stockholm conference, reveals that his "LAV" ("HIV") test is positive (*Eve*, 134–39) This hair-rising scene, a veritable coup de theatre revealing Hocquenghem's uncanny sense of timing, breaks the novel at its midpoint.

Like characters out of Voltaire's *Candide*, Hocquenghem's protagonists are swept onward by fate and coincidence to the New World. Forced to leave their island paradise after they murder Boy, they are pursued by his avengers to Kadmon's native Argentina. Their encounter with the darkly baroque world of Adam's family—perhaps an echo of Hocquenghem's visit to Argentina with Copi in the mid-1980s—begins to reveal the reason for Adam and Eve's strange resemblance. They are identical twins, products of a Nazi experiment in which Adam's mother had taken part near the end of World War II. The second embryo produced by the experiment—the future Eve—had remained frozen in a Parisian hospital until Judith discovered it in 1968.[37]

Responding to criticism that his thesis is too fantastic, Hocquenghem later told one interviewer,

Pour émouvoir, de nos jours, il faut faire plus fort, plus réel, plus brut que les journaux et la télé. Tous les grands romans sortent des faits divers. J'ai toujours eu le fantasme de me prolonger à travers un clone féminin de moi-même. . . . Je rêve d'une société où les pères et les fils pourront appartenir à la même génération grâce aux manipulations génétiques. . . . C'est certainement la parenté qui est à l'origine des guerres et de la société hiérarchique.[38]

In order to move people these days, you have to make things seem stronger, more real, more hard-core than what they read in the newspaper and see on T.V. The greatest novels emerge from items in the news. I've always had the phantasy of extending my own existence via a feminine clone of myself. . . . I dream of a society in which fathers and sons will be able to belong to the same generation. . . . Wars and social hierarchy no doubt derive from [vertical] kinship.

In Uruguay, Adam and Eve encounter Seth, the last survivor of a Black tribe descended from escaped slaves. Under Seth's aegis, Adam undergoes a powerfully narrated ritual burial and resurrection. Once again in flight, the trio make for Seth's tribal homeland in Senegal. But that mythical paradise has been decimated as well. In the midst of utter desolation stands a Club Méditerranée surrounded by thick cacti on which starving children impale themselves in an attempt to reach a garbage dump. Again tracked down by Boy's associates, the three steal a yacht and make for France. During a storm at sea, the terrible truth emerges. Eve, who had double-crossed Boy, has been using Adam's medical condition as a front in order to transport suitcases of cocaine back to France. Impenitent, she reveals that she is 15 weeks pregnant.

Up until this point in the novel, AIDS has largely loomed in the background. The novel's action has been punctuated by a series of dream sequences and allegories. One of these evokes the role of Eve (Sophia, Hawa, Norea) in the Gnostic account of the Creation (*Eve*, 145–47). Another fantasizes about the existence of a neo-Gnostic cult founded by a disciple of nineteenth-century French physiologist Claude Bernard.[39] This cult, celebrated in the Church of "Saint-Juste et Marie Curie," is, of course, a parody on the religion of modern medicine. Its adherents swear to the precepts of "Hygiene," "Knowledge," and "Truth" (*Eve*, 190–92). A third allegory chronicles the fate of a utopian community founded in the remote Italian countryside. Devoted to free love, physical beauty, and the destruction of "moral prejudice," this community thrived for five ("Or was it ten?") years. One evening a beautiful stranger arrived among them and ended up making love to all the utopians. The following year the first cemetery had to be opened:

Ils étaient étonnés et profondément atteints; ils n'avaient pas pensé à la mort. . . . Quand ce devint une épidémie, ils jetaient [les morts] dans les fosses et refusaient d'en parler; et la vie et les chants et les chambres d'amour continuèrent, jusqu'à ce que la maladie qui leur rongeait les entrailles eût fait son oeuvre, et les eût détruits jusqu'au dernier. (*Eve*, 115–16)

They were surprised and profoundly afflicted; they had never thought about death. . . . When it became an epidemic, they flung [the dead] into common graves and refused to talk about them; and life, and the singing, and the orgy-rooms continued, until the disease, eating away at their insides, had done its work and destroyed every last one of them.

The final 85 pages of *Eve* are explicitly and brutally invaded by the subject of AIDS. Allegory gives way to a realism that would have delighted the Goncourt brothers. Adam lies mortally ill at the Hôpital Pitié-Salpêtrière ("a name which makes even Parisian taxi drivers slightly uneasy") (*Eve*, 225). Life in the hospital, Adam writes to Eve, is also a "voyage": "Voyage sur place, voyage entre les services, voyage dans la souffrance et la mort" (*Eve*, 265; A journey while standing still, a journey between departments, a journey into suffering and death).

Hocquenghem evokes the dehumanizing daily rituals of the cult of the hospital. Its high priests, professional and detached, subject their initiates to an interminable series of "petits gestes" (little procedures). Among the most terrifying is Adam's liver biopsy. On a television monitor, he watches a steel thread descend downward through a vein in his neck. Once in contact with the organ, the sound bears its teeth and tears away a bloody piece of tissue. Adam, reliving the torture of Prometheus, realizes that doctors have fulfilled the inquisitor's ultimate fantasy: "turning the body inside out like a glove so as to render an individual's most intimate parts entirely visible, to spread them out and palpate them at leisure" (*Eve*, 275).

But worse is yet to come. Another "petite biopsie . . . sans grandes conséquences" (little biopsie . . . of little consequence), imposed to document an obvious diagnosis of *Pneumocystis carinii* pneumonia, turns out to be a torture of the damned from which Adam never really recovers (*Eve*, 297–304). His worst fears, articulated during the first week of his hospitalization, are realized: "Je ne crains pas la mort, je crains la souffrance. . . . J'ai peur de l'acharnement thérapeutique; mon corps, mon pauvre corps douloureux, crucifié, demandera la paix" (*Eve*, 269; I don't fear death, I fear suffering. . . . I'm afraid of treatments undertaken out of desperation; my poor hurting, crucified body will cry out for peace).

Hocquenghem dedicated *Eve* to AIDS specialist Willy Rozenbaum, "dont l'action mérite certainement mieux que l'humour amer de mes dernières pages" (*Eve*, 7; whose efforts merit more than the bitter humor of my final pages). By distancing his own doctor from his portrait of physicians in *Eve*, Hocquenghem reminds his readers that he is not writing an autobiographical novel. Hocquenghem's personal experience, of course, provided grist for his fictional mill. But Adam Kadmon is not Guy Hocquenghem. Adam is a character with an existence all his own, a rare achievement in French AIDS literature to date. As if to emphasize this, Hocquenghem suppresses Adam's narrative voice in the course of his last surgical ordeal and switches to a disarming use of the third person.[40] Adam regains his voice—but only as a character, not as narrator—only once in the novel's final pages. Hocquenghem permits him to say good-bye to his doctor, who is leaving France to take a more lucrative post in America. Fear of abandonment by the caregiver, evoked with such black humor in Copi's *La Visite inopportune*, here takes on another face. Dr. Samael, suddenly more human, places "deux baisers discrets" (two discreet kisses) on the cheeks of his dying patient (*Eve*, 309).

In the maternity ward of the Salpêtrière, Eve prepares to give birth. She is attended by Judith and Anne, certain that the baby will be of the feminine sex. Meanwhile, Adam, slipping in and out of a coma, hears a voice murmuring a prayer in Spanish:

> *Passe donc de corps en corps*
> *Subis des tourments nouveaux*
> *Brebis perdue loin du père . . .*

> Go now from one body to the next
> Submit to new torments
> Lost sheep far from the Father . . .

Feeling the end near, Adam is granted a mystical vision: "cette vie éternelle dont son corps n'avait été qu'un hôte provisoire, le phénotype apparent, cette ligne de gènes qui s'étendait devant lui et continuerait après, royalement indifférente, immortelle, insensible" (*Eve*, 311; that eternal life of which his body had been but a provisional host, the visible phenotype, that line of genes which stretched out before him and would continue after him, royally indifferent, immortal, insensible"). In the maternity ward, his infant son is being born: a being perfectly identical to him yet separated from him by 40 years. In the instant of his last breath, Adam's soul leaps out of his hollow chest, traverses the hospital, and enters the tiny body of another Adam.

Hocquenghem's final vision in *Eve* turns on the ancient doctrine of the transmigration of souls, a belief that separated many of the early Gnostic sects from orthodox Christianity. In *La Colère de l'agneau*, Hocquenghem imagines his distinctly Gnostic Christ as having heard the ancient teachings of the Buddha during his sojourn among the Essene community.[41] It is perhaps not surprising that Hocquenghem's final religious and philosophical position was the subject of considerable speculation at the time of his death. Parisian readers have long demonstrated an inordinate interest in the subject of deathbed conversions. Two hundred years later, controversy still surrounds Voltaire's purported reception of the Catholic last rites. Hugo Marsan, evoking the spectacle of a largely atheist Parisian intelligentsia finding themselves at a Catholic funeral service for a gay activist and writer "connu pour sa libre pensée" (known for his free thought), argues that Hocquenghem's request for a religious ceremony was a final militant act aimed at forcing the Church to confront AIDS and homosexuality (Marsan, 84–85). Certain of Hocquenghem's friends, on the other hand, recall that the writer's desire to receive symbolic last rites was the product of a deep personal (albeit unorthodox) mysticism.[42]

From a literary perspective, the details of Hocquenghem's final philosophical thoughts are perhaps less important than the fact that his penultimate novel[43] transcends the autobiographical constraints limiting so much of the new literature of AIDS. Brilliantly renewing the genre of the philosophical novel, *Eve* sets the problem of suffering within the context of the founding myths of European culture. In its quest to overturn the established hierarchy of parents over children, it is a very radical book indeed. In its rereading of Gnostic thought via the optic of modern genetics, it points the way to a genuine mysticism of modernity.

Hocquenghem's teacher, philosopher René Schérer, recalls his student's favorite aphorism: "Vivre allégoriquement" (live allegorically). According to Schérer, the conflict between the aesthetic and utopian dimensions of the homosexual ethos and the reality of the modern world had always been a major theme in Hocquenghem's works. Hocquenghem, the most celebrated gay militant of his day in France, never thought of homosexuality as a simple sexual orientation but as a "vision du monde" (vision of the world). And between homosexuality and mysticism, Schérer insists, there exists an inevitable analogy: "L'homosexualité est, contre ce monde, ou en marge de lui, un état de perpétuelle contestation: elle espère, elle entrevoit un ailleurs"[44] (Homosexuality, inscribed in the margins of the world, exists in a perpetual state of contestation against it. It hopes. It catches a glimpse of the Other).

January 1991

Hervé Guibert's last two works—L'Homme au chapeau rouge (Gallimard) and Cytomégalovirus: Journal d'hospitalisation (Seuil)—appeared less than a month after his death on 27 December 1991. La Pudeur ou l'impudeur, Guibert's film chronicle of his final illness, was broadcast on French television on 30 January 1992, provoking controversy within the Parisian AIDS community. Contrary to

Hugo Marsan's prediction, the NAMES Project ("le Patchwork des noms") did catch on in France in the course of 1991. With the dramatic worsening of the AIDS crisis in Paris during the past year, the massive denial among that city's gay community described in the foregoing essay now seems as remote as that of San Francisco or New York in 1984.

9

"All the Elements of a Good Movie": Cinematic Responses to the AIDS Pandemic

KEVIN J. HARTY

> AIDS has all the elements for a good movie—drama, passion, tragedy.
>
> —*Vito Russo*

The late Vito Russo's comment[1] notwithstanding, those who make films in Hollywood and for television have hardly rushed to provide general audiences with films about AIDS and AIDS-related issues.[2] Indeed, Hollywood could be accused of virtually ignoring AIDS as subject matter for film. The Academy of Motion Picture Arts and Sciences did award *Common Threads: Stories from the Quilt* the Oscar for best documentary in 1990 and did subsequently nominate Bruce Davidson for an Oscar as Best Supporting Actor in 1991 for his role in *Longtime Companion,* but no major studio has released a film that treats AIDS—"better *Batman* than the boy next door dying of a sexually transmitted disease" (Goldstein 1990, 300).

Television has had a slightly better record in dealing with AIDS.[3] Primetime shows from *St. Elsewhere* to *thirtysomething* have developed continuing story lines that touch on AIDS, and even sitcoms have not totally shied away from the topic.[4] AIDS, too, has been the subject of a number of "disease of the week movies" on both American and British television. Yet, given the enormity of the AIDS pandemic, the length of time that the pandemic has raged and will doubtless continue to rage, and the myriad problems—medical, legal, religious, social, psychological, and emotional—that accompany the pandemic, filmmakers generally continue to ignore AIDS.[5]

Billed as "the first dramatic movie" about AIDS when it premiered on September 12, 1985, at San Francisco's Castro Theater, Arthur J. Bressan, Jr.'s *Buddies* uses a familiar enough cinematic device—the eventual coming together of an odd couple—in an attempt to dispel the at times still current myth that AIDS is solely a sex-related matter. Written in five days and filmed in nine, *Buddies* was first shown as part of a benefit for the Shanti Project, a San Francisco–based organization that provides support for people with AIDS. The film's two main characters are David Bennett (David Schacter), a typesetter working on a book about AIDS, and Robert Willow (Geoff Edholm), a longtime political activist. While not that far apart in age, David and Robert are at least a generation apart in their attitudes about their gayness and at first about AIDS. David volunteers to be an "AIDS buddy" and initially appears in Robert's hospital room wearing a surgical mask, gown, and gloves to offer Robert an attractively gift-wrapped box of candy. Robert in the midst of a relapse of PCP is frank about his sexual preference and adamant about the importance of gay politics. In contrast, David is almost still in the closet.

Robert slowly begins to convince David to change his attitudes. As Robert's condition worsens, David brings some of the cherished items from Robert's apartment to his hospital room, where together they watch home movies of past Gay Pride marches and of Robert and his former lover Edward. As his involvement with Robert increases, David gradually starts to imagine himself in Edward's place. Asked what he would do with 24 hours of good health, Robert quickly answers that he would make love with Edward and then catch a plane to Washington to picket the White House for increased AIDS funding.

David is soon telephoned by a reporter doing research for an article about people with AIDS and their buddies, but he at first panics about coming out so publicly about his gayness and his involvement with AIDS. Robert convinces him that the article will be beneficial to everyone who is affected by AIDS, and David goes ahead with the interview. When David subsequently arrives at the hospital to show Robert a copy of the printed interview, he finds that Robert has died. David then hops the first plane to Washington and stands alone outside the White House with a sign protesting the government's indifference to AIDS.

Buddies presents the lives of two ordinary people confronted by an overwhelming obstacle, AIDS. At first almost polar opposites, the two men come to understand, support, and respect each other. By the film's end, the two have almost become one, united by a double tragedy: the tragedy of those who die from AIDS and the tragedy of those who support the dying and live on after them. But most significantly, *Buddies* is unapologetic in its treatment of a wide range of gay issues, not just sex. Richard Goldstein notes in his review of the film that it is sexually explicit but that Bressan "won't succumb to the lure of self-hate: he refuses to blame either the actors in the film or the men watching it for the fate that's befallen them. Instead, he suggests that desire remains a bond between us, even in the face of death."[6]

In contrast NBC's *An Early Frost*, American television's first film to deal with AIDS, could not be more "closeted" in its treatment of homosexuality.[7] The movie first aired on November 11, 1985, and has been subsequently released on videotape. *An Early Frost* is one in a long line of telemovies using disease as a plot that goes back to *Brian's Song*, a 1971 factual drama about a football player's fight against cancer. While *An Early Frost* gets points for being factual about AIDS, it quickly loses them for its lack of frankness about homosexuality. The telemovie presents the story of Chicago attorney Michael Pierson (Aidan Quinn), a person with AIDS who happens to be gay, rather than a gay person who has AIDS. Nowhere does the film make allowance for an expression of affection between gay characters. Michael and his lover Peter (D. W. Moffett) never touch, never even share an emotional moment together, let alone kiss.

In allowing him to make the film, NBC gave the film's director, John Erman, three precautions:

- The picture shouldn't throw the country into panic.
- The medical facts should be accurate and up-to-date—right up to air time.
- There should be a balanced view of the homosexual life-style—the film should not endorse it or knock it.[8]

The writers and directors did not really take the second precaution entirely to heart. Key scenes in the film, such as the one in which Michael's doctor tells him he has AIDS, were shot in such a way that new dialogue could be inserted if medical advances were made before air time, but a reference to the fact that AIDS is transmitted by the exchange of bodily fluids had to be deleted from the script.[9] The scene between Michael and his physician frames doctor and patient, although Peter, Michael's lover, is sitting at his bedside. By ignoring Peter in this key scene, the film denies its audience an experience of his reaction. Instead, in the next scene, Peter boldly struts out of Michael's hospital room "to talk with the doctor," as if somehow such a macho display of nonemotion will set things straight—pun intended. Later, when Michael returns to their home, Peter's reaction is limited to his bringing Michael a sandwich to eat so that he can keep up his strength. The telemovie's only emotional scene between the two lovers shows Michael throwing Peter out of the house, after Peter confesses that he has not always been monogamous in their relationship. The confrontation is less than subtle in its moral under-pinnings: Peter's promiscuity may have been responsible for Michael's infection with the AIDS virus; some people are, after all, just "carriers" of the virus.

Although Michael, the central character, is clearly gay, the telemovie deals with this potentially problematic fact by classifying gays into categories. Michael, the respected lawyer who has fast-tracked to be a partner in his firm, does contract PCP, which leads to his first hospitalization, and suffers from a Toxoplasmosis-related seizure, which leads to the second; but for the most part, other than weight loss, which is noticeable even to his family, he is spared the ravages of AIDS-related diseases. However, one of the telemovie's minor characters, Victor (John Glover), gets less antiseptic treatment. More flamboyant than Michael, Victor, a former cook, who once he is diagnosed with AIDS is fired from his job, thrown out of his apartment by his roommates, and abandoned by his family, battles PCP, Toxoplasmosis, and Kaposi's Sarcoma (KS), an ailment that plagues other members of the PWA support group who briefly appear in one scene in the telemovie. (To the script's partial credit, that support group includes a straight man, a former IV-drug user, and a person of color, but there are no women with AIDS.) Victor does have a message to deliver about the possibility of dignity in the face of death that is not lost on Michael, though the effect of that message on the members of a typical television audience would probably be counterbal-anced by what they would doubtless see as his "stereotypical" gay flamboy-ance.

An Early Frost is not without its educational value. Michael's mother (Gena Rowlands) reads all the appropriate weeklies in which stories appear seeking to dispel the increasing number of myths about AIDS. And she gets to put her reading to good use when she must, time after time, almost platitudi-nously tell people—her husband, her daughter, the paramedics who refuse to transport the ailing Michael to the hospital—that AIDS cannot be contracted through casual contact. Indeed, the women come off somewhat better in the telemovie than do the men. Faced with Michael's simultaneous revelation of both his sexuality and his illness, his father (Ben Gazzara) lashes out at him, almost striking him. The two paramedics are men, and the bedside manner of the doctors (all male) in the telemovie pales when compared with that of the film's nurses (all female). Michael's sister (Sydney Walsh), after some initial fears for the safety of her child and the baby in her womb, comes to embrace Michael; and his grandmother (Sylvia Sidney) demands more than a simple peck on the check from Michael, reminding him that her own husband faced ostracism by the ignorant when he battled cancer years ago.

An Early Frost's sympathies clearly lie with the traditional family. An article in *People* trumpeted the film as "a shattering AIDS TV movie [that] mirrors a family's pain."[10] Although its main character has AIDS, *An Early Frost* really examines the effect of the illness on Michael's family—to the exclusion of his lover—rather than on Michael himself. The telemovie celebrates the resilience of the traditional family in the face of this, and by extension, any other tragedy or challenge. At the film's end, Michael goes back to Chicago to die, and one can only guess if he is also going back to Peter. His family has, however, healed itself of any rifts; indeed, the final credits roll over a family Christmas portrait from happier times, when they were all healthy in body, heart, and soul.

Director William Freidkin said of the negative reaction in gay circles to his 1970 movie *The Boys in the Band*: "This film is not about homosexuality; it's about human problems. I hope there *are* happy homosexuals. They just don't happen to be in my film."[11] Bill Sherwood's 1986 film *Parting Glances* presents us with gays who are as happy as their straight counterparts. *Parting Glances* is a different kind of AIDS movie than either *Buddies* or *An Early Frost*. Although one of the main characters, Nick (Steve Buscemi), does have AIDS, the film is more generally an examination of the world of upwardly mobile Manhattan gays in the mid-1980s.[12]

Parting Glances chronicles 24 hours in the lives of Nick and two of his friends, Robert (John Bolger) and Michael (Richard Ganoung). Michael and Robert have been more or less happily coupled for six years. Michael, a "Ken doll" clone, works for a world health organization and has just had himself posted for two years to Africa because, we eventually learn, he fears that his relationship with Michael is becoming routine.

Michael's past, however, involves Nick. When Michael first moved to New York from Wisconsin to attend NYU, he met Nick, who introduced him to New York's gay subculture. Nick, now a successful rock musician, clearly offered Michael a road not taken, a road that Michael just as clearly at times seems to regret not having taken. Although he is genuinely in love with Robert, Michael has still not abandoned the love he had for Nick. Indeed, he confesses at one point in the film that Nick has been his only true love.

Nick, while looking gaunt enough, shows no visible signs of the disease. He clearly understands the seriousness of his situation, but he is at times able to laugh in the face of death. The film includes a wonderful parody of the visit of the Commendatore at the end of Mozart's *Don Giovanni*: here the Commendatore appears to Nick not to urge repentance but to report that heaven is not all that it is cracked up to be. If nothing else, *Parting Glances* argues that the anguish of AIDS need not preclude the joy of life. Nick is too busy trying to live to worry very much about death. His friends seem to worry more about him than he worries about himself. Nick remains for Michael a road not taken, a road that could have led to happiness but that could have just as easily led to AIDS. But, in *Parting Glances*, all is not doom and gloom. Happiness is still there, albeit there is a cloud hanging over everyone's head. Nick is, however, unapologetic about his life and the choices he has made, and he teaches Michael, eventually Robert, and by extension the film's audience, a valuable lesson in the face of the AIDS pandemic—the importance of a life without regret.[13]

British television exhibits much greater frankness in two telemovies about AIDS—ITV's *Intimate Contact* (1987) and BBC2's *Sweet As You Are* (1988)—which share qualities woefully missing from a telemovie such as *An Early Frost*. Both, however, focus on heterosexuals with AIDS.[14]

Intimate Contact tells the story of a middle-class wife, Ruth Gregory (Claire Bloom), who must confront ignorance and prejudice when her husband Clive (Daniel Massey) contracts AIDS after a liaison with a New York prostitute while away on a business trip. In chronicling Clive's gradual deterioration, *Intimate Contact* also chronicles the personal growth the couple experiences as they come to accept the inevitable: Clive's death.

When first informed of his diagnosis, Clive reacts with arrogance; Ruth, with dismay, first believes her husband is homosexual and then wishes he had cancer instead. But the enormity of the problems they soon face transforms them as they become heroic in their own separate, simple ways. When Ruth seeks comfort from friends and family, that comfort is not always readily forthcoming. Their daughter Nell (Abigail Cruttenden) stands by her parents but must drop out of school because of the taunts of her schoolmates. Their son Martin (David Phelan), a recent university graduate who has his eye on a political career under the auspices of the Tories, decides political loyalties outweigh familial ones and rejects first his father and then his mother. Bill Stanhope (Mark Kingston), longtime friend and company physician, indiscreetly reveals Clive's illness, and Stanhope's business associates and clients drop him one after another. In an especially appalling scene, Clive shows up for a luncheon meeting only to have all his workmates leave him sitting alone at the table. The local vicar is a sanctimonious cad who hints that AIDS may be a form of divine judgment. Ruth's golf club members stab her in the back and caution others not to drink out of Ruth's glass; eventually they ask her to resign from the club.

Intimate Contact is in many ways the most catholic movie to deal with AIDS. It gives voice to a wide range of people upon whom AIDS has had an effect, and it shows the full range of stupidity and prejudice that they must endure. The main story line—how Ruth and Clive deal with his diagnosis, deterioration, and death—is constructed broadly enough to allow for a series of secondary story lines involving other characters in similar situations. A young hemophiliac who has contracted AIDS from a blood transfusion suffers ostracism at school. His father and Ruth form a special bond and eventually become lovers. A fellow golf club member is a recovering alcoholic trying to regain custody of her children. A former IV-drug user who now has AIDS provides Clive with an opportunity to overcome his self-pity and to share his fears and expectations with someone else. A gay man whose lover is dying of AIDS offers Ruth his friendship as they desperately pool their efforts to keep their mates alive.

Most impressively, *Intimate Contact* does not hesitate to suggest that the AIDS pandemic presents society at large with a moral obligation to react to the disease with compassion and humanity. Too often, however, as the film shows, ignorance and prejudice win out. Parents give into their hysteria and attempt to bar a child with AIDS from school. Social clubs and business organizations bar the doors to those with AIDS and even to those close to people with AIDS. The church offers condemnation rather than comfort. Even in death, Clive is not spared indignity. The pallbearers must be paid off before they will take his casket out of the hearse. *Intimate Contact* suggests that moralizing has no place in the pandemic, and the telemovie offers a wealth of facts to counterbalance the all too readily available pious posturing.

Sweet As You Are is a more modest telemovie. The seemingly happy marriage of college lecturer Martin Perry (Liam Neeson) and his wife Julia (Miranda Richardson) is shattered when Martin receives a postcard telling him to report to a public health clinic; a former student whom he bedded has contracted AIDS. Martin learns that he is HIV positive; Julia tests negative. *Sweet As You Are* does not take Martin's medical condition any further; rather it uses his HIV status as a way of examining straight middle-class values. The telemovie's director, Angela Pope, points out that the straight middle class thinks of marital infidelity as an issue plain and simple and ignores the implications such infidelity has in the age of AIDS.[15]

In a sense, *Sweet As You Are* simply replays the time-honored battle of the sexes with new and more frightening stakes. Julia first denies Martin any contact with their daughter, and then, in a tirade, she sees the danger he has exposed her to in terms of a whole pattern of male abuse and exploitation of women ("It's men who buy the pornography. It's men who rape" [*SAYA*]). There are fewer villains in *Sweet As You Are* than in *Intimate Contact*, though a clinic that promises quick results from HIV antibody tests and charges exorbitant fees for their services is held up to particular scorn. Rather as in *Buddies, Sweet As You Are* traces the disquieting effect AIDS has on the lives of quiet, ordinary people and shows how in their ordinariness they have depths of strength on which they can rely in the face of the pandemic.

Theater rather than film has led the way in producing cultural responses to the AIDS pandemic. Three plays—William Hoffman's *As Is*, Harvey Fierstein's *Tidy Endings*, and Terrence McNally's *Andre's Mother*—have been adapted for and shown on television. Both *As Is* and *Tidy Endings* survive transfer to the screen intact. For broadcast on television, *Andre's Mother* becomes a different and even better teleplay.

As Is originally shared the New York theatrical spotlight with Larry Kramer's *The Normal Heart*.[16] It was, in contrast to the Kramer play, the less angry one, the one without self-hatred, the one that said sexual relations between men were still okay. *As Is* tells of the effect AIDS has on Saul (Jonathan Hardary) and Rich (Robert Carradine). Former lovers who separated, they are now reunited when Rich is diagnosed with AIDS. Their story is played out against a background of friends, family, and medical personnel who provide a context for the story. In *As Is*, Hoffman provides a wealth of information: information about medical developments and breakthroughs, about the politics of AIDS, about the social history of gay New York, and about the array of emotions that AIDS can produce, both in the people who have it and in those who care for them.

Hoffman asks us to view AIDS and those affected by it (actually and potentially) *as is*, without apology or pity. His characters are fallible human beings who make no moral judgments about their lives, and Hoffman asks us to do the same. In an almost Brechtian way, *As Is* offers a suggestion of hope in the face of admittedly overwhelming obstacles, a hope tempered by a challenge to the audience that solutions to the AIDS pandemic lie not within the play or its teleplay but within themselves. Without denying the toll that AIDS has already taken and will continue to take and without brushing off the very real nightmare of contracting a disease for which there is no known cure, Hoffman suggests that where there is life there is hope. The last words in both the play and the telemovie belong to a former nun who works in an AIDS hospice (Colleen Dewhurst in the teleplay): "[I]t's a privilege to be with people when they are dying. Sometimes they tell you the most amazing things. The other night Jean-Jacques—he's this real queen, there's no other word for it—he told me what he misses most in the hospital is his corset and high heels. I mean he weighs all of ninety pounds and he's half-dead. But I admire his spirit. . . . Last night I painted his nails for him. . . . Flaming red. He loved it" (*As Is*, 96–97).

The teleplay of *Tidy Endings*, originally part of Fierstein's trilogy *Safe Sex* in which it is entitled *On Tidy Endings*, adds an initial scene to the play's script during the opening credits in which Arthur is pointedly excluded at the cemetery from the mourning rituals and at Marion's apartment when the gossip about the cause of Collin's death is less than sympathetic.[17] Both play and teleplay present a meeting between Arthur (Harvey Fierstein) and Marion (Stockard Channing) to tidy up the affairs of Collin Redding, who has recently died of AIDS-related causes. Arthur is Collin's lover; Marion, his ex-wife. *Tidy Endings* becomes a battle between the two for the right to mourn, with society systematically denying Arthur the right to mourn. During the opening credits, he is not allowed to scatter dirt upon the grave, his name is omitted from all of Collin's obituaries, and Marion takes it upon herself to answer all the notes of condolence addressed to them both and to draw up a list of which of Collin's possessions should go to whom as mementos. Unlike the other films discussed so far, *Tidy Endings* focuses only on those who mourn and wonders how they can possibly survive their tremendous losses.

From society's point of view, Marion's lot is the easier. Society respects the rights of former wives to mourn; divorce is no impediment to grief. But society is less kind to surviving same-sex lovers. (A quick survey of the obituaries in both the gay and the straight press shows there is not even any agreement about what to call the survivor—longtime companion, partner in life, primary partner, or the more euphemistic "friend" all appear in death notices.) Arthur demands the right to mourn, and he demands recognition of his loss. "This is not your moment of grief and loss," Arthur yells at Marion. "It's mine!" (*Tidy*, 95).

Complicating Arthur's problems is Jimmy (Nathaniel Moreau), Collin and Marion's 11-year-old son. In some ways wise beyond his years, he is obviously confused about his father's death and resentful of Arthur, whom he naturally blames for that death. "He's been looking for a scapegoat since the day you and Collin first split up. Finally he has one," Arthur tells the incredulous Marion (*Tidy*, 85). In *Tidy Endings*, Fierstein argues that common emotions unite all people, gay and straight. Even more, AIDS affects all people, gay and straight. Although no one in either the play or the teleplay actually has AIDS, in an ironic twist, the script reveals that Arthur has tested negative for the AIDS virus, whereas Marion is HIV positive. Because she is afraid of infecting either her new husband or the child that they plan to have, she, like Arthur, has invested in "rubber futures." In the final analysis, *Tidy Endings* is a plea for definition and recognition, and Jimmy finally brings both elements to the play and teleplay (*Tidy*, 112).

Terrence McNally's *Andre's Mother* also focuses on those who are left behind. Here the issue is not who has the right to grieve but who has the capacity to grieve, and unlike *Tidy Endings*, *Andre's Mother* offers no catharsis to its title character. On paper, the play is just three pages long and takes fewer than 10 minutes to perform. As a teleplay, it runs just under 50 minutes.[18] The play and teleplay focus on a memorial service for Andre Gerard. Andre, an actor with, we are led to believe, extraordinary talent and great potential, died of AIDS-related causes and was buried back in Dallas in the family plot. The memorial service, held in New York, takes place several weeks after the funeral.

In the play, Andre never appears; in the teleplay, we see his back, his leg, his arm. In both, we learn about Andre from others. The play takes place in Central Park where Andre's mother has reluctantly joined his lover—Cal— and Cal's father and sister in a ritual that early on came to be associated with people mourning loved ones who died of AIDS-related causes. Each of the four holds a white balloon. Cal explains to Andre's mother that "They [the balloons] represent the soul. When you let go, it means you're letting his soul ascend to Heaven. That you're willing to let go. Breaking the last earthly ties" (*Andre*, 192).

The teleplay begins inside a church where friends and family have gathered to remember Andre. In a series of flashbacks, the teleplay introduces us to

Andre's life and shows us the first meeting between Cal (Richard Thomas) and Andre's mother (Sada Thompson). Other flashbacks include encounters between Cal, Andre's mother, and her mother—Andre's grandmother (Sylvia Sidney). In one scene as mother and daughter squabble in a restaurant, Cal excuses himself, announcing he has never had a more unpleasant meal in his life. Mother and daughter continue arguing and are dressed down by a gay waiter who tells them not to be patronizing or condescending to him or to anyone else about being gay. Andre's mother, we learn, has never acknowledged her son's sexual preference, and her failure to do so has put an insurmountable barrier between her and her son. Her failure to connect with Andre follows him to his grave.

Cal is more than valiant in his attempts to placate her, both before and after Andre's death. But she remains immovable: "[Cal:] Do you remember the comic strip *Little Lulu*? Her mother had no name, she was so remote, so formidable to all the children. She was just Lulu's mother. 'Hello, Lulu's Mother,' Lulu's friends would say. She was almost anonymous in her remoteness. You remind me of her. Andre's mother" (*Andre*, 193). Because they can open up to each other, Arthur and Marion in *Tidy Endings* attain an inner peace that Andre's mother is incapable of finding. Although they are both still scared by Collin's death, Arthur and Marion have healed a sufficient number of wounds to be able to get on with their lives. As Cal releases his balloon quoting *Hamlet*, Andre's favorite play, Andre's mother stands alone quivering, on the verge of a breakdown, but ultimately defeated by denial. Cal is at least shored up by his grief, and his father (Richard Venture) and sister (Haviland Morris) by their acceptance of the life Cal and Andre had with each other, a life that enriched all who took the trouble to know the two as lovers. In *Andre's Mother*, AIDS is a mirror in which the full tragedy of what McNally describes as "missed opportunities" and an "inability to connect even in the most primary relationships" can be viewed.[19] Here the only victim—an offensive term when applied to a person with AIDS—is Andre's mother.

All the cinematic treatments discussed so far are nothing if not tasteful. *Ein Virus Kennt Keine Moral* (*A Virus Knows No Morals*) by German director Rosa von Praunheim (longtime *nom du cinéma* of Holger Mischwitzki) makes no pretensions of being tasteful. Von Praunheim shares Larry Kramer's anger. His film is agitprop, sprinkled with a generous dose of gallows humor.

A sinister researcher, Dr. Blood (Maria Hasenaecker), visits Africa to find the cause of the epidemic. Bitten by a monkey, she contracts the disease. Marxists proclaim that AIDS brings power to the proletariat. A group of drag queens stages Poe's *The Masque of the Red Death*. Later they return dressed as nurses to sing "You have your fate in your hands" to the tune of "He's Got the Whole World in His Hands." A woman journalist (Eva Kurz) who works for a scandal sheet plays to the hysteria and prejudice that surround the pandemic by turning her camera on the worst of human excesses. Later, wearing a dildo, she attempts to spy on her son (Christian Kesten) in a public restroom frequented by gays in search of sexual liaisons. Still later in the film, she catches her son masturbating while gazing at a photograph of tennis star Boris Becker. A primal scream therapist (Regina Rudnick) brings her gay patients tiny pink coffins, so they can shrink into them and experience their own deaths. A sex-crazed woman screams she wants a child by a gay man "before they all die out." The government quarantines everyone infected with the HIV virus in a death camp known as "Hellgayland," where Christmas will be celebrated once a month in recognition of the detainees' anticipated demise. The film's central character, Rudiger (played by von Praunheim himself), runs a gay bathhouse and lives off the potential infection and misery of others by distracting his customers with the latest safe sex pornography imported from America. Himself infected, alone, and abandoned by his mother (Thilo von Trotha) and his lover (Dieter Dicken), who tells him "Everyone is going to die in a nuclear war anyway. You're just going to die a little sooner," Rudiger blithely cruises a wooded area where the branches of trees and bushes hang heavy with used condoms. Three night nurses on duty in an AIDS ward roll dice to see who will die first this evening: "Mr. Lulu Patabooloo will go first. The die is cast." A German radio program delivers a chronicle of the pandemic that includes the following tidbits: "AIDS patients thrown from the fourth floor. . . . Gay-beating becomes a sport. . . . Theatres [are] closed around the world. . . . [There are] no lights on Broadway."

There is, of course, much to be angry about in the AIDS pandemic, but this very dark film has an additional, and unnecessary, dark subtext. Almost all the villains in the film—the therapist, the researcher, the journalist—are women who are portrayed as hysterical monsters. Von Praunheim's misogyny seems to know no bounds. Taken to task for it in Toronto during a discussion that followed a screening of the film, von Praunheim is reported to have said that "'gay men have the right to portray women this way,' particularly their mothers, whose sons try so hard to please them, 'and all you get is shit.'"[20] The larger message of von Praunheim's film is that a virus may have no morals, but people do. The director himself could use a lesson in morals.

Von Praunheim's fury and frustration spill over again in two documentaries—*Positiv* (*Positive*) and *Schweigen = Tod* (*Silence = Death*)[21]—neither happily marred by even a hint of misogyny. *Positiv* views the AIDS pandemic through the eyes of artists affected by it. Specifically, it features playwright Larry Kramer, documentary film director Phil Zwickler, and singer Michael Callen, who are clearly in von Praunheim's view among the pandemic's heroes. The villains, the documentary argues, are much more numerous. The film castigates government for its murderous inaction and society at large for using AIDS as a means of tapping into its long-standing bigotries. The film's focus is broad, encompassing the issues of safe sex, homophobia, the meaning of death, healing techniques, and AIDS-related drama. (The film includes scenes from a production of Robert Chesley's *Jerker*.) *Positiv* also contains some interesting juxtapositions. As members of ACT UP (the AIDS Coalition to Unleash Power) are shown shouting at do-nothing politicians, members of a healing circle sit around tickling each other to release their pain.

Schweigen = Tod follows a similar tack by examining the pandemic through the visions of writers and artists who have made AIDS the subject of their work. The film opens with a piece of performance art designed to shock even the most blasé audiences. Emilio Cubiero, playing someone with AIDS, announces he has become a victim of both germ warfare and those who say he deserves his lot in life. Faced with such a no-win situation, he announces he will kill himself. Vowing to die the way he lived ("I've always been an asshole in one sense, so there's no better way to go out"), he bares his rear end, sticks a gun up his rectum, and shoots a fake bullet. As blood gushes out, he falls over dead.

Other artists who appear in *Schweigen = Tod* include poet Allen Ginsberg and painters Keith Haring, who has since died of AIDS-related causes, and David Wojnarowicz. Ginsberg announces that the whole world has AIDS and that we must all "practice safe sex with Mother Planet." Haring is shown working feverishly on a complicated erotic mural: "This painting is about nostalgia. It's not about anything that could happen now." Wojnarowicz claims the lion's share of the film's attention. His comments are made against a background of disturbing visual collages he has created depicting a world out of control. At one point, he appears with his lips sewn together; at another he announces he wants no memorial: instead, his dead body, he declares, should simply be dropped on the front steps of the White House.

ABC's telemovie *The Ryan White Story* takes a decidedly safer approach to the AIDS pandemic with no intent to offend. Basically a morality play, this fact-based telemovie pits Ryan (Lukas Haas) and his mother Jeanne (Judith Light) against the citizens of Kokomo, Indiana, the most disagreeable single-minded group of yahoos one can imagine. The telemovie spans a four-year period from 1984 to 1987. Ryan, a hemophiliac, contracts AIDS through a blood transfusion. The citizens of Kokomo quickly ostracize him and his family. Ryan is soon banned from the local high school. Faced with her son's death, Jeanne tries to comfort him, asking him what more than anything else in the world he wants. His response, "I want to go to school," galvanizes her to take the school board to court.

The press quickly picks up on the story and soon rivals the local citizenry in its insensitivity to Ryans' plight. Banned from attending classes or public activities, Ryan is forced to take classes by phone. In one touching scene, Ryan throws the telephone that is his only link to school across the room. His mother, in her own disconsolation, presses her face against a window in Ryan's bedroom to hide her tears from her son, only to find the faces of the members of the press corps, with cameras running and notebooks and pens at the ready, staring back at her. George C. Scott plays the lawyer who takes

Ryan's case against the school board. Ryan's grandparents (Mitchell Ryan and Grace Zabriskie), as well as a sympathetic school nurse (Sarah Jessica Parker), offer all the support they can. Ryan's sister, Andrea (Nikki Cox), at first jealous that her brother is the center of the family's attention, eventually rallies to his support. White himself appears in the telemovie as Chad, a fellow hemophiliac who has contracted AIDS. The strength of *The Ryan White Story* lies in its celebration of the small victories in the lives of the title character and his mother. They finally win their lawsuit but decide to move to another town in Indiana, where they are welcomed with open arms. The telemovie ends in a freeze-frame of the actors playing the White family that fades into an image of their real-life counterparts. In that last scene, Ryan, who looked sickly when playing the role of Chad, beams the smile that became his trademark up to the time of his death. The happy ending is underscored by the telemovie's soundtrack in which Elton John defiantly sings his "I'm Still Standing."

While is is almost impossible to find fault with *The Ryan White Story* itself, the television networks cannot escape their continuing fair share of criticism. Without diminishing in any way the genuine courage and nobility that Ryan White displayed in his life, it would be less than ingenuous not to point out that what attracted ABC to his story is clearly the fact that Ryan was one of the "innocent victims of AIDS," a phrase heard too often on the lips of those in the media and in public life. The implication is, of course, that others may be "not so innocent victims." The telemovie does provide a forum for public education. But what about the people for whom television is unwilling to feel compassion? What about the majority of those who contract AIDS for reasons other than a blood transfusion? Where did the tainted blood that infected Ryan come from? Television is clearly capable of manipulating its audience's emotions;[22] regrettably, it does so only with safe AIDS-related issues.

Selecting a situation to portray is, of course, necessary in any artistic response to an issue. My criticism of *The Ryan White Story* is not directed at its selecting Ryan White as subject (the plight of hemophiliacs diagnosed with AIDS needs to be told), but I object to the reasons behind that selection: telemovies such as *The Ryan White Story* pander to heterosexual audiences for whom it is a safer story to film than stories about others who suffer from AIDS. Two commercially distributed films, *Men in Love* and *Longtime Companion*, both of which trace the effects of AIDS on two different communities of gay men, are also selective in their response to the AIDS pandemic, but with very different results.

Despite its director's good intentions, *Men in Love* may be the silliest movie yet to deal with the AIDS pandemic. The film opens in San Francisco as Steven (Doug Self) gathers with friends to mourn the death from AIDS-related causes of his lover Victor. As one of its strong points, the film rightly suggests that in the age of AIDS, in an attempt to deal with the pandemic's overwhelming toll, communities of friends have replaced more traditional family units. As in *Andre's Mother*, the mourners soon move outside to release balloons signifying that they have let go of their grief. In accordance with Victor's wishes, Steven then flies to Hawaii to scatter Victor's ashes. There Steven encounters Robert (Emerald Starr), Victor's former lover, now chief guru in a New Age gay commune. The tension of their first meeting is in no way dissipated when Steven criticizes Robert for failing to come to Victor's bedside when he was asked to do so, and Robert replies that he did indeed visit Victor's deathbed spiritually through a "vision quest." Most film audiences would doubtless share Steven's skepticism and anger about all this mumbo jumbo. When told of the balloon ceremony held back in San Francisco, Robert replies with seemingly unintended bathos that when the balloons fall to earth, they will be swallowed by dolphins, which will then choke on them and die.[23]

Robert and Steven eventually reconcile their differences, and another caring community gathers in Hawaii to scatter Victor's ashes. The dialogue here, though, is again likely to cause eyes to roll. While Steven's journey to Hawaii clearly marks an ending, it also signals a beginning. True to form, *Men in Love* raises some significant issues only to undercut them with strained or silly dialogue. At the commune, Steven meets Peter (Joe Tolbe), a gardener, and the two begin a courtship. The film gets high marks for addressing issues with which Steven's viduity presents him. How soon after Victor's death should he start dating? Should he have the AIDS antibody test? And if he tests positive, will someone still love him? In turn, can he still love someone if he finds out that a potential new lover is HIV positive? The sexual encounters between Peter and Steven are done tastefully, and they provide valuable education about safe sex techniques. But when Steven runs off to a cave to undertake a Polynesian ritual of self-discovery and subsequently emerges covered with mud but healed, the audience is simply led to believe, in the words of *Variety*'s reviewer, "that overacting [is] apparently good for the soul."[24] The film's director, Marc Huestis, defended the film's spirituality in an interview: "There are going to be people who will roll their eyes when they see this film and say 'Oh, God, this is completely out there.' . . . But I also think there's a large element, particularly in the gay community, that would be really refreshed by seeing it. There's definitely a lot more of a spiritual movement in the gay community because of AIDS and what we have been through."[25] Whether that spirituality is so easily reduced to Tantric chants is, however, a matter of some debate.

Longtime Companion has been the closest thing to a mainstream film about AIDS that has been made so far; it was produced by PBS's American Playhouse but distributed by Samuel Goldwyn. In some ways a cinematic counterpart to Randy Shilts's *And the Band Played On*, but without the weight of statistics or the overt outrage, the film chronicles the effects of the AIDS pandemic on a group of New York gay men and their friends. The film covers eight years from 1981 to 1989 but focuses on what happened on one day in each of those years. The film opens on July 3, 1981, the day when the *New York Times* ran its first major story about a then rare disease spreading among gay men. A year later, John (Dermot Mulroney), a friend of the film's central character Willy (Campbell Scott), lies in a hospital ward violently ill and soon dies. Soon one after another of this group of attractive, bright young men is affected by the disease. Some die; others watch those they love die. By the time the film ends, the number of AIDS-related deaths in the United States alone had reached 80,000.

Longtime Companion charts gay awareness of the growing pandemic through Willy's eyes. At first horrified, then concerned, then paranoid, Willy comes of age in the face of AIDS. If criticisms can be lodged against the film, they are that the world the film portrays is exclusive and that the film suffers in its attempts to resolve the issues it raises.

The characters in the film all belong to the Fire Island set. They are all white, good looking, well off, and successful. While John must suffer the indignities of a public ward and overcrowded emergency rooms, the other hospitalized characters enjoy semiprivate and even private rooms. There is only one female main character; the lone black in the film appears marginally as a home health-care worker; and the only Hispanic is an understandably angry AIDS patient who must listen to a dressing down from Willy, his AIDS buddy, about how he does not have the right attitude about his condition.

The film's ending sequence is problematic. It depicts a gathering on the beach at Fire Island where the living and the dead join for one more happy time, as if the events of the past eight years had never occurred. If, as Bruce Davidson has said, the film is about more or less "ordinary people in extraordinary circumstances who have no choices," the never-never land ending ultimately runs counter to the film's real theme.[26] The painfully complex issues raised by the movie remain disappointingly unresolved by its sentimental ending.

These criticisms aside, *Longtime Companion* is unflinching in its honest depiction of the effects of AIDS on the lives of the characters. The most moving events in the film involve Dean (Mark Lamos), a television script writer), and his lover, David (Bruce Davidson). David's wealth enables them all the luxuries—except good health—that money can buy. After Sean gets sick, we see him gradually deteriorate in scene after scene, until David helps him to die or, as the film as it, "to let go." AIDS activates others. The actor Howard (Patrick Cassidy), who had previously feared being typecast if he took gay roles, becomes the master of ceremonies for a show written and performed by actors with AIDS. Willy's show business lawyer-lover, Fuzzy (Stephen Caffrey), staffs the telephones at a support group for people with AIDS, dispensing free legal advice and offering free legal assistance. If selective, the accumulated losses depicted in the film are nonetheless as staggering as the bravery and endurance of those who care for the sick and dying are inspirational.

The Oscar-winning documentary *Common Threads: Stories from the Quilt*, narrated by Dustin Hoffman, is built around the AIDS Memorial Quilt made by the San Francisco–based NAMES Project. The quilt consists of hand-made, decorative panels memorializing those who have died of AIDS-related causes. *Common Threads* sees the political indifference of the Reagan (now Bush) administration as tantamount to criminal negligence and criticizes society at large (and Eddie Murphy in particular) for its insensitivity to those who are affected by AIDS. As the documentary's codirector Jeffrey Freidman noted, "[O]ne of the things we have to learn about AIDS is that trying to assign it some larger meaning is off the point. The enemy is the virus."[27]

While railing against the many things there are to rail against in the AIDS pandemic, *Common Threads* tells the stories of five people. Sara Lewinstein, a lesbian, recalls her life with Dr. Tom Wadell, a former Olympic athlete and one of the founders of San Francisco's Gay Games. After they had had a child together, Wadell discovered he had AIDS, and the documentary shows him preparing audiotapes for his daughter to listen to after his death. Sallie Perryman stood by her husband Robert while he tried to kick his drug addiction. By the time their child was born, Robert had developed full-blown AIDS. Sallie has since tested HIV positive. Vito Russo became an AIDS activist after his lover, Jeffrey Sevcik, died from AIDS-related causes. Twelve-year-old hemophiliac David Mandell, Jr., contracted AIDS from a blood transfusion. He appears in the documentary along with his parents, Suzi and David, Sr. Navy commander Tracy Torrey, who made a panel for his dead lover David Campbell, discovers he, too, has AIDS and begins work on his own panel. While *Common Threads*, like the quilt itself, speaks volumes through its moments of silence, its strongest message against bias and hatred comes from the young David Mandell: "'We didn't come from a different planet. We're still the same beings that they are. We just have . . . a little difference in ourselves. And I don't see why anyone should put some person down for that.'" *Common Threads* shows the quilt in all its massiveness displayed on the mall in Washington, D.C., a city of memorials, and celebrates the quilt's unique role as a living memorial (unfortunately, new panels continue to be added daily) to those who have died during the pandemic.

All the films surveyed here simply show how much more needs to be done to provide a cinematic record of the many faces of AIDS and those it affects: children and adults; men and women; gays, straights, and bisexuals; people of all colors; IV and injectable drug users; hemophiliacs; residents of the new and old worlds and the third world. In contrast to the cinematic response to AIDS, the theatrical one has, as I indicated earlier, been more immediate and forceful. As Don Shewey notes:

Compared to television's live coverage every night of the latest election campaign or hostage crisis, theater may seem like a cumbersome form of communication lagging behind in dealing with urgent issues of the day. Yet theater can also lead, asserting its ancient function as a public forum in which a community gathers to talk about itself. The best contemporary example is the theater's response to the AIDS crisis. . . . [It] took the lead in promoting education on AIDS and concern for the afflicted, a social obligation that the press, the government, even made-for-TV movies were slow to pick up on.[28]

The Hollywood film and made-for-TV movie industries have yet to weigh in with their equivalents of Larry Kramer's *The Normal Heart*, William Hoffman's *As Is*, Harry Kondoleon's *Zero Positive,* or Robert Chesley's *Jerker*.

10

AIDS Enters the
American Theater: *As Is*
and *The Normal Heart*

JOEL SHATZKY

When William Hoffman's *As Is* opened in early March 1985 at the Circle Repertory Theatre, followed a month later by Larry Kramer's *The Normal Heart* at the Public Theatre, they were not the first plays on the subject of AIDS produced in this country. Jeff Hagedorn's monologue *One* was performed earlier, and in 1984 Seven Stages Theater of Atlanta produced *Warren* which was performed in Hawaii and San Francisco. *The Aids Show*, which originated in San Francisco, also preceded the New York debuts of *As Is* and *The Normal Heart*.[1] But, as with most other shows that do not become "visible" to the national media until they are given a New York production, it was the latter two that established the basic approaches to the dramatization of the AIDS epidemic: personal reaction and public outrage.

By the time *As Is* opened, the AIDS epidemic had finally become widely recognized because it had already claimed 5,000 lives. This number was mentioned in several reviews of the plays[2] as if to legitimize the anger expressed in both plays. Jack Kroll in *Newsweek* seemed, in fact, to be apologetic in explaining that "these plays, however, are not 'homosexual' plays; they enact situations and raise questions of universal concern for everyone, straight or gay, male or female" (Kroll, 87). William Henry, in *Time*, commented that "these AIDS plays reach out to heterosexuals, both for help in combatting the disease and to warn that it is spreading into the 'straight' population" (Henry, 85).

Of course, both *As Is* and *The Normal Heart* are very specifically about gay relationships, the problems that straights have in understanding and accepting gay sexuality, as well as the problems gays face in trying to deal with the disease that is destroying them. For although there are stylistic differences between the two plays, they are quite similar in their expression of the feelings between the lovers whose tragedy provides the emotional thrust of both dramas.

The relationship between Rich and Saul in *As Is* is at the center of the play. The play begins with their "divorce" when they decide on who is to take which pieces of furniture from the apartment they have shared. The bantering tone, however, is punctured when Rich reveals, after the two catalogue the deaths of their friends who have been victims of AIDS, "I have it."[3] The rest of the play records the progression of the disease, Rich's anger and denial, his wish to kill himself, and his coming to terms with his illness. At the end, the two men, now emotionally lovers again, wish to consummate their relationship with "something safe" (*As Is*, 60). The play ends with the two together in Rich's hospital bed, the curtain drawn by a sympathetic hospice worker.

Although the love between two men in *The Normal Heart* is not nearly the central focus of the play as in *As Is*, there are a number of parallels in the development of the relationships of the lovers in each play. Ned Weeks, the protagonist of *The Normal Heart*, is not the jilted lover who must be reconciled; instead he begins a relationship with Felix, a man very reticent about his gayness and fearful he might lose his job. Felix, in fact, had been formally married, and Ned chides him for not fighting to see his son: "That means you're ashamed. So he will be too."[4] But in many ways the plots of the two plays are similar. Just as Rich reveals his illness to Saul, Felix confides in Ned his suspicion that he is coming down with the disease. Just as there is a scene of rage and denial between Rich and Saul, there is one between Felix and Ned, who laments, "Whoever thought you'd die from having sex?" (*TNH* 2: 116). And just as Rich and Saul consummate their love for each other at the end of *As Is*, Felix and Ned go through an informal marriage ceremony just before Felix dies (*As Is* 2: 122).

In both plays there is an estrangement and a reconciliation between one of the men and his brother. In *As Is*, the brother has found it extremely difficult to cope with Rich's gayness, but he embraces him in his hospital bed (*As Is*, 1: 52). *The Normal Heart* ends with an embrace between Ned and his brother, Ben (*TNH*, 2: 123). The act of reconciliation is significant in both plays because it indicates the protagonists' need to "connect" with their families while asserting their own conviction in who and what they are. Despite Kroll's and Henry's observations, these family connections are the only gestures the authors make toward the straight world. The consummation scenes, however, are a more clear indication of the assertive stance presented by Hoffman and Kramer; this stance is more difficult to maintain than twenty years ago because although the triumphs of the sixties and seventies established gays with the right to their own life-style, the public's attitude toward AIDS has put many gays on the defensive.

These structural parallels aside, however, the plays are very different in their approach to the problems of AIDS. This difference is reflected in the critics' reactions to these two dramas. In contrasting them, one critic notes, "There's no trumpet call to action in *As Is*, instead merely—merely!—an effort to accept impending death."[5] Another remarks on the play's "softness" and criticizes it for its upbeat ending "sentimentality"[6]; whereas a third praises *As Is* for being more than "a documentary account of an AIDS victim's grotesque medical history . . . [the play] reaches out to examine the impact of AIDS on hetero- and homosexual consciences as well as to ask the larger questions (starting with 'Why me?') that impale any victims of terminal illness."[7]

The critical reaction to *The Normal Heart* is far more contentious, not only because of the play's polemical content and harsh tone, but also because of the playwright's willingness to "name names" of those he feels should be confronted with their callousness and cowardice because they did not act even when the magnitude of the disease became obvious. Although one critic agrees that Kramer's indictment of the Koch administration is valid because the city failed to respond more quickly and seriously to the epidemic, he also dismisses the play as "a pain in the neck," "a long rant from a pamphlet on AIDS," and having "an amateurish script" (Berman, 569). Another observes that "Kramer's play . . . is less literate and poetic than *As Is*, but more rousingly polemical, more politically and morally challenging."[8] *New York Times* critic Frank Rich reacted to Kramer's accusations in the play by defending his paper: "Some of the author's specific accusations are questionable, and, needless to say, we often hear only one side of inflammatory debates." He adds, "The writing's pamphleteering tone is accentuated by Mr. Kramer's insistence on repetition—nearly every scene seems to end twice—and on regurgitating facts and figures in lengthy tirades."[9] On the same page as the review, the *Times* even included a denial of Kramer's accusation that the *Times* had failed to cover AIDS and the defense that the newspaper had sent a member of the science staff to cover the story as soon as it had been informed of the existence of the disease (Rich, *"The Normal Heart,"* 17). In an article several weeks after this review, Mel Gussow in the *Times*, although observing that *The Normal Heart* "mixes fact, fiction and dramatization in the manner of a Costa-Gavras movie," also concedes that "Mr. Kramer's play has a historical perspective both in its treatment of homosexuality and its attitude toward public apathy."[10]

Other critics praised Kramer for his polemics, for example, "Like the best social playwrights, Kramer produces not a series of debates but a cross-fire of life-and-death energies that illuminate the many issues and create a fierce and moving human drama" (Kroll, 87). Another critic felt that Kramer "dishes up highly imaginative invective, not least toward a character based upon himself" (Henry, 85). Both plays were given praise for the courageousness with which they approached the subject, but because of the political nature of Kramer's work, it created a greater variance of opinion among the critics.

These reactions from the New York critics indicate that unlike many plays that are judged on the basis of aesthetic qualities in terms of script, production, and performance, *As Is* and *The Normal Heart* had created an audience that attended as much to the political and social content of these works as to their dramatic vitality. As Mel Gussow observed, "Though English dramatists from John Osbourne to David Hare to Caryl Churchill have been concerned—and in some cases, obsessed—with questions of public portent, American dramatists have generally tended to neglect this area while contemplating questions of a more psychological and behavioral nature. When they have explored politics, it is often through a smoke-screen of symbolism" (Gussow, 3). Arthur Miller's "The Crucible" could be cited as such an example; the play uses the Salem Witch Trials to create a parallel to McCarthyism. But in the case of the two AIDS plays, as Gerald Weales concedes, "Neither work seems to me a particularly distinguished play, but the enthusiastic and obviously moved audiences are not simply expressing their approval of the plays and the performances, which are fine in both cases. They are responding to subject matter" (Weales, 406). It is precisely because neither playwright tried to treat the AIDS epidemic in symbolic terms or to compromise his portrayal of gay men that these dramas have had such an electrifying effect on their audiences. This forthrightness is characteristic of gay literature of the last decade and is an active expression of the gay community's political as well as social agenda: to go beyond a request to be "accepted" by straight society to an affirmation of their own cultural and sexually identity. *The Normal Heart* and *As Is* share this assertiveness.

When one compares the two plays, however, it is clear that the authors have contrasting responses to AIDS. Hoffman's play, although tinged with anger, is very much a nostalgic—and, at times, satiric—look at the "good old days." The character Saul recalls, "I was at the gym soaking in the hot tub when I first heard about AIDS. It was how many years ago?" (*As Is*, 1: 27). As the disease progresses, Rich becomes more nostalgic, remembering his youth: "I was a good kid, but I was lonely and scared all the time. I was so desperate to find people like myself that I looked for them in the indexes of books—under H. I eventually found them. . . . And then I found you in a porno theatre." (*As Is*, 2: 48).

In addition to Rich's wistful remembrance of his past, Hoffman also presents a satirical view of the gay scene in the late seventies before the AIDS epidemic rendered that world desolate:

CLONE 2: Thought you were this guy Chip I met here on Jockstrap
    Night.
CLONE 1: Haven't been here since the Slave Auction. (*As Is*, 1: 20)

The main point of Hoffman's play is to reach the audience through depicting the humanity and suffering of the two central characters as well as other, more anonymous figures who share in this suffering. One critic found in Rich the "Camille image" of someone's "gentle . . . wasting away" (Weales, 407). But there is also anger in Rich: "I can't afford to be noble. The only thing holding me together is rage. It's not fair! Why me?" (*As Is* 2: 58).

Not confident that he will make his point by focusing solely on his central characters, Hoffman intersperses the scenes depicting Rich and Saul's relationship with monologues of a hospice worker, two men responding to panic calls on an AIDS hotline, and several anonymous men and women who reveal "the first time I heard about it" (*As Is* 1: 27–29). None of the characters other than Rich and Saul are really developed, so despite the nonpolemical focus on them, Hoffman feels obligated to try to expand and extend his emotional territory to include a cross-section of those members of American society who have been affected in one way or another by the disease. It is as if he has an impulse to be polemical, but his method dictates that he reveal his main theme through a love story.

The Normal Heart takes much the opposite approach. It is a roughly autobiographical account of the circumstances surrounding the beginnings of the AIDS epidemic in New York and Kramer's activity in the Gay Men's Health Crisis, which helped counsel and comfort those who were stricken with the disease from its outset. In the three years chronicled in the play, 1981–84, Kramer takes on such members of the Establishment as the *New York Times*, Mayor Koch, the Centers for Disease Control in Atlanta, and the entire medical profession. Kramer is criticized for "almost smother[ing] his play by dropping great chunks of now unnecessary information on its opening section," and because the "rhetoric of accusation begins to get silly when the foot-draggers, from Mayor Koch to the members of the NIH committees, are presumed to be acting out of their fear of being found out as closet gays" (Weales, 407). Yet the play always proves to be lively, fast paced, witty, and dramatically effective when the playwright is dealing with issues and ideas as in the following encounter between Ned, several other members of his organization, and the Mayor's assistant.

NED: We have been trying to see the mayor for fourteen months. It
    has taken us one year just to get this meeting with you and you are
    an hour and forty-five minutes late. Have you told the mayor there's
    an epidemic here?
HIRAM: I can't tell him that!
NED: Why not?

HIRAM: Because it isn't true.
BRUCE: Yes sir, it is.
HIRAM: Who said so?
TOMMY: The government.
HIRAM: Which government? Our government?
NED: No! Russia's government!
HIRAM: Since when?
MICKEY: The Centers for Disease Control in Atlanta declared it.
TOMMY: Seventeen months ago.
NED: How could you not know that?
HIRAM: Well, you can't expect us to concern ourselves with every little
   outbreak these boys come up with. And could you please reduce the
   level of your hysteria? (*TNH* 2: 86)

This rapid-fire banter both is dramatically effective and contains some of the
information the playwright wants the audience to know about the callousness
of the mayor of a city that has a grossly disproportionate number of AIDS
cases, in part, undoubtedly, owing to the mayor's inaction when the epidemic
began. Even a critic who found much to object to in the tone and
presentation of the play admitted, in referring to Mayor Koch, "And lest
you're tempted to let him off the hook, the walls of the theater are covered
with damning statistics about AIDS and government response, and drawing
and quartering [of them] is the least that should happen" (Berman, 569).

Throughout the play there is conflict, with Ned Weeks as the focal point.
The conflict with the "outside" world of city officials and unresponsive
doctors, who even reject the application for a grant from the courageous
woman physician who pioneered research into AIDS, is mirrored by Ned's
conflict within his organization. Near the end of the play, he is told by the
organization's president that he is being relieved of his position. Bruce
regards Ned as "a bully" because Ned is so insistent in having his way in
dramatizing the horrors of the disease and the urgency with which it must be
met. Ned, however, feels that the organization is being "strangled" by the
timidity of the leadership and its reluctance to fight against the indifference
of the general public and, particularly, the mayor of New York (*TNH* 2:
113).

The momentum created by conflict, argument, even rhetoric, gives the play
an immense vitality, yet Kramer feels obliged to include the personal
relationship between Ned and Felix. But the repartee between the two seems
forced when Ned is not discussing his "cause."

FELIX: I have something to tell you.
NED: You're pregnant.
FELIX: I was married once.
NED: Does that make me the other woman? (*TNH*, 2: 75)

There are, in fact, only four scenes between Ned and Felix out of sixteen after they become lovers; the most dramatic is the one in which Ned tries to help Felix deal with his illness. But, structurally, the relationship between them is dealt with episodically, while the play's main thrust is the developing urgency of the AIDS crisis and Ned's increasing frustration in trying to get his colleagues and adversaries to deal with the epidemic as he thinks they should.

The contrasting approaches to the AIDS epidemic in these two dramas are reflected in later works, but the approaches are also prototypical of the dramatic treatment of other social and political issues. The most tempting analogy to AIDS, and one that I make with some reluctance because it has been so inappropriately overused, is the Holocaust. Certainly, there appears to be no evil antagonist who is deliberately killing the innocent victims of AIDS; nor is there the sense that the deaths of the victims are due to the arbitrary fact that they share a religious background.

Yet there are two significant characteristics of AIDS victims that make them similar to victims of the Holocaust: they are treated with apparent indifference by those who would seem to be able to mitigate the situation; and they are a "minority" group in some way, easily misunderstood, regarded as "different from the rest of us."

In the play, Ned makes the analogy to the Holocaust when he complains to Felix of the lack of coverage the papers have given the epidemic and points out that the *New York Times* and the *Washington Post* had buried the story of the Final Solution even though both newspapers were owned by Jews (*TNH* 1: 50). His feelings of rage at the cowardice and timidity of the leaders of the gay community bring him to see the connection between the victims of AIDS and the victims of the world's indifference to Hitler's barbarism.

Dramatic treatments of the Holocaust do reflect the two basic modes of presentation exemplified by *As Is* and *The Normal Heart*. The personal approach can be seen in such plays as the dramatization of *The Diary of Anne Frank* (1955) or *I Never Saw Another Butterfly* (1979) about the children of Theresienstadt. The more public, polemical approach can be seen in a confrontational play such as Hochuth's *The Deputy* (1963), which accuses Pope Pius XII of acquiescence in the murder of the European Jews. There are, of course, a vast array of dramas about the Holocaust that do not neatly fall into either category, but as Kramer suggests, aspects of the suffering of the victims and the indifference of the outer world that one finds in dramas about AIDS have echoes in Holocaust literature. One might find similar prototypes in African-American drama—the confrontational works of Ed Bullins and Amiri Baraka (LeRoi Jones) in contrast to the more personal approaches of Lorraine Hansberry and August Wilson. But repetition of this prototype only reflects that people who are oppressed will respond to their oppression in some basic ways: the impulse to humanize themselves so that others can understand them and the contrasting desire to indict those whom they feel are the cause of their suffering. What makes the analogy between AIDS and the Holocaust particularly apt, as Kramer sees it, however, is that danger not only comes from the common enemy; it also can be found within the victimized group in their fear and temporizing.

In their different approaches, *As Is* and *The Normal Heart* reflect the confusion, frustration, and anger the gay community faces in dealing with the AIDS epidemic. A recent anthology of plays about AIDS, *The Way We Live Now*,[11] shows that these two approaches have been adopted in a variety of ways.

In *Safe Sex* (1987), Harvey Fierstein bitterly satirizes the sexual lives of two gay men in the post-AIDS era. As the play opens, the lovers, Ghee and Mead, seem to be making love in the dark, but when the lights come up, it is revealed that they are lying flat on a balancing board, only their feet touching, a parodistic comment on Kramer's crusade for "safe sex." Ghee waxes nostalgic about "different times" (*TWWLN*, 93) and the play ends in an embrace. But the approach, although satirical, is meant to humanize the dilemma of the gay male faced with making a choice between physical love and physical safety.

In contrast, in a scene from *Angels in America* (1989), Tony Kushner re-creates an encounter between Roy Cohn, the notorious lawyer of the McCarthy era and his doctor. In indicting Cohn's hypocrisy in persecuting homosexuals while being a practicing homosexual who succumbed to AIDS, *Angels in America* is similar to *The Normal Heart* because it targets an important historical figure who should have helped bring attention to the disease instead of denying his connection with it. Cohn's rationale for his sexual behavior demonstrates his elaborate self-deception: "I bring the guy I'm screwing to the White House and President Reagan smiles at us and shakes his hand. Because *what* I am is defined entirely by *who* I am. Roy Cohn is not a homosexual. Roy Cohn is a heterosexual man . . . who fucks around with guys" (*TWWLN*, 134).

A number of plays in the anthology include a mixture of private reaction and public outrage. Terence McNally's *Andre's Mother* (1988) is a poetic elegy to a departed victim; Susan Sontag's *The Way We Live Now* (1989) combines elements of elegy with criticism of the casual attitude of doctors toward the disease. Although none of these works has the polemical energy and urgency of *The Normal Heart*, the changing attitudes towards AIDS have made such a play less appropriate than it was several years ago. Yet even today, indifference and ignorance about the disease still manifest themselves, particularly since it has now become less of an exclusively gay illness and more a disease of less articulate and well-connected victims—drug addicts and their spouses and lovers.

The theatrical response to AIDS by the gay community has been powerful and effective in bringing to the attention of the general public the dangers and tragedies that this disease has created. The two basic approaches to it have been evident from the outset: personal reaction and public rage as exemplified by *As Is* and *The Normal Heart*. But these responses are typical of articulate people who have been set apart from the rest of society because of society's ignorance and fear. The story of those who have no William Hoffmans or Larry Kramers or Susan Sontags among them is yet to be told, for they, too, have their tragedies but have not yet found the voices to cry out for them.

11

Rage and Remembrance: The AIDS Plays

D. S. LAWSON

As the incidence of Acquired Immune Deficiency Syndrome has spread, the literature dealing with or focusing on the disease has burgeoned. Ironically, at the same time that the virus is killing many men and women around the world, the body of literature surrounding AIDS seems to be growing with alacrity; as people sicken and die, the words flourish and live.

Early on in the plague, two plays—Larry Kramer's *The Normal Heart* and William Hoffman's *As Is*—established twin avenues of dramatic reaction to the situation. Borrowing terms from the subtitle of gay American composer John Corigliano's first symphony, I call these reactions rage and remembrance. Kramer's invective typifies the rage many feel at this microscopic killer and at the society that for so long ignored (and continues to ignore) the health and destiny of its gay brothers and sons and fathers and friends. Hoffman's nostalgic play defines a mode of remembrance, of sadness over freedom and innocence and pleasure lost; it is a wistful elegy for a world we can now only remember and hope to recapture. Of course, often these modes of dramatic reaction are mixed together in any given play, but I hope to show that many plays are primarily either rage or remembrance plays.

Since these two plays first attracted attention, many others have taken the epidemic and those it affects as subject matter—too many, in fact, for a coherent consideration in a short amount of space. Therefore, I would like to trace the threads of rage and remembrance in a small group of plays that have had New York productions and were written by gay male American playwrights. Lest these boundaries seem arbitrary or capricious, I would hasten to point out that, in America at least, gay men have borne and are continuing to bear the brunt of the disease and that New York, along with San Francisco, has been the site where the epidemic began and where attention to it has been focused.

The notoriety of Larry Kramer's *The Normal Heart* was responsible for one of the earliest encroachments of the disease into the dramatic culture of the United States. Certainly Kramer is a very angry man with many axes to grind in his play; the anger (sometimes vicious, sometimes righteous) gives *The Normal Heart* its power. The anger of gay men—whether caused by their oppression, their marginal position in society, the physical danger they often face, or the immediacy of death by AIDS—is a deep vein of ore for a playwright to mine. The rage surfacing in contemporary protest groups (most famously in ACT UP) is already present in Kramer's play.

The prevailing ideology of our times is anti-gay; the centrality of family, patriarchy, bourgeois values, heterosexuality, of work and money in society cannot be denied. In his play, Kramer indicts various aspects of society that are responsible for maintaining and inculcating the dominant ideology. The then nearly helpless medical profession, the legal system, and the press all come under merciless critique. Even good, caring doctors cannot cure or ease the pain of men who only quite recently were young and healthy; the refusal of the main character's brother—a high-powered lawyer—to do pro bono work on behalf of gay causes reveals the failure of the legal process and the family to help those victimized equally by homophobia and by microbes; the "marriage" ceremony at the play's climax underscores our society's unwilling-ness to give sanction to same-sex relations; the refusal of the "newspaper of record" for the United States—the *New York Times*—to give early, timely, and thorough coverage to gay issues foregrounds a tendency to ignore and exclude homosexuals and the issues which they confront from the public discourse. The death of a *Times* reporter from AIDS at the play's end only serves to highlight how the official organs of society (in this case, the press) are ignorant of the situation and plight of gay men (even those whom they know directly).

The play shows the state functioning in a variety of ways that exclude and marginalize its gay citizens. A reader can easily see the play as accusing American society—through all the state apparatuses depicted in *The Normal Heart*—of being directly complicit in the deaths of so many gay men. Given the powerful sanctions society places against homosexuality, as portrayed in Kramer's play, the wonder is not that gay men are dying, but that there were ever any gay men in the first place.

From its very title *The Normal Heart* seeks to challenge the dominant ideology. In citing W. H. Auden (virtually a gay icon), the title holds up an image of homosexual men contrary to that shown by society to itself.[1] These men are compassionate, they suffer and love, they get angry and take action, they fail or succeed much as straight people would, and they live or die in very ordinary, nonthreatening ways. Only when their rage prompts them to battle those elements of society that try to define them negatively or oppress them do Kramer's characters threaten; significantly, they do not molest children, camp up the national culture, or weaken the morale of the armed forces—in short, they threaten, but not in any of the ways society typically expects of gay men. They threaten only in hopes of obtaining a "normal" life. Even the specious "freedom" from commitment or familial responsibilities so accusingly thrown at homosexuals is absent here; these men care about each other in enduring, formalizing ways and must, of necessity, become a family for each other as there is no other real family for them to appeal to for help, succor, celebration, advice, or any other of the myriad functions allegedly served by heterosexually based, typically patriarchal family units.[2] In the words of the title, Kramer depicts his gay characters as having normal hearts—not as the sex-driven monsters of ideologically based stereotypes.

The play also treats gay issues figuratively. The famous scene in which a carton of milk splatters accidentally to the floor and ruins a sack of groceries is a case in point. Read abstractly, this scene features prominently the wasting of valuable, necessary, nourishing resources. Certainly on one level this might represent the waste of human potential as society first ignores and then allows the deaths of a large group of men who have a lot to contribute. On the other hand, the scene also depicts the inability of gay men to find the nourishment they need to live. Either reading of the scene makes clear the motivation for anger.

Kramer's abandonment of conventional stage realism—of a trompe l'oeil set—serves his interests well. The isolation of his characters and their actions from a recognizable landscape both allows a Brechtian distancing, whereby the audience can react critically and objectively to the play and formulate a politically correct response to it, and projects an image of homosexual men as pariahs, outcasts from a world whose ideology is so well perpetuated in literary and dramatic Realism.

In all western literary genres the realist mode has long been the most popular one. In direct ways, the dominance of realism on the stage threatens gay people and inculcates homophobia. The middle class, the family, the workplace and the home, and the subjugation of persons other than bourgeois, white, Christian males have been the almost exclusive focus of realism on the stage. If audiences over and over again see plays that depict this way of life (even if some individual realist works critique that way of life), would they not conclude that this way of life is somehow the proper one, perhaps the only one to be considered, perhaps even the only one available? Kramer wisely jettisons conventional realism; since he wishes to indict the society in which he places his characters, he does not wish to support that society by using a set of dramatic conventions that have long served that very society's interests.

The rage created by the AIDS epidemic is also present in Alan Bowne's play *Beirut*, the production of which caused a scandal even greater than that of Kramer's play. Certainly *Beirut* tells us many unpleasant and frightening things about both ourselves and the society we live in. Otherwise open-minded and perceptive theater critics responded to the New York production of *Beirut* with incomprehension and accusations; one reviewer even deemed the play a danger to society.

Perhaps a critic strictly oriented to gay theoretical matters would find *Beirut* a disappointment: Bowne has transferred AIDS to a heterosexual context; the characters seem in no important way to resist or resent their imprisonment by society; and the play ends with a genuflection to tradition-ally romantic (and, hence, heterosexist, patriarchal, and homophobic) no-tions of the primacy of a man/woman commitment despite overwhelming odds.

In Bowne's play, the Lower East Side of Manhattan has been transformed into a prison for people suffering from a nameless, sexually transmitted disease. The main action of the play involves an illegal (and initially unwelcome) visit from Blue (an uninfected young woman) to her boyfriend Torch. The play exploits the stereotype that domestic violence is inherent in relations between lower-class, relatively uneducated people as Torch and Blue repeatedly scuffle and push each other, while constantly firing off barrage after barrage of vituperative insults filled with personal attacks and curse words.

Certainly the characters are undesirable types. The only other character to appear on stage is a sex-starved guard who attempts to watch Blue and Torch having sex and is finally frightened off by fear of infection. In the outside world, sexual relations have been prohibited: pornography is rampant, and reproduction is accomplished exclusively in test tubes. The guard is uniquely in a position where he could have direct, immediate access to human sexuality, and he attempts to exploit this situation at the first opportunity.

It seems germane to note that one early conservative response to AIDS was to propose quarantining those infected with AIDS. In the play, disease victims are even tattooed in a private place so that those who potentially would have sex with them will be forewarned; this extreme measure was also proposed as an appropriate reaction during the early days of the AIDS crisis.[3] Bowne's fantastic, dystopian play twists this frightening suggestion around, applying it to young straights. Rather than seeing the heterosexual context of *Beirut* as a sell-out, I view Bowne's purpose here as pointing an accusing finger at the dominant heterosexual culture, the ideology behind it, and the power it wields; Bowne is asking, "What if this were to happen to men and women and not to men and men?" The strategy here is counterattack; Bowne tries to make the heterosexuals face the possibility that it could happen to them (as seemed likely at the time the play was written).

Obviously the title links the AIDS crisis to the situation in Lebanon during the time the play was written: various middle eastern factions fought for control of a once beautiful and cosmopolitan but now ruined and dangerous city. At the time, the Americans were involved in Beirut variously with naval forces deployed off shore, with marines occupying part of the embattled city, and with hostages held by several of the battling factions within the city itself. In a way, the Lower East Side never adequately becomes literally like Beirut, but the figurative connection is powerful and meaningful. Just as decades of failed, misguided U.S. policy toward Arabs in the middle east (significantly, like homosexual men, a group usually despised by the American public and often given highly negative stereotypical portrayals in vehicles of popular culture) helped to create the mess in Beirut, years of oppression and ignorance and fear of gay men—all of which was reflected in public policy—helped to fuel the AIDS crisis once it began in earnest. Like Kramer, Bowne blames the government and the society whose interests it represents for the explosion of the epidemic. Although the title *Beirut* is in some ways sensationalistic (and in purely literary terms cannot be seen as a total success), it does help to serve Bowne's purposes here and is another means for Bowne to express his rage at society.

The play's ending is undeniably disturbing: Blue forces herself on Torch so that they cannot be separated in the future; as she will have been exposed to the illness, she thus must be quarantined. Her desire to stay with the man she loves, to experience him sexually, and to share her life (and death) with him reeks of a romantic sensibility. In the face of a widespread epidemic that is killing thousands of people annually, the implication that some people willingly contract it and others willingly spread it in significant ways serves the prevailing ideology that this play seeks so strenuously to subvert.

Unlike Kramer's play, *Beirut* in no way abandons conventional realism. One might legitimately ask whether a play that coopts, uses, and projects techniques that for so long and so powerfully have served the bourgeois, phallocentric, heterosexist, patriarchal society could be a "gay" play. The best that can be said of Bowne's dramaturgy is that he attempts to use realism to accuse and to reject the type of culture and ideology that have made his work possible and necessary in the first place.

Joe Pintauro's *Raft of the Medusa* is another instance of the "rage" response to AIDS. Dramaturgically, the play is somewhat of a muddle, but undeniably it has important things to say about the crisis, those who suffer from it, and the society in which it is happening. The play suffers from rampant tokenism: there is one example of every kind of person likely to contract AIDS (a homosexual man, a prisoner, an intravenous drug user, a heterosexual woman with bisexual partners, a homeless person). Among Pintauro's characters there are men and women, anglos and Hispanics, blacks and whites, middle- and lower-class people.[4]

Pintauro organizes his play around a support group for PWAs headed by a heterosexual psychiatrist. Ideologically, one might object to Dr. Rizzo as a representation of the patriarchy and, indeed, he functions in certain respects as the paterfamilias to this group. Despite these negative elements, however, he is presented as enlightened and compassionate. He gives clean needles to Nairobi, a homeless, deaf, black woman addicted to drugs and infected with HIV. Like the doctors in *The Normal Heart*, though, he is utterly unable to cure those he seeks to comfort and help.

The realism of the support group scene is violated, however, by an apparently gratuitous frame of a deathbed scene at the opening of the play featuring the death of one member of the group (whose lover will remain in the group) as his parents watch in helpless sadness and regret. The ghost of the young man will periodically appear in the early parts of the play, but he is quickly dropped from the scheme later on. Pintauro seems not to know what to do with this frame once he has established it; it seems to belong to an early conception of the play that might best be abandoned in favor of a strictly realist format based on one particularly dramatic meeting of the support group.

Although the antirealist elements of Pintauro's dramaturgy would seem to serve the interests of a radically new, gay theater, in this particular instance they in fact weaken the play by confusing and obscuring the primary plot line and by pulling the audience in two directions at once as they try to integrate the surreal magic of the ghostly presence with the detailed realism of the support group. In this respect the play is hopelessly flawed. Notwithstanding these very real problems, *Raft of the Medusa* is a worthy addition to the "rage" plays.

Pintauro's rage, as might be expected, focuses on the society that permits (and even encourages) the epidemic. Among the group members is a man who contracted the disease in prison and a young woman who contracted it from her abusive, drug-addicted boyfriend. Certainly Pintauro means for the audience to connect the society's failure to deal with the problems of crime and drugs with the presence and spread of AIDS. Just as society's problems manifest themselves in a vastly overcrowded prison system and in violence against women, society's problems are also manifest in the AIDS crisis in which once again a small, relatively weak and helpless minority segment of society has been allowed to suffer while the majority refuses to help or even to acknowledge the problem.

As in Kramer's play, one character in *Raft of the Medusa* is a reporter. In this case, the reporter is merely posing as a person with AIDS to obtain information on a soap opera star who becomes a member of the group but who is not publicly out and whose antibody status is known to neither his fans nor his employers. Certainly this plot device is Pintauro's indictment of the media's attitude and response to AIDS; rather than informing and educating, the media in *Raft of the Medusa* seek to exploit and expose. Of course greed is the underlying motivation: "exclusive" news of the star's homosexuality and illness would sell papers in a way that reports on research or articles on safe sex would not.

When the reporter's true purpose for attending the group is revealed, in a genuinely effective and horrific scene Nairobi sticks him with a needle and allows him nearly to go mad with fear before acknowledging that she has pricked him with one of the clean needles just given to her by Dr. Rizzo. Is Pintauro here advocating or approving of extreme, potentially violent ways of forcing society to recognize and deal with the AIDS crisis? Certainly he condemns those who would exploit the epidemic, but his other purposes remain unclear.

Once again, the title of Pintauro's play is important. By citing the Gericault painting, Pintauro attaches his artistic response to a horrifying situation to another, more famous work of art with social significance. He may be arguing that art is a perfectly appropriate response to an ugly and deadly circumstance; also he seems clearly to hope that his art will awaken public awareness and raise concern for AIDS. Perhaps Pintauro also believes that his characters are like these people who were on *The Medusa*—adrift in an inhospitable world with precious little hope of survival.[5]

Another play that might aptly be described as a "rage" play is Ed Cachianes's *Everybody Knows Your Name*. Rather than directly attacking various "public" apparatuses in anger, Cachianes takes on the more difficult task of depicting the "private" rage of individuals whose lives are ended or disrupted by the epidemic. Most of the play's dialogue is written in a campy, "queeny" language utterly appropriate to the New York gay subculture. The language of *Everybody Knows Your Name* is one of its chief beauties and the main source of its power. Just as an antirealist mode can help to reject the bourgeois culture that oppresses homosexual men, a gay dialect also rejects that culture by denying the power of its language to define and circumscribe discourse.

In fundamental ways, our language controls what we think since, after we acquire language in childhood, except for primitive and basic thoughts, most of our thought occurs in language. If the language of the prevailing ideology dominates the thought and discourse of those people whom that ideology rejects and oppresses, then, by using that language, the oppressed prop up the very society that is set on their destruction. Cachianes's use of gay dialect permits a radical dislocation of the dominant discourse and thus frees gay men to use gay language and not thereby contribute to their own oppression. Certainly it is not stretching the point to view the queening dialect as a manifestation of rage: men who consciously choose not to use the mainstream language might do so as a result of anger with the system that perpetuates and is perpetuated by it.

The characters' use of gay language is crucial in redefining themselves. When they feminize their names, call each other "girl," or puncture the balloons of those outside their private linguistic world, they not only redraw the boundaries of the discourse that delineates their lives, but they also impinge on that dominant, public world whose language they distort. Whenever they coopt the language for their own purposes, or twist it into new patterns of meaning, or attribute new signifieds to its old signifiers, they build their own frame of reference that is beyond appeal to the language's standard use. Much as the sexuality of gay men diverges from the prevailing heterosexual mainstream, their language is part of a private world where the grounds of meaning and interpretation are different.

Cachianes also rejects conventional stage realism in favor of a more flexible dramaturgy. He is quite successful in presenting the narrative elements of his plot in a nonrealist mode. The play shifts between dreaming and waking states, between contemporaneous action and past memories, and between various locales—chiefly apartments and a hospital room. The characters not only include a man dying of AIDS, his friends, a New Age AIDS buddy, and a nurse, but also the man's long-dead mother who appears in the nonrealist guise of a stand-up comic.

Everybody Knows Your Name also uses surrealistic transformations of ordinary and mundane scenes to highlight the play's themes. Early on we see a dream of Andrew, a man in his mid-thirties who is dying of AIDS; in this dream he and his longtime friend Carl prepare for a night out in the preplague days. As they primp in front of the mirror and apply makeup, trashing mutual friends all the while, the transforming power of the dream begins to take effect. Recurrently in a voice-over above the diagetic dialogue we hear Andrew screaming for himself to wake up, thus introducing and subsequently reinforcing the notion that Andrew is having a nightmare. Later on, Andrew will incomprehensibly find his hands covered with blood and not be able to wipe the blood off his robe. The scene shifts into and out of disco music and dancing—presumably moving from "home" to "disco" at will.

Scenes such as this one and the later appearance of Andrew's mother with her rapid-fire and often cutting humor help to dismiss the realist mode from the stage in this play. When otherwise familiar and realistic characters are confronted with incongruous shifts of location, associative trains of events, and other characters who violate the rules of the realist conventions, the stage becomes ripe for presentations of action and theme that will fall as far outside the purview of realism as urban gay life falls outside the middle-class lives that realism depicts; similarly, the agonies and fears of AIDS lie far beyond the comfortable, insulated world of the bourgeois living room that so often provides the set for realist drama.

The rage of these characters manifests itself not only in how their actions are presented and in how they speak, but also in what they do and in what they say. Although the rage is caused by the circumstances of a minority population under attack from society, politics, and microbes, these characters vent their anger at whatever is at hand. They curse, they verbally attack each other, they torture themselves in nightmares and memories of the past—all as a result of anger over their helplessness at the hands of the dominant society and their powerlessness to alter the progress of the virus that is shattering their lives. Not only are Andrew's verbal assaults on his AIDS buddy Ray, on his overweight friend Ellison, and on his nurse often hilarious, but they are also usually quite frightening at the same time: Andrew is turning humor (and the language it uses as a vehicle) into a weapon, and thus we laugh at the same time that we blanch with fear.

Gay drama's other main response to the AIDS crisis has been remembrance, fond nostalgia and wistful longing for a return to a world that can no longer exist. The play that first defined this mode of response is William Hoffman's *As Is*. Certainly Hoffman's characters feel rage (as is demonstrated in the scene in which Rich is in the hospital and refuses to cooperate with his nurse and insults the Hispanic janitor), but the primary mood of *As Is* is one of regret.

The play follows two men, Saul and Rich, past lovers, who at the start of the play are dividing up their possessions because Rich has moved out to live with his new lover Chet. The scene serves to introduce the audience to the main characters, and it also contains Rich's announcement to Saul that he has tested positive to HIV and now has swollen glands.

Hoffman chooses to abandon the realist mode. The play has recognizable playing areas (a living room that is later transformed into a hospital room, and a bar) but the action shifts in and out of chronological sequence. One trick Hoffman often employs is shifting the action to some other locale whenever something that transpired outside the main playing area is remembered or discussed. In this way, we see Rich attempting to pick up men at bars, we see the past when he and Saul were lovers, we see him first meeting Chet, and we hear how news of his illness affects his friends and family. We see some characters merely identified with numbers, First Woman, PWA 5, Clone 2, and so on. These characters serve important functions in various scenes, but they are not individuated (for example, the clones' names all begin with "Ch"—Chad, Chuck, Chip—perhaps in a dig at the callow and selfish Chet for whom Rich leaves Saul; in the course of the play Chet dies of complications brought on by AIDS). They cannot be seen as characters in the realist sense of the word, and thus, they add to the abandonment of realist techniques.

One of the most beautiful moments in *As Is* occurs when Saul and Rich are remembering the past: public sex in a hotel window while crowds in the street below watch and cheer; late nights at famous New York City gay landmarks; orgies at the baths; trips to porno bookstores; a vacation in Morocco; simply talking dirty with other men. The past is presented as a kind of dream world of plentiful, pleasurable sex with little more to worry about than how to get rid of an undesirable partner tactfully. Hoffman also utilizes a scene in which various persons (some of whom are characters, some of whom are simply a kind of witness and never reappear in the play) remember when they first heard of AIDS. At the end of this dreamlike scene with its nondiagetic characters and overlapping dialogue, the actors simply recite a long list of male first names, implying that these people have died and are now part of that remembered past.

These strikingly nonrealist elements contribute to the mood of remembrance and show dramatically that the world being fondly remembered is patently not part of the "real" world of the play's here and now. Certainly this wistful remembrance of the past is meant to convey a positive gay image—a time when the gay men of New York were happy and more or less carefree. One is left hoping that somehow, miraculously, this world could return.

As Is ends with Saul and Rich's attempt to regain part of that lost world: they have sex for the first time since the onset of Rich's illness. The question of whether having sex will help resolidify their troubled relationship is left unanswered, but their attempt to have some sort of intimate, sexual life in the troubled times of *As Is* is admirable. Indeed, the ending of the play is hopeful and optimistic: yes, the past is irretrievably gone and the present is frightening and dangerous, but we must take the present and those in it "as is" if we are to find any pleasure, any way of life with meaning and value.

In contrast to the rage plays, the anger in Hoffman's play is subordinated to an overwhelming nostalgia. In the rage plays we see the characters as the victims of many wrongs—only one of which is AIDS. In the remembrance plays, on the other hand, the presence of AIDS is seemingly the only thing that prevents gay men from being happy and leading fulfilling lives. Perhaps this is a bit reductivist given the richness of the remembrance plays, but none of them takes on societal and political wrongs wholesale in the direct and confrontational manner of the rage plays.

Harvey Fierstein's three short plays grouped together under the title *Safe Sex* are best seen as part of the remembrance mode as well. The plays are linked by a shared set of themes: love and loss, the potential health risks of sexual activity, the nature of enduring relations between gay men (both with each other and with the "outside" world). The first two one-act plays, "Manny and Jake" and "Safe Sex," are definitely part of an antirealist stage practice appropriate to gay subject matter.

"Manny and Jake" features dialogue that is almost poetic in its rhythmic progress and often elliptical subject matter. The play depicts two handsome young men who might have had sex together in the past. Jake is willing, but Manny is not. Manny meditates on his life, on the world situation, and mostly on the past. He looks forward to a new world, without the specter of AIDS, in which he will know what to do because he will *remember* it from before. At the breathtaking end of the play, Manny rhapsodizes about a future time when he can return to spontaneous sex with as many partners as he pleases and promises to have learned nothing during the plague—rejecting overtly that anything of value could come from something so deadly, so unfair.

The second play of the trilogy, "Safe Sex," concerns two lovers, Mead and Ghee, who interrupt themselves in the middle of making love because their passion has tempted them to be unsafe. The interruption sparks a conversation about what is possible for gay men to do together and what is necessary for their survival psychologically; after all, if gay men cannot or will not have sex, how can they be overtly gay? They may certainly continue to exhibit many of the signs of being gay, but they stand to lose a defining characteristic of homosexuality—the desire for and commission of sexual acts with other men. The play takes on the fear of loss of selfhood and identity if sexuality is lost or too long denied. Through Ghee, Fierstein accuses some gay men of using AIDS to avoid sex, for what they are afraid of is not disease, but homosexuality itself.

As Ghee and Mead rehash past grievances with each other, they remember a world without AIDS. They remember sex as fun, as dirty, as something they actually did. They remember worrying about herpes, or the clap, but not about dying. The world has transformed itself into a hostile, dangerous place where everything must be checked against the safe list, where intimacy is a potential source not only of argument and frustration or of pleasure and satisfaction, but also of horrible death.

The set of "Safe Sex" is a giant seesaw or teeter-totter—which is utterly appropriate as a set for the action of two men arguing and making up, trying to balance their needs and desires against what is possible and safe. The teeter-totter's potential for large swings might also represent the radical shift in the lives of gay men. Certainly Mead's standing on the edge of the board at the play's end and his daring and coaxing Ghee to do the same is meant to demonstrate the nature of "danger" and the necessity to face it and come to terms with it. The antirealist stage practice of this play is brilliant: the seesaw works on a symbolic level in addition to being an original alternative to the living room or kitchen set of the realist mode.

The final play, "On Tidy Endings," features a man, Arthur, whose lover, Collin, has recently died of AIDS. As he packs to vacate their apartment, Arthur must deal with the man's ex-wife, Marion. The play is basically a domestic comedy in which the characters solve some serious problems (surviving the loss of a beloved, sorting out their feelings, negotiating a relationship with each other) while trading a stream of one-liners. In high realist fashion, the living room of the apartment is the set.

"On Tidy Endings" is the longest, most fully developed and ultimately most disappointing of the three plays. The play's only gay character, Arthur, exhibits unswerving loyalty to heterosexually based modes of behavior. He and his late lover have had a sort of marriage and family that even included the lover's 11-year-old son, Jim, who called Arthur "Uncle."

Not only does the action of "On Tidy Endings" ideologically mirror prevailing, heterosexual notions of human relations, but Fierstein's realist stage practice also reinforces that ideology. A critic oriented to theoretical matters might term the play a sellout to the dominant ideology in both theme and technique. Arthur is presented throughout the play, however, with compassion, understanding, intelligence, and humor. Although the end of the play (a presumably continuing connection with the ex-wife and child of his beloved) reeks of bourgeois heterosexuality, Arthur maintains his wit and dignity throughout the action. On the other hand, the ex-wife gets all the perquisites, benefits, and problems of a relationship with Collin: she is selling the apartment; she has his son; her name was mentioned in the newspaper obituaries; she was surrounded by friends and family at the funeral; and even she, not Arthur, is HIV positive. Though the play itself is meant to be critical of the society that has displaced a man's male lover at such a difficult time, the techniques through which that criticism is presented tend to reinforce the values of that society.[6]

Victor Bumbalo's *Adam and the Experts* can also be classified as a remembrance play. It, too, however, contains a generous amount of rage, especially from Eddie (a PWA friend of the title character) who vents his fury with the system (particularly with the politicians) in one especially memorable and effective scene. Nevertheless, the central mood of the play is remembrance. Adam has reacted to the AIDS crisis by retreat and retrenching. He has put his sex life (and with it parts of his emotional life) on hold indefinitely. He is frequently assailed by The Man, a nondiagetic character who is an embodiment of all those things Adam has denied or repressed in himself. The Man is a visual reminder of all that used to be in Adam's life and, as a result of AIDS, is no longer there. As such, The Man constitutes the chief vehicle for remembrance in *Adam and the Experts*.

The Man is by turns hilarious, demanding, and wistful. By the end of the play, Eddie has died and Adam has come to a sort of reconciliation with The Man—acknowledging his need for a whole life, even in the time of plague. Thus, as in *As Is*, there is a faint element of hopefulness at the end of *Adam and the Experts* that some happiness and pleasure can still be salvaged from this world. The note of sad remembrance for the past in Bumbalo's play is extended by inference to the present and the future; toward the end of the play The Man speculates on what might have happened if Eddie had lived and met a nice young man at a party who might have been his lover. Bumbalo's characters are not merely remembering a lost past but mourning a future never to be.

Obviously through employing a device such as The Man, Bumbalo departs from realist practice in his play. The play's set is flexible and contains several locales important to the action, but it is not overtly designed to represent any of them with realist detail. Like Hoffman, Bumbalo uses a small group of actors to double all the minor roles. The action shifts back and forth from location to location and some of the characters (particularly a priest and two ersatz maharishis) are treated with a great deal of often funny satire, which renders them frankly nonreal. Bumbalo's dramaturgy helps to reinforce the thematic material of his play. Ultimately, *Adam and the Experts* is one of the most satisfying of the remembrance plays.

Jean-Claude van Itallie's *Ancient Boys* uses a gathering of the friends of the late Reuben, an artist who has recently died, as the basis for its nonrealistic plot. The friends remember Reuben (who essentially kept them separate from each other), and their memories are acted out and interspersed into the relatively thin main plot of the "memorial ceremony" itself. Van Itallie's achronological treatment of his material is a great strength in *Ancient Boys*, for we see Reuben at various stages in his life and can put together for ourselves a holistic picture of him.

Van Itallie's use of a continuing series of projected slides (scenes from Reuben's life, famous works of art, pictures of the characters in amusing situations) further violates the realist stage and thus solidifies this remarkable play's wholesale rejection of the realist mode. By the end of the play the stage is dominated with a large example of Reuben's art, which serves as a powerful reminder of the great potential wasted by this man's death.

Reuben himself is a problematic character. At times he seems to succumb to homophobic notions about the nature of AIDS, arguing that the thymus glands of people who have died of AIDS are often shrunken; since the thymus is located near the heart and plays a role in the onset of puberty, Reuben concludes that gay men are misusing their heart energy—their love—and suffer health consequences as a result. At one point he even says he is tired of being gay and actually prefers women to men. In one scene, Reuben imitates his mother and remembers the comforts of her garden and her telling him that the world outside the garden was a terrible place. It is not stretching it to read this as heterosexist ideology: if you stray from the idyllic garden, you face utter nothingness and might as well end your life.

On the other hand, Reuben offers positive images of gay people when he argues that gay native Americans were usually the powerful and respected medicine men of their tribes; he even goes so far as to compare the gays to the Jews as a group of God's chosen people. Reuben's dichotomy is quite real: he clearly rejects his mother and her ideology, but he is marked for life by it and has coopted and internalized various elements of the very ideology that seeks to thwart his happiness.

Part of what is going on in *Ancient Boys* is an exploration of Reuben's problems (of which AIDS is the most life threatening, but not the only one): his compartmentalization of his life, his partial retreat from or denial of his artistic abilities, and finally his inability to accept himself fully. Certainly Reuben in these regards is typical of many gay men, but ideologically this portrait (and its equating disease with certain stereotypical elements of gay male psychology) is disturbing.

The ending of the play is troubling as well. Reuben opts for suicide rather than living through a horrible and depersonalizing death. One could easily imagine a play in which this kind of decision was treated as a positive, self-affirming act, but *Ancient Boys* is not such a play. Reuben's final words (directed to his mother who is not physically present at the time) indicate that, rather than feeling that he is taking a positive step, he thinks he is doing something shameful or naughty, something for which he needs his mother's forgiveness.

In *As Is* at one point Rich asked Saul to get him enough depressants to kill himself. Saul goes to buy the drugs and ends up throwing them in the gutter when he has the realization (on an unpleasant street in ugly weather) that there is still beauty in the world; the idea that there could still be beauty in life even with AIDS is obvious. Reuben in *Ancient Boys* is never afforded a parallel kind of realization and thus cannot find any reason to deny himself a suicide.

One further play—Craig Lucas's *Prelude to a Kiss*—warrants consideration here and seems most nearly to fit the remembrance category, so I have included it as a sort of epilogue to my discussion. The play is lyrical and magical; it has a great deal of beauty in it, but its relation to the themes discussed herein is ambiguous. AIDS is in no overt way the subject of the play; *if* the play is about AIDS, it is only in a figurative sense.

The action of the play consists of the heterosexual courtship, marriage, and minor marital problems of a young, urban couple, Peter and Rita. At their wedding, Rita is kissed by a mysterious old man whom no one knows, and somehow the two exchange souls. Peter, who had married a young, beautiful, healthy person, finds himself instead in love with a sick, dying old man (whose body contains the soul and personality of his beloved). Certainly a symbolic representation of AIDS can be seen here: in the gay world many men like Peter fall in love with someone young and healthy only to have HIV turn their lover into a dying old man.

If this reading is accepted, then *Prelude to a Kiss* is a remembrance play, since Peter expends so much energy trying to recapture the world he thought he had won. Peter relentlessly tries to understand what has happened and attempts to undo the exchange, to reorient the souls into their proper bodies so that his life can continue on as he had envisioned it. Certainly many gay men feel the desire to be able magically to return the world to what they had hoped it would be.

Dramaturgically the nonrealistic plot devices are reinforced by a nonspecific stage setting that shifts through various locations including apartments, a suburban home, a honeymoon vacation spot, a bar, and so on. Ideologically, the thematic material of the play is thus underscored by the dramatic techniques used on the stage. As is the case with Bowne's *Beirut*, one might object to the heterosexual context in which Lucas places his action, and one might also see the fairy-tale motifs that he employs (the magic kiss, the Prince Charming, the lonely maiden, the happily-ever-after ending) as serving a homophobic ideology. Although Lucas does not overtly take on the AIDS epidemic in his play, *Prelude to a Kiss* does have connections with the plays I have been discussing and thus must be seen as at least a cousin of the family of plays considered here.

AIDS plays continue to be produced in increasing numbers. Several plays have gone beyond New York to touring companies, or to local productions throughout the United States, or to West End productions in London. Early on in the history of dramatic representations of AIDS written by gay American men for the New York stage, two broad categories of response to the crisis—rage and remembrance—were codified by important productions. In their ground-breaking plays, Kramer and Hoffman defined the parameters for treating AIDS on the stage that would be used in many later plays, not just those plays discussed here. The response to AIDS in both of these initial plays is coupled with a radical departure from realist stage practice, which, as I have argued, is appropriate, given that the plays are highly critical of the prevailing ideology and, in fact, place much of the blame for the AIDS epidemic and the deaths of thousands of gay men squarely on the shoulders of the society that perpetuates itself through the dominant ideology. Whether raging against the lot of gay men in the contemporary world or sadly remembering the free and beautiful past, those plays are most successful that reject the theatrical techniques of dramatic realism and strike out into territory unknown on the popular stage; in very real ways, gay men in their lives have been abandoning the familiar and exploring the new throughout human history. It is only appropriate that theater that celebrates them or mourns their passing or erupts with anger over their situation should itself break new ground.

12

AIDS to Remembrance: The Uses of Elegy

GREGORY WOODS

Simon Watney has said, "The frequent emphasis on death in AIDS commentary is at best sentimental, and at worst simply morbid."[1] Given that he is calling for an activist, interventionist literature of AIDS, committed to such tasks as health education and the agitation for effective and urgent government responses to the epidemic, Watney is right. The dead have died. The past can wait; aesthetics can wait. Douglas Crimp has underlined the point: "We don't need a cultural renaissance; we need cultural practices actively participating in the struggle against AIDS. We don't need to transcend the epidemic; we need to end it."[2]

However, since people are dying, there are times when you have to speak of death. One such time is when a person you love has died. If the bereaved are to survive, they must deal with their grief even while they are gathering the strength to withstand their own possible infection with HIV. It is the eventuality of loss—no trivial matter, even when there is health care for the living to be fought for—that I am about to address. Inevitably, my subject is death. I do not apologize for feeling the need to speak of it.

Let me begin with a sequence, in random order, of quotations and brief narratives. Socrates kills himself by taking hemlock when charged with the corruption of minors. The Maenads dismember Orpheus for the evangelical fervor of his sexual interest in boys. The Theban Band, lovers of men to a man, fight to the death lest they be discredited to one another's eyes. The cultures of the Cities of the Plain attract the divine Final Solution: genocide. "Each man kills the thing he loves" (Oscar Wilde). Dennis Nilson dismembers and boils the meat off the bones of the boys he has strangled. A gentleman convicted of "indecency" takes his pistol into a private room to "do the decent thing." "Kill a queer for Christ" (Florida bumper sticker). "If a man also lie with mankind, as he lieth with a woman, both of them have committed an abomination: they shall surely be put to death" (Leviticus 20:13). "AIDS is a pain in the ass" (toilet wall graffito). "When I was in the military they gave me a medal for killing two men and a discharge for loving one" (epitaph of Leonard P. Matlovich, 1943–1988).

Gay culture has, for a long time, been acquainted with death. More than any of the other so-called "high-risk groups," gay men were well prepared, albeit unwittingly, to cope with the AIDS epidemic. It was not the first time we had died for no good reason. Even our poets, whom we might have expected to be a relatively privileged and protected species, had not escaped danger: Verlaine shot Rimbaud in the wrist; Wilde was given hard labor, from the effects of which he eventually died; Owen was shot dead, at age 25, in November 1918; Crane threw himself off the stern of a liner; fascists assassinated Lorca, giving him a homophobic coup de grace up the ass; Pasolini was beaten to death by a hustler and then repeatedly run over with his own car.

Throughout this century—or, to be a little more accurate, since the Wilde debacle of 1895—homosexual men have been thought of as inherently tragic figures. Think of homophobic reactions to the recent reappropriation of the word "gay": there's nothing *gay* about a queer. Look at how we were marketed on the black covers of paperback novels in the fifties and sixties. Think of how those novels, and the films based on them, almost invariably ended in murder or suicide. Many homosexual men and women internalized this opinion of themselves and set about living out the tragic destiny of loneliness and shame.

But in the literature of gayness, the new homosexuality of the last three decades, the tragic motif came to be seen as redundant and reactionary. Novelists made a conscious effort *not* to end their plots with death. Only when politically justifiable, in terms of the aims and complaints of the gay movement, did death enter the most right-on of our narratives. The suicides of scared teenagers or exposed adults, for instance, often resonated in gay verse lamenting homophobic malice. Certain events, caused by accident, or by chance, could not go unrecorded: the death of Frank O'Hara, run over by a beach buggy on Fire Island in 1966; the disastrous fire at the Everard Baths, New York, on 25 May 1977.

It is easy to forget that a lot of writing from the Golden Age between Stonewall and AIDS was filled with foreboding. Larry Kramer's novel *Faggots* (1978) is an obvious example. Another is Michael Rumaker's *A Day and a Night at the Baths* (1979), which starts with a clear suggestion that the bad old days are not yet over. Heading for his first visit to the Everard Baths, Rumaker's narrator passes the scene where a suicide has landed after jumping off the Empire State Building. He comments, "As I turned away, heading down Fifth, my first impulse was to suppose, intimate with suicide among us, that the victim had perhaps been gay."[3] His subsequent sojourn in the baths is heavy with as much dread as desire, with constant negative references to the stale reek of bodies, poppers, chlorine, and marijuana. Even the healthiest looking bodies remind him of the likelihood of disease. One passage is representative:

> The shapely posteriors parading by in the hall I imagined rampant with hepatitis, the penises that flamed with passion flaming with spirochetes as well; and scabies, and yaws, and all the other parasites carried here, along with desire, by the sailors of love from every port of the globe, the lonely and flesh-hungry from every corner of the nation and from every borough in the city; carrying here centuries-old infections of the fathers, their gay sons infected hosts, carriers in blind desire of invisible flesh-eating stowaways on bodies innocent of contaminating, and, in imperative yearning riding out the fears of infection, driven to this contagious harbor again and again, myself among them now, there are so few unrestricted havens, no ports free of the contaminating fathers. (*A Day*, 27–28).

In spite of this reaction, the narrator enjoys what he came here for—sexual intercourse—and stores it up against an indistinct but unpromising future: "I could hold all the unexpected visitations throughout my day here, like gifts, always, in any dark times to come" (*A Day*, 78). This is ambiguous; he seems to mean memories of sexy moments; but he could just as well be speaking, again, of viruses or germs. The novel ends with a note by the author, referring to actual events:

> Dedicated to the nine who died,
> and to those injured,
> and to those present,
> in the fire that destroyed the Everard Baths
> on West 28th Street in Manhattan on the morning
> of May 25, 1977.
> And, out of the ashes and ruin of all despair,
> and in spite of it,
> to the spirit of the rainbow gay and lesbian phoenix, rising.
>   (*A Day*, 81)

This novel, then, shows a clear awareness, even when dreaming of its future "phoenix," of dangers past and to come. Bathhouses catch fire; bodies catch diseases. Rumaker offers no secure emergence, for gay men, from the "tragic" nightmare of their past. It may be that we are facing, in some texts, evidence of undercurrents of guilt: a lingering suspicion that, just as our straight critics were never missing an opportunity to state, we were having too good a time of it. The sweatshirt slogan "So many men, so little time" was our contemporary version of *carpe diem*: seize the day; eat, drink, and be merry, for tomorrow you die. It was a covert acknowledgment that, even at the heights of physical pleasure, we were nonetheless conscious of mortality.

If this is true of the sexually celebratory life-style and literature of the Golden Age, it should come as no surprise to find, in the subsequent era of the AIDS crisis, that gay men have started referring back to those homophobic myths of their own tragic status. As Bill Becker says, punning on his own first name at the start of one of his poems about living with AIDS,

> For years
> I've been billing myself
> as a tragic figure
> Now it seems
> I fit the bill.[4]

It is Becker's task, in the rest of his book, to deny this suggestion. His main concern is not an acceptance of inevitable death but, as his acronymic title puts it, *An Immediate Desire to Survive*.

In an appalling way, just as AIDS has returned us to the position in which hostile straights are most happy to confine us, it has returned many of us—particularly those of older generations—to a place where we once felt, if not happiest, most at home. It is where so many of us were brought up, a place we call the "closet," a lonely space where nothing is (in the "old" sense) gay. It is not a new place; we recognize it. Some never ceased to be nostalgic about it. One of the central purposes of a seriously reflective gay literature is to reach such readers and win them back to the outside world. Writing poetry is not a waste of time. The notorious volatility and inaccuracy of written responses to AIDS—notably in the press and on toilet walls—have underscored, in the eyes of those whose communities have been affected, the need for a considered and considerate literature of the crisis.

It is not easy—perhaps it is not even possible—to convey in measured tones the sense of betrayal gay men feel as a result of the way AIDS has been used against us. It is not just the open glee of bigots, wreaking their revenge for the years of gay liberation, that has hurt. Equally painful is the way even humane and liberal eyes have discreetly turned away from the crisis as though it did not really exist. (This was always easy with regard to drought or earthquake victims in the so-called Third World; but what theatrical gestures of indifference are needed when the problem exists right under one's nose!) People have ostentatiously been waiting for AIDS to spill over into the "general population" before engaging their care. And then, of course, they will have gay scapegoats to blame for the heterosexual catastrophe.

In reaction to these reactions, gay men have made a gay cultural festival out of our acts of remembrance. The emergency role of gay culture is clear. While giving his account of the illness and death of his own lover, Paul Monette has made the appropriate point very cogently:

> Loss teaches you very fast what cannot go without saying. The course of our lives had paralleled the course of the movement itself since Stonewall, and now our bitterness about the indifference of the system made us feel keenly how tenuous our history was. Everything we had been together—brothers and friends beyond anything the suffocating years in the closet could dream of—might yet be wiped away. If we all died and all our books were burned, then a hundred years from now no one would ever know. So we figured we had to know and name it ourselves, tell each other what we had become in coming out.[5]

Simon Watney has written of how "gay men have learned to celebrate the achievements of the living, and mourn our dead, *on the terms of our own culture*. Anyone who has heard the frequent juxtaposition of disco music by Grace Jones or Donna Summer played at AIDS funerals alongside arias from the *Verdi Requiem* or *Der Rosenkavalier* will appreciate this point very well."[6]

It is in this context that we should site all elegiac cultural productions that have emerged from the epidemic. It may be that such poems—for it is with poetry that I am, at present, primarily concerned—turn out to be sentimental, nostalgic, backward looking and, in a narrow sense, conservative. That is, perhaps, their first function. But the most thoughtful of them will, while refusing to forget, turn to the requirements of the present and forge, out of the disappointments of the past, hopes for the future.

By speaking of elegy, we invoke, at once, a classic sequence of sentimental friendships, which some would call love affairs, cut short by loss. From their readings of the Alexandrian poets Theocritus, Bion, and Moschus, and of Latin poets like Vergil, English writers shaped their own distinctive tradition of pastoral laments. In "Lycidas," John Milton grieves the death, in 1637, of his friend Edward King. Thomas Gray's "Elegy Written in a Country Churchyard" was motivated by the death, in 1742, of his 25-year-old friend Richard West. Percy Shelley's "Adonais" commemorates the death at 24, in 1821, of John Keats. Matthew Arnold's "Thyrsis" memorializes Arthur Hugh Clough, who died in 1861, at age 42. Alfred Lord Tennyson's *In Memoriam* commemorates Arthur Hallam, who died in 1833, at age 22. Even so public a poem as Whitman's "When lilacs last in the dooryard bloom'd," written on the occasion of Abraham Lincoln's assassination, sticks to homoerotic convention at least to the extent of referring to the dead President as "him I loved." Similarly, Allen Ginsberg's "Elegy Che Guevara" is at pains to present Guevara as a potential sexual partner.[7]

The gender of the loved one in this tradition is neither immaterial—as one modern, liberal argument would have it—nor proof of mere "friendship." A number of ancient laments take the fact that the dead man was male as being central to the nature of the intimacy that once existed between mourner and mourned. In the Bible, David sings, "I am distressed for you, my brother Jonathan; very pleasant have you been to me; your love to me was wonderful, passing the love of women" (2 Samuel I:26). In the epic known by his name, Gilgamesh sings, "Hear me, great ones of Uruk, / I weep for Enkidu, my friend, / Bitterly moaning like a woman mourning / I weep for my brother."[8] For all the male-male love affairs recorded in the ancient world, there were no formally defined literary conventions writers could employ. David has to compare his love with heterosexual relations, or with those of mother and son. Gilgamesh runs swiftly through the friendship-widowhood-brotherhood gamut to give some impression of how he feels. But these comparisons are also, crucially, contrasts. It is *because* the dead loved one was male that the lover's grief is so intense. Their shared gender is understood to have intensified the degree of their identification with each other.

In its consolatory role, as I have already suggested, elegy is required to perform a change of mood, from grief, through fond remembrance, to hope. This process is generally achieved by simple means: a sequence of changes of tense. Typically, an elegy will pass through four stages: (a) *present* (he is dead); (b) *past* (I loved him); (c) *present* (but he is dead); (d) *future* (but he will live hereafter). Even when, in Bion's "Lament for Adonis," the mourner cries out, "Let all nature die, / now Adonis is dead," his curse is of limited duration. The flowers he calls for, to be strewn on the boy's grave, represent the year's descent from summer into fall. An unspoken future springtime is understood. The mourner curses the natural world, not to an eternal death, but to six months' mourning in an uncomfortable winter.[9]

So, the most stupendous miracle of the traditional English elegy—the breath-taking revelation on which the change of mood from grief, through resignation, to hope is hinged—occurs when the poet understands that the loved one *will live again*: if not here and now, "hereafter." (This can come as a slow realization or as a dramatic flash.) An orthodox version of this occurs in Spenser's "Astrophel," in which he mourns the death of Sir Philip Sidney. Spenser says of Sidney's spirit: "Ah, no, it is not dead, ne can it die, / But lives for aye in blissful paradise." The same transition from loss to confidence in eternal life happens, in Milton's "Lycidas," between the forlorn declaration "Lycidas is dead, dead ere his prime" (line 8) and "Weep no more, woeful shepherds weep no more, / for Lycidas your sorrow is not dead" (lines 165–66). A far longer and more difficult transition happens in *In Memoriam* between the moment when Tennyson imagines himself as a distraught girlfriend in her lover's absence, crying "all is dark where thou art not" (8:12), and the consoling confidence of "Dear heavenly friend that canst not die / Mine, mine, for ever, ever mine." (128:7–8). It is then not long before the poet realizes that even his own future death will not end their friendship:

> Far off thou art, but ever nigh;
> I have thee still, and I rejoice;
> I prosper, circled with thy voice;
> I shall not lose thee tho' I die.
>
> (129: 13–16)

In "Adonais," *In Memoriam* (126) and in "When lilacs last in the dooryard bloom'd" the mourned men reach their respective apotheoses as stars in the firmament.

A predominantly secular age such as—in the industrialized West—our own clearly does not offer easy opportunities for statements of faith in an eternal afterlife. It may be that we must piece together our eternities out of temporal fragments far more mundane. Curiously, in his poem "Kip," which elegizes the well-known American porn star Kip Noll, Marc Almond does not take up this opportunity.[10] One could argue, after all, not only that Kip lives on in glory, naked and at his best, on our video screens, but also that he may thereby be helping to preserve the lives of those of us who "love" him, by inspiring us to the safest form of sex—in a salutory solitude gladdened by his company—solo masturbation. The poem conspicuously fails to give Kip the "immortality" that his own videos do. Andrew Holleran has ironically lamented the fact that "The Mayans left temples in the Yucatan; we seem to have left pornography."[11] However, in my opinion, pornography may not be such a poor legacy as he imagines.

There is also, of course, a second type of elegy, less numerous but no less important than the first. This is the elegy, not on an individual who has died, but on a way of life. A good example of this sort is Oliver Goldsmith's "The Deserted Village" (1770) which argues passionately against the enclosure of common land by landowners; deserted villages are the consequence of such action. A controversial recent example of the general elegy is Tony Harrison's *v.* (pronounced "versus"), in which the poet complains about the daubing of his parents' gravestone with obscene graffiti. Modelled on Gray's elegy, the poem widens out from family concerns to a critique of the social and economic reasons for such vandalism.[12]

In its accumulation of types, and taken as a whole, Robert Boucheron's *Epitaphs for the Plague Dead* (1985) becomes an elegy of this second sort, commemorating an era. Its contents page lists such poems as "Epitaph for a Bodybuilder," "Epitaph for an Atheist," "Epitaph for a Disco Bunny," "Epitaph for a Bureaucrat," "Epitaph for a Stammerer," and so on. All are modeled on the measure of Tennyson's *In Memoriam*, and each works as a discrete unit, a record of one life: unique in its idiosyncracies, yet representative of others. Like fictional characters, each person is an individual and a type. But, taken together as a series, the poems acquire broader significance as records of an era. This strikes me as a somewhat embittered collection, with a strong undertow of retrospective moralizing. Suspicions on this score are confirmed when one encounters a poem about a baby that was infected before birth, by a mother who had been infected, in turn, by her hemophiliac husband. The poem is called "Epitaph for an Innocent"—an apparently unironic reflection on the other lives the book outlines.[13]

No matter which type of elegy a poet chooses to write, the nature of AIDS prevents an entirely conventional lament. Death by water, the most common origin of the traditional elegy, does not place the poet himself at risk; it is not transmitted sexually (unless you count, say, the death of Ophelia as an instance of venereal drowning). In poems about AIDS, on the other hand, the mourner may know that he is, or must suspect that he may be, infected with the HIV that, apparently, led to or hastened his lover's death. His elegy may, therefore, become, to some extent, reflexive: grieving for his own death to come—yet, perhaps, all the more willing to accept his fate, since his lover has gone ahead of him.

Roy Gonsalves, in a poem called "The Photograph," consults a photo of himself and two friends at Christmas, and concludes: "Benny died last year./ Les died last month. / Tomorrow I go for the results of the blood test."[14] At its most negative, the implication of this characteristically stark sequence of facts is that by this time next year all three of us will be dead. (And, indeed, some of the poets with whom I am here concerned have already died.) Much of Paul Monette's book of elegies Love Alone consists of the poet's realization of the need to prepare for his own death. The poem "Readiness" speaks of his arrangements for his own funeral and for his interment in his lover's grave; the poem includes the epitaph he has written for himself.[15]

The very nature of desire has, of course, become embroiled in the crisis. Thom Gunn's "In Time of Plague" starts with another expression of this awareness of personal vulnerability:

> My thoughts are crowded with death
> and it draws so oddly on the sexual
> that I am confused
> confused to be attracted
> by, in effect, my own annihilation.[16]

To an extent, then, desire itself, fixed on the future, becomes prematurely elegiac, morbidly anticipating a time when the encounter desired will be in the past and the desirer will have died of its effects. One overcomes this dread not by turning away from the object of desire and sublimating one's physical and emotional needs in good works but by negotiating a safe sexual encounter with him. This is how we release our desires into a viable future.

Nor is it only from AIDS itself that the living are under threat. Those who mourn require our attention, to be protected from despair. Therefore, in "Elijah and Isaac," John McRae expressly turns from the dead to the living—though with no intention of forgetting the dead. The poem ends as follows:

> This June Elijah died of AIDS.
> This is not a poem about Elijah dying of AIDS.
> I love the memory of him.
>
> But God I weep for Isaac.[17]

One weeps for the weeping. Lamentation concerns the living as well as the dead—or even the living *rather than* the dead: to lament is to negotiate a mode of survival. Lamentation is itself an acknowledgment that the one who sheds tears *has a future*.

Most of these writers know of AIDS as an inscribed cluster of social texts, with no immunity to issues like sexism, homophobia, and racism. Their work is often concerned to emphasize the continuity and contiguity of such issues. Craig G. Harris's poem "Our Dead Are Not Buried Beneath Us" (*"for Marc-Steven Dear, 1953–1986"*) implicitly demonstrates how the dying enter history in the following observation:

> I noticed the tribal markings
> of his face
> multiplied
> grown larger than when I'd last seen
> constant reminders of
> dimly lit liaisons.[18]

One can take these markings as literal scars, on an African face—tribal markings accentuated by the lesions of disease—or as a metaphor for lesions on a face previously unmarked. Either way, the point is that the illness brings the ill man ever closer to his African roots, perhaps stigmatizing him even further than his black skin, in American society, already does. The man's origins and his AIDS are associated here, but not in the bigot's manner ("he is African; therefore he has AIDS"). What connects these two aspects of his being is, on the contrary, racism itself. Having AIDS makes him, in the eyes of a racist society, *more African* (where the name of the continent is meant as a term of abuse). So, as a matter of defense, let his lesions proclaim him to be, in racist eyes, defiantly more African indeed (where the name of the continent connects with a long and proud history of civilizations predating those even of Europe, let alone of white America). Let him wear his identity, though it kills him, with pride.

As on Washington's memorial to the dead of the Vietnam war; as on so many patches of the NAMES Project's quilt: a naming of names may be sufficient commemoration. The quilt itself—that massive artifact whose symbolism reminds us both that it was beneath our bed covers that we loved those who have died, and that gay men symbolically *know how to embroider*—is fast becoming a mobile yet immovable monument, inscribed not merely with the names of those we have lost but also with certain chosen aspects of their personalities. Even if words fail us, we can ensure that our dead do not, like those of the Black Death or the Holocaust or the Killing Fields, go anonymously to mass graves. Andrew Holleran has said, "Someday writing about the plague may be read with pleasure, by people for whom it is a distant catastrophe, but I suspect the best writing will be nothing more, nor less, than a lament. . . . The only other possible enduring thing would be a simple list of names—of those who behaved well, and those who behaved badly, during a trying time" (*GZ*, 18). This highlights one of the weaknesses of Robert Boucheron's book. None of his characters have names. They are all identified by occupation, or habit, or quirk; it may not be enough. In contrast, section 3 of Sam Ambler's "After the Howl" (following in the wake of Allen Ginsberg's "Howl") is all the more powerful for the straightforwardness of its strategy. Each three-line unit consists of the clause "I will not let you die," followed by the name of an individual; a second line bearing only the birth and death dates of this person; and a third, more expansive line, briefly outlining some unforgettable aspect of his/her life. The accumulation of names and lives takes on the character of a formal act of remembrance, a litany of ordinary saints.[19]

One does not have to make a roll call of the dead, though, to open out from the particular to the general. So many of the elegies about named individuals seem, as if by unavoidable accident, to become the more general sort of lament. For instance, Michael Lassell's "How to Watch Your Brother Die" includes an account of the brother's funeral, attended by "several hundred men / who file past in tears, some of them / holding hands." And one says to another, "I wonder who'll be next." The funeral, like the poem itself, is centered on the loss of the individual but is also acutely aware of the wider crisis. Not just one man is dying, not just one generation, but whole ways of life.[20] Honor Moore's "Memoir" ("*For J. J. Mitchell, dead of AIDS 4/26/86*") ends with a revealing, retrospective scene of dementia:

> Jimmy said
> your last days the virus at your brain had you
> in summer at the door on Fire Island
> offering refreshment as guests arrived,
> beautiful men, one after another.
> (Morse & Larkin, 260–61)

Here, even before his own imminent funeral, the demented subject revisits lost friends—or rather, he allows them to visit him—for a valedictory house party on Fire Island, the *locus* of the Golden Age, gay urban America's Arcadia, a place that can now only support nostalgia. Dementia takes the dying man back to the past. The suggestion is, perhaps, that any similar regression on *our* part (we being the living) would signify a comparable descent into dementia. To remain sane, while not forgetting the past, we must look to the present and its future.

In the middle of his poem "Readiness," which I have already mentioned, Paul Monette's consideration of his own gravestone and epitaph leads to a brief vision of such a future. He imagines a chance visit to his and his lover's grave, at some indeterminable point in the distant future:

> if we're lucky some far-off
> men of our sort generations hence a pair
> of dreamy types strolling among the hill graves
> for curiosity's sake this well may be
> in a time when dying is not all day and every
> house riven and they'll laugh *Here's 2 like us*
> won't that be lovely Rog[?]
>
> (*Love Alone*, 28)

That anything could still prove "lovely" *in the future tense* is indicative of a sort of triumph here. The epidemic will end. Love will, after its own dreamy fashion, prevail. It is an act of real courage for a man with HIV to reach this conclusion.

Without that sense of a future, perhaps only silence would beckon. It might have seemed that the best reaction to despair would be an elegy for rational speech—something keened to the melody of John Cage's "4′ 3″." Yet although a Francis Bacon scream or the self-denying mouth of Beckett's *Not I* were felt to be appropriate modes for the late modernists, the very fact that we have not been reduced to minimalist silence is itself a triumph of eloquence. Silence = Death.[21]

The future tense is a mode of resistance in itself—as is the act of commemorating the past for the sake of an implicit future generation. What rings false about the ending of Norman Rene's film *Longtime Companion* (1990), in the absence of any religious dimension, is that it is the dead themselves who rise again and go disco dancing in some hypothetical future beyond AIDS. What is now emerging, in a confident, gay literature of the crisis, is that if future generations of gay men can go dancing, freely and healthily, that is enough. That *is* our future. This is not a trivial matter, not some frivolous question of making the future safe for disco bunnies. It is a question of the survival of—to use a dated phrase—gay liberation.

Simon Watney, with whom I began this essay, says that "we need to avoid mythifying AIDS. The situation of the person with AIDS is not poignant, not at all like a poem by Cavafy, or a Donizetti opera, or a Gershwin song."[22] While I take Watney's point and see that it needed to be made, it relies on an assumption that the arts do not serve useful purposes in their manipulations of human emotion. Poignancy may, in fact, be a pad from which action may be launched; it is, at least, a *reaction*, all the better than a turning away. As Watney would probably agree, there is no need for us to harden our hearts, so long as we do not allow our hearts to distract us from the need to act. Every elegy should bear a caveat: tears alone make a soggy memorial.

13

The Repression of the Returned: AIDS and Allegory

JAMES MORRISON

In 1987, an AIDS education comic book was designed by the Gay Men's Health Crisis, funded with money provided by the U.S. government. One noteworthy scenario contained in the comic book, illustrated by the well-known gay artist Donelan, depicts a plumber's visit to the home of another man who, as the first frame makes clear, is much attracted to the workingman. Not surprisingly, the attraction is found to be avidly returned, and in short order this dark-haired representative of the bourgeoisie joins the blond object of his desire—a genial, submissive emblem of the proletariat—in the cozy bower afforded by the underbelly of the kitchen sink. The scenario bluntly reconstitutes, without apology, a set of conventions associated with gay porn of the seventies: the fantasy of a reconciliation of social classes in sex; the opposition of physical types coyly designated by different hair colors but self-consciously subverted by the presentation of both figures as identical, idealized, pumped-up "clones"; the placement of the trick within a presumably nonsexual, quotidian context that becomes gradually sexualized in the course of the narrative. To be sure, the trade-off here—both fetishizing plumbing and renewing or replenishing sexual possibilities by transferring the discourse of plumbing to that of sex—participates in a recognizable rhetoric of indirection, a style of metaphoric thinking endemic to pornography. Thus, the figures in the comic strip speak not of penises and anuses but of *pipes* that need fitting or, with the bright leer of *double entendre*, of a "plumber's helper" that turns out to be—and here's the novelty—a condom.

167

Indeed, the figures in the comic strip ecstatically instruct one another in the rudiments of safe sex, and the pamphlet as a whole depends for its project of fetishizing the elements of safe sex on a layering of metaphor, of systematic strategies of concealment or of circumlocution, invested thereby with erotic significance. However, when this surely dubious but equally harmless text came within the disbelieving purview of Senator Jesse Helms, as it was bound to, the Distinguished Senator from North Carolina (as Charles Laughton might have called him if he were, as he certainly should be, a character in *Advise and Consent*) saw none of this dense rhetoric of indirection, this sly resort to metaphor accompanying the line drawings of body parts that so outraged the senator. Hence the second tableau of this large social narrative: on 14 October 1987, Helms rises to his feet in the Senate, red faced (probably), husky voiced (no doubt), unsteady with righteous indignation (certainly), brandishing a copy of the comic book, and delivers himself of the following utterance: "The comic-book promotes sodomy and the homosexual lifestyle as an acceptable alternative in American society. . . . I believe that if the American people saw these books, they would be on the verge of revolt. . . . Without exception, the Senators were revolted by [the books], and they suggested to me that President Reagan ought to know what is being done under the pretense of AIDS education."[1] Helms's statement not only provides illuminating evidence of the circumstances under which Helms finds it possible to conceive of revolution in the United States but amply illustrates at work the thesis of Simon Watney's important study of AIDS representations, *Policing Desire*: "AIDS is not only a medical crisis on an unparalleled scale, it involves a crisis of representation itself, a crisis over the entire framing of knowledge about the human body and its capacities for sexual pleasure."[2]

Taken together, these scenarios vividly define the crude dialectic of acceding and retrenching, the severe, painful crisis of representation engendered by the effort to speak of AIDS within overdetermined cultural conventions. The comic book may well have not been designed for an audience of Jesse Helmses, but its rhetoric of indirection anticipates, in part, the existence and response of such an audience. Thus, a representation directed from one institutionalized group of gay men to a second, generalized group finds itself mediated by a hostile interpreter. Although that representation cannot say fully what it would say, uninhibitedly, if Helms were not watching or reading, still Helms reads it as saying too much, as requiring further restriction, and he appeals to the bugbear of public funding to assure such restriction. The only rhetorical indirection Helms sees at work here is a simple form of deviousness, the "pretense" of pornography disguised as AIDS education.

Unless one were willing to grant to all pornography, seemingly the most revelatory of modes, a heavily allegorical component, it would not do to categorize the GMHC pamphlet as exemplary of a form of incipient allegory.

Still, though addressed to the most high profile of high-risk groups in the AIDS lexicon, the comic book lambently reflects a number of the conventions of AIDS representation presumably directed, to borrow another term from that lexicon, to the "general population"—which means, of course, to the white heterosexual middle class. Forced underground, AIDS as a topic in popular culture reemerges in much the way critiques of McCarthyism did in popular culture of the fifties—the obvious examples are *The Crucible* and *The Invasion of the Body Snatchers*—recognizable only behind a dense hermeneutical camouflage, subordinated to a complex of symbology. Because of its repression and emergence in this sort of altered form, at least, the subject of AIDS in its current representations takes on a number of the classical attributes of the genre of allegory. In his book on allegory, Angus Fletcher offers a provisional, wide-ranging definition that encompasses both the indirection and the stark moral schematism characteristic of allegory: "Allegory says one thing and means another. It destroys the normal expectation we have about language, that our words 'mean what they say'. . . . Pushed to an extreme, this ironic usage would subvert language itself. . . . In this sense we see how allegory is properly considered a mode: it is a fundamental process of encoding our speech. For the very reason that it is a radical linguistic procedure, it can appear in all sorts of different works."[3] According to Fletcher, allegory is a series of metaphors arranged in sequence. To be sure, Coleridge distinguished metaphor, an unconscious process, from allegory, the conscious arrangement of metaphors into an artistic pattern, but Fletcher revises this formulation, claiming that modern allegory with its accumulation of fragments toward no strict goal resembles nothing so much as obsessional neurosis with all its pockets of unconsciousness and unexplored psychic territory. If popular culture responds to the "threat" of AIDS in this vein of allegory, academic criticism claims to recover the reality of AIDS experience, to articulate the mythologies on which these allegories are based. I am concerned here not with the allegorical shapes into which the experience of AIDS is forced in American popular culture but with the complicity of academic criticism—specifically of poststructuralism—in such representations. I am concerned, that is to say, with showing the connection between styles of expression in popular culture and the claims to authority of academic discourse.

It is now clear to most writers on the subject that representation of AIDS creates an implacable paradox: while the association of the disease with gay men—with the "homosexual life-style" and with, in fact, certain facets of gay sensibility—has been certified as forcefully as has any tenet of contemporary culture, the same culture that schematically certifies it simultaneously discourages any explicit identification of that association in popular representations of AIDS. Thus the association emerges subtextually, as a multiply-coded allusion, as the "something other" toward which postmodern allegory gestures. A cultural history of mainstream American representations of AIDS would surely reveal homosexuality as an absent force that actually shapes those documents. The off-screen bogey of the gay man's body, the site of the disease's fiercest emergence in this country and, ipso facto, its implicit cause, is negatively exploited as a source of narrative pathos in the sundry "after-school specials" or disease-of-the-week treatments of AIDS on American television. The suffering children or untainted hemophiliacs of these tales are set against the (usually absent) gay man, and the sympathy elicited for the "innocent" derives precisely from the encodement of *that which they are not*—a figure, that is, of insidious otherness whose voracious appetites and perverse rejection of the "natural" social order have led to his logical fate. This convention has become so firmly installed that even genuinely compassionate representations, such as Alice Hoffman's novel *At Risk* (1987), perhaps unwittingly participate in it. One of the first attempts to deal with AIDS in mainstream American culture, the television film *An Early Frost*, was widely praised even at the time of its first showing in 1986, for presumably defying the convention.

As the evolution of such conventions makes clear, the issue of cultural constructions of disease, especially of AIDS, is a troubling one for both the specific modes of popular culture itself and for the forms of poststructuralist discourse—overwhelmingly the dominant discursive practice of contemporary academic intellectuals—that claim to analyze popular culture from a distance. Without wishing to set these tendencies against one another in schematic opposition, I note that since both operate in the sphere of allegory in their efforts to construct and to understand the intense problematics of AIDS, they are potentially accomplices in stigmatizing those who suffer from the disease. Poststructuralism claims to expose the endlessly ramifying assumptions of, not least of all, popular culture; even the thorough indifference of popular culture (in poststructuralism's version of it, in any case) to articulating assumptions of any sort is merrily used by the poststructuralist chorus to advance its own program of political and cultural dissent. The kind of division I have set out here is familiar enough in contemporary criticism, but the rhetoric of AIDS construction offers a vehement challenge to such divisions, clearly demonstrating the strategies many of the main lines of poststructuralist discourse share with what they seek to analyze and demystify and must therefore, despite repeated disclaimers, claim superiority to.

Again and again in the critical writing on the phenomena circling around AIDS, the reader is reminded that the disease is inseparable from the practices that signify it. The journal *October* devoted a special issue to AIDS in 1987, and although the conclusions of its contributors are varied, even a casual reader must note that these conclusions tend to proceed from an identical assumption articulated at the outset by the number's editor, Douglas Crimp: "AIDS does not exist apart from the practices that conceptualize it, represent it, and respond to it. We know AIDS only in and through these practices."[4]

It is clear that the "we" here who know the disease "only in and through" these practices must be distinguished from the "they" who suffer from the disease and therefore know it in a manner more immediate than as the chain of signification Crimp proceeds to trace. If Crimp's ruminations, wholly sympathetic in tone (Crimp is a gay man), implicitly promote the divisive categories he claims to critique, the overlay of metaphor at work elsewhere in the issue has much the same effect. The very titles of the essays by Leo Bersani or Paula Treichler, for example—"Is the Rectum a Grave?" or "An Epidemic of Signification"—suggest the complicity of poststructuralist discourse in generating a version of AIDS that is defined as radically *other* in crucial ways: a disease of *others*, and a disease that is *something other*, that must be understood by means of figures, extended tropes, free-playing semiosis— something to be looked at, examined from a distance, a *spectacle* of representation.

The poststructuralist denial of the body in pain—or its denial of bodily pain as a legitimation of anything but the authority that social, signifying systems claim over the body, "inscribing" it with textual reference—is especially disturbing in the context of a disease that is, quite literally, so inflammatorily subject to the intervention of social formations. To take the process of semiosis to some kind of conclusion, figuring, for example, the lesions of Kaposi's sarcoma as indexical signs on the surface of the body as text is to see that no critic, especially among those who concern themselves with AIDS representations, would broach such a conclusion. Yet the phenomena of AIDS representation are fully conducive to poststructural analysis in their foregrounding of the human body's fate as a site of the articulation of power, in their attention to the regulatory functions of social order, and in their placement of the illness as the latest in an intertextual series of allegorized, socially constructed diseases. So clearly is this the case that the "AIDS essay" has become a localized genre within poststructuralist criticism. If, as one of the conventions of that genre insists (rightly, of course), AIDS provides a handy pre-text for right-wing backlashers to re-situate AIDS within an allegorical realm of contagion and impurity, it is no less true that Crimp, Treichler, Bersani, and others *represent* AIDS as a pre-text for opposing agendas. To be sure, with its ready assimilation to prior symbolic structures, AIDS may well be the disease that poststructuralism would have had to invent if it did not, in all its horror, already exist.

In a recent issue of *South Atlantic Quarterly* called "Displacing Homophobia," Lee Edelman reflects on the problem of appropriating the figure of AIDS as material for poststructuralist criticism, decrying the possibility of the disease's serving as fodder for the "intellectual arabesques" of writers operating within the "neutralizing conventions of literary criticism."[5] Until this expression of concern at the essay's conclusion, Edelman's piece is unapologetically deconstructionist in its bent, critiquing the activist organization ACT-UP's slogan "Silence = Death" on the grounds that its rhetorical equivalency locks it into an endless, chiasmic exchange that renders its terms not only interchangeable but amenable to substitution: DISCOURSE = DEFENSE = DISEASE = DISCOURSE. Edelman's claim is that the slogan's defensiveness "deployed—in the realm of discourse or disease—to combat agencies of virulence may [itself] be informed by the virulence [it] is seeking to efface" (Edelman, 307). Although Edelman does separate discourse from disease, grants each term some integrity apart from the other, his sense of the "field of metaphoric contention" that renders the rhetoric of political action redundant or merely answerable to the power it claims to combat suggests that, within the terms of his own formula, the alternative equation he posits might just as well read "Discourse = Disease," or vice versa. Moreover, Edelman's *virtuosity*, unfolding from the text "Silence = Death" a complex, eclectic reading that fully intends to exceed that text (rather like Barthes's production of *S/Z* from a comparatively laconic story), is paradigmatic of the deconstructionist valuation of the *bravura reading*, by no means undermined by Edelman's conclusive meditation on the *ethics* of basing such a reading on a pre-text of disease.

In the context of deconstruction, Edelman has no problem recuperating what might otherwise appear to be a rhetorical glitch, the irrepressible hiccup of a bad conscience, under the auspices of his conceptual framework. After all, deconstruction typically welcomes such glitches with what joviality it can muster as evidence of textual doubleness or self-contradictoriness. The "social constructionist view of sexual identity"[6] advanced by Steven Seidman, writing in *Social Text*, is less easily reconcilable, after initially claiming that representations of AIDS enact "a symbolic drama of pollution and purity," with the sudden, ungainly lurch at the essay's end into a notably bizarre vein of empiricism: "It is, then, possible that AIDS may have a long-term beneficial effect. AIDS requires credible empirical knowledge of homosexuality. This will stimulate and legitimate research on homosexuals, much of which will challenge stereotypes. Finally, this knowledge will be disseminated throughout society and will be taken seriously because of its link to a health crisis."[7] The Foucauldian underpinnings of Seidman's analysis up to this point in his argument raise the obvious question of how these "credible" researches will be carried out triumphantly free of the social constructionism Seidman sees elsewhere in his work as "transfiguring sexual identity." Seidman's claim that this future research will manifestly "challenge stereotypes" patently and obviously contradicts his own methods, because he fails to ask such basic questions as who will conduct such research and in what manner? how will its dissemination "throughout society" proceed? and why should the culture "take seriously" this "knowledge" instead of understanding or dismissing it as yet another installment in the "symbolic drama"?

As exemplars of the poststructuralist analysis of AIDS construction, these essays have much in common. Recognizing the allegorical force of AIDS representations, these critics simultaneously recognize the impossibility of detaching the topic from allegory. Sounding the common issues of poststructuralist discourse, they also admit into that discourse such terms as "ethics" or "empiricism," both here granted a degree of legitimacy, usually excluded from poststructuralist discourse, incurring the risk knowingly or not of undermining it altogether. If AIDS causes a crisis of representation within the culture, then it also faces poststructuralism with a crisis in the very terms with which that tradition seeks, like the culture at large, to *represent* AIDS.

The manner in which poststructuralist thought complies with larger cultural trends in its representations of AIDS may be illuminated by turning to an important essay by Craig Owens, "The Allegorical Impulse: Toward a Theory of Post-Modernism." Predating the identification of AIDS as a virus in America, the essay nonetheless provides a way of understanding the predispositions from which current representations of AIDS arise. In an effort to construct a "coherent" understanding of postmodernism, Owens turns to what he takes to be among the *least* coherent of symbolic modes—allegory—and develops a sustained comparison between the traditional elements of allegory and the forms of postmodernism: discursivity, hybridization, appropriation and accumulation of imagery. Owens's sense of the allegorical image in the context of postmodernism is that it is supplemental to *essentialized* versions of the image: "In [the allegorist's hands] the image becomes something other. He does not restore an original meaning that may have been lost or obscured; allegory is not hermeneutics. Rather, he adds another meaning to the image. If he adds, however, he does so only to replace: the allegorical image supplants an antecedent one."[8] This supplemental quality, the sense of coexistent, nondialectical imagistic possibilities within a single text is linked, for Owens, to the poststructuralist—Baudrillardic or Derridean—assertion of the uncertain relationship of the sign to an antecedent reality: that relationship too may be *additive*, transformative, supplemental, even allegorical. The patterns of thought Owens sees as perceptibly inhering in postmodernism are themselves, for Owens, decidedly allegorical in their loosening of sign from referent, in their assertion of the arbitrary connection of event or action to concept, in the amenability of those patterns to symbolic structures: "The manipulations to which [allegorical artists] subject such images work to empty them of their resonance, their significance, their authoritative claim to meaning" (Owens, 205). Consequently, the formulation of nature, or of the natural as a concept, in the allegorical postmodern is as "wholly domesticated by culture; the 'natural' can be approached *only through its cultural representation*" (Owens, 223).

As the diagnosis of a cultural symptom, Owens's thesis, echoed in the claims of such critics as Crimp, Seidman, and Edelman, has been prophetic of trends in AIDS representation. Nowhere in the discourse on AIDS do we find the plethora of minute physiological detail, culturally coded to be sure but overwhelming in its amplitude, of—to choose an example from seemingly far afield—Defoe's *Journal of the Plague Year*. Such a text of an earlier epidemic is sometimes cited as the origin of an aesthetic of bourgeois realism, but the modes of modernist nihilism and postmodern despair culminate in the grave distance between spiritual reference and technological reality, yielding the generalized, nonbiological, overtly allegorized "plagues" of Camus, Kafka, Céline—or, more recently, a work like André Brink's *The Wall of the Plague* (1984)—all clear descendants of this modernist tradition and ancestors of current AIDS representations. Postmodernism's abandonment of the "ideal" of the organic, of an assured connection between "essence" and "symbol," reveals here a liability of the humane when confronted by a phenomenon, such as AIDS, that must be understood *from the standpoint of its sufferers* as, at least in part, organic. If the narrative of twentieth-century culture can be understood as the trajectory from High Modernism's reactionary defense against the vulgar, the commercial, the industrial, to postmodernism's half-ironic incorporation of these elements (as Jürgen Habermas, for example, asks us to understand it), the palimpsestic, neutrally layered texts remaining in modernism's wake are inscribed with illegible messages that appear to negate or at least to find it impossible to articulate *one* of the imaginable responses to AIDS: identification with the dying.

Owens claims that the postmodern mining of allegory is in part a reaction to the modernist *rejection* of allegory. Inherited uncritically by the moderns from the romantics, this disrepute of allegory grew, according to both Fletcher and Owens, from its association with didacticism, a tendency many modernists believed themselves to be rejecting. Despite this generally accepted critical history, however, it should be remembered that one of the most vociferous critics of the modernist sensibility based his criticism on what he took to be a blinding vein of allegory in modernist art. In the crucial essay of his book *Realism in our Time*, Georg Lukacs argues that the nature of modernism is essentially allegorical: Lukacs goes on to trace the link between allegory and the rejection he sees at the heart of modernism of the historical consciousness that he so highly valued. The resurgence of allegory in postmodernism/structuralism cannot, of course, be understood as a rebirth of the didactic impulse since the radical hybridization of postmodern allegory—its production, part playful, part terrorized, of "signifiers" without "signifieds"—"proposes the idea of a new, unreadable allegory."[9] In the absence of *readable* allegory, though, we require new *ways* of reading allegory that may prove capable of subverting or reinscribing it. If representation of AIDS is to present an authentic challenge to homophobia, cultural conservatism, and the excommunication of the ill, we need not reject (must see that we *cannot* reject) the "seduction" of metaphor.[10] Rather, we need to attend closely to the metaphors themselves, in an effort to divest them of their mythic power and invest them with the understanding of self-consciousness.

14

Larry Kramer and the Rhetoric of AIDS

DAVID BERGMAN

Just as "the love that dare not speak its name" became the love that won't stop talking about itself, so, too, the disease that no one wished to discuss has become the subject on everybody's lips. The bibliography on AIDS has grown geometrically, creating what Paula A. Treichler has called "an epidemic of signification."[1] To the silence that was death now comes the babel that is itself a plague. I embark on this effort, then, with a good deal of trepidation, and I want first to address the compulsion to add to the growing discourse on AIDS. ACT UP, the political action group devoted to AIDS issues, has appropriately adopted the Beckett-like slogan "Silence = Death," suggesting that what is said is far less important than the fact of speaking. We may judge its wisdom by hearing the CEO of the Kellogg company, Bill LaMothe, who having been criticized at stockholders' meetings for approving allegedly homophobic advertising, said, "When the noise level reaches a certain point, then perhaps that's a noise level we have to address."[2] LaMothe judges gay criticism not on its merits but on its loudness.

But the benefit of speaking about AIDS may more properly belong to the speaker than the listener. For the mourner, words both release and relieve grief. For those who feel the moral obligation to do something, writing may fulfill such an obligation. There is also the irrational feeling that by speaking about AIDS, one wards off the disease. Much of the vehemence of AIDS rhetoric may be attributable to the belief in language's magical prophylactic powers.

Not everyone, of course, thinks that the ceaseless discussion about AIDS is helpful or desirable. Susan Sontag, for example, longs for a day when AIDS will become as "ordinary" as leprosy has become in our own time, a subject rarely discussed and free of stigma.[3] "But the metaphors cannot be distanced just by abstaining from them," she acknowledges: "They have to be exposed, criticized, belabored, used up" (Sontag, 94). Lee Edelman worries that since gay writers will always find their discourse "subject to appropriation by the contradictory logic of homophobic ideology," and since "there is no available discourse on AIDS that is not itself diseased," he suggests following Freud's advice on how to respond to the Nazi threat and remain quiet.[4] Most writers, however, have come to believe that the urgency of the epidemic requires neither the austere objectivity of Sontag, nor "the verbal terrorism" Frances Fitzgerald lamented in her study of the Castro, but a pragmatic language that motivates people to helpful action.[5]

No one is more responsible for the rhetoric of AIDS than Larry Kramer, whose various works seemed ubiquitous in the early years of the epidemic. He has secured himself a place in the history of AIDS as a writer; as a founder of the Gay Men's Health Crisis (GMHC), the largest private service organization dedicated to helping people with AIDS; and as an organizer of the community protest group AIDS Coalition to Unleash Power (ACT UP). Kramer is a controversial figure more for his delivery than for the content of his statements. Are his methods successful? Without his confrontational tactics, AIDS services and research might possibly have developed more quickly, but it is more probable that his methods hurried things along. And in *The Normal Heart*, he not only addressed the social responses to AIDS before audiences that usually ignore such issues, but he also created one of the more powerful artifacts of its period. Kramer once described himself as not an artist, but "a message queen."[6] I wish to discuss his writings in that light: not as art, but as action. Did he make something happen, or were his tools unfit for the job? Is he the queen of the message queens or their ugly stepmother?

To answer such questions we must look at the three or four stages Kramer has passed through as an activist. Initially he focused the gay community's attention on AIDS and raised money for research and patient services. His early broadsides also attacked every perceived enemy in sight, including Mayor Koch, The *New York Times*, the Centers for Disease Control (CDC), and the National Institutes of Health (NIH) (*RH*, 32). After his break with the GMHC, Kramer entered his second stage, targeting the GMHC along with the Mayor and the *Times*. In the third stage, Kramer directed his attacks primarily on Washington and the Federal bureaucracy, especially NIH, its program director Dr. Anthony Fauci, and the FDA's Dr. Frank Young. Finally, *Reports from the Holocaust* ends with a recent essay—less strident than the earlier writing—that sets down the logic behind Kramer's political positions. However, with the possible exception of this final stage, Kramer's style has changed little and displays a striking uniformity; his attacks on

Fauci, Reagan, and Koch as "megalomaniacs playing God," recapitulate a theme first announced in his screenplay for *Women in Love*.

Kramer's consistent style is typical of the rhetoric surrounding AIDS, which has struck most analysts as predictable rehashing of traditional tropes. "It is almost impossible to watch the AIDS epidemic," Allan M. Brandt comments, "without a sense of *déjà vu*."[7] Sander L. Gilman finds the representation of AIDS "clearly repeats the history of the iconography of syphilis."[8] The depiction of AIDS "reminds" Charles E. Rosenberg "of the way in which society has always framed illness,"[9] and Martha Gever bemoans that the public is "reassured" by "the containment of knowledge . . . within familiar structures" and does not seek more appropriate ways of understanding AIDS.[10] Virtually all the writers on AIDS are prisoners of long ingrained ways of looking at disease, and Kramer's writing is at once symptomatic of that cultural problem and heroic in its struggle to free itself from such tropes.

Kramer responded to the first announcements of AIDS with an alacrity that can only be partially explained by his friendship with some of the first identified cases. The first official notice of the disease appeared on June 5, 1981, in the CDC's *Morbidity and Mortality Weekly Report* (*MMWR*) (30:21, 250–52). On July 3, the same day that *MMWR* reported cases of both Kaposi's Sarcoma and *Pneumocystis carinii* pneumonia in New York and California, the *New York Times* reported, "Rare Cancer Seen in 41 Homosexuals." Kramer weighed in with his first article in the *Native* in the August 24–September 6 issue. Thus three months after the first obscure report in a journal read by a handful of specialists, Kramer was already making "A Personal Appeal" to the gay men of New York City, warning them that "the many things we've done over the past years may be all that it takes for a cancer to grow from a tiny something-or-other that got in there who knows when from doing who knows what" (*RH*, 8). Kramer could address AIDS with such speed and force because the disease served as an objective correlative of many ideas and attitudes he already had; AIDS merely triggered a set of preexisting responses.

If Kramer's "Personal Appeal" was a knee-jerk reaction, so too were the responses the article drew from gay readers. In a letter to the *Native*, Bob Chesley immediately recognized that Kramer's response to the crisis merely continued his earlier criticisms of the gay community. For Chesley, Kramer's emotionalism only thinly disguised his guilt for being gay. Chesley insists that the subtext of Kramer's works is always the same: "the wages of gay sin are death" (quoted in *RH*, 16). Kramer answered Chesley's attack at some length in a subsequent *Native* article; nevertheless, Chesley's charge contains more truth than Kramer admits, even as it fails to grasp the correctness and urgency of much of Kramer's analysis.

Like Chesley, Andrew Holleran also finds the roots of Kramer's response to AIDS in his 1978 novel *Faggots*.[11] *Faggots*, a would-be Waughian satire of the New York homosexual life, is a phantasmagoria of rape, incest, drug addiction, coprophilia, pedophilia, and torture. I have difficulty imagining how Kramer could think readers would find his mordant comedy amusing. Like Thackery's *Vanity Fair*, *Faggots* has no hero; its protagonist, Fred Lemish, Kramer's alter ego, is a successful screenwriter in love with Dinky Adams, a handsome, charmingly manipulative, and utterly self-destructive nonentity. We follow Fred and Dinky and dozens of drugged and barely differentiated characters on a four-day odyssey that takes us through bus station tea rooms, gala openings of discotheques, S-M sex clubs, steam baths, Manhattan luxury apartments, and finally to the opening of the Fire Island season. Lemish keeps himself aloof from most of the orgy of sex, drugs, and violence, but in the end, despite the fact that he believes that "one of these days we must stop shitting on one another," Fred defecates in defiance and disdain in a garden Dinky designed.[12]

Chesley's contention that Kramer blames promiscuous gays for their own death is best supported by a relatively tame episode in which Dinky argues that the scarcity of happy couples should tell Fred that friendship is better than love. Fred replies, "Yeah . . . It tells me no relationship in the world could survive the shit we lay on it. It tells me we're not looking at the reason why we're doing the things we're doing. It tells me we've got a lot of work to do. A lot of looking to do. It tells me that, if those happy couples are there, they better come out of the woodwork fast and show themselves pronto so we can have a few examples for unbelieving heathens like you that it's possible. Before you fuck yourself to death" (*F*, 265). Though Kramer strenuously denies it, such a passage does come perilously close to saying "the wages of gay sin are death." His alternative to "fuck[ing] yourself to death" is a marriagelike relationship between men, suggesting that gay survival relies on approximating heterosexual behavior. Kramer blames the victims of lovelessness for their own predicament, and their death on a life of mindless, unrestrained sexuality. In *The Normal Heart*, Ben, the heterosexual brother of Ned Weeks, says "You guys [homosexuals] don't understand why there are rules and regulations, guidelines, responsibilities," and Ned lamely agrees.[13] For Kramer, gay sexual behavior is "the equivalent of eating junk food." (*TNH*, 79), irresponsible because it disobeys the rules governing heterosexual relations. He fears, as I will discuss later, its very uncontrollability.

If Kramer's insistence that gay men temporarily forgo all sexual activity could be justified in the early stages of the health crisis as a reasonable response to a disease whose cause and mode of transmission were unknown, his continued sexual abstinence cannot be so easily explained and suggests rather strongly that beneath his earlier position lies a latent antipathy toward sex. In *Reports from the Holocaust* he freely admits that he has difficulty making love, even safely because the act is firmly tied in his imagination to death. Even kissing is forbidden because he fears some slip-up might occur (*RH*, 227). Such neurotic fears of contagion, exacerbated by his early refusal to be tested for HIV antibodies, further support those who argue that Kramer uses

AIDS to mask his sexual discomfort. Yet, attacking Kramer for internalizing homophobia and antieroticism is an empty charge since we all to some extent internalize the values of a society that considers sexuality sinful and homosexuality worse. Kramer can be faulted because by denying such latent tendencies, he can neither root them out nor make allowances for their persistence in his thinking, and so he allows his homophobic feelings to color not only his attitudes but the very style of his polemic.

Kramer believes that the criticism leveled against *Faggots*, as well as the rest of his writing on AIDS, is an angry response to the truth he dared to report: the lovelessness that lay behind homosexual license. Yet the anger Kramer arouses cannot be so easily explained away. Much of it came from sensitive and discerning writers such as George Whitmore—the writer of one of the best and most moving accounts of the epidemic, *Someone Was Here* before dying from the disease—who urged his readers to boycott *Faggots*. Moreover, 1978, the years *Faggots* was published, also saw the appearance of Edmund White's *Nocturnes for the King of Naples* and Andrew Holleran's *Dancer from the Dance*, works that shared Kramer's critical attitude but aroused wide approval. What separates White and Holleran from Kramer and what freed them from an angry backlash is that they possess a lyric sympathy for their wayward characters; whereas Kramer, at best, musters an angry identification. Whereas White and Holleran are sweetly elegiac; Kramer is bitterly censorious.

Kramer's practice of responding to political events as personal affronts, of transforming impersonal bureaucracies into individual bogeymen, of subsuming all conflicts into a version of the Freudian family romance is the source of both the power of and the problem with his political polemics. His broadsides derive much of their creepy insistence from their intimacy. So often does Kramer remind readers that the GMHC was born in his living room that we come to feel that he felt betrayed when it left his apartment. In *The Normal Heart* and *Reports from the Holocaust* Kramer weaves in his conflicts with his brother as if the AIDS epidemic were an episode in a continuing family squabble. Indeed, both *Normal Heart* and *Reports* end not with Kramer addressing the gay community but with him embracing his brother and sister-in-law. Placing the gay community within the bosom of the heterosexual family is, I think, one reason why his work speaks so powerfully and uneasily to gay readers, for it suggests a vision of reconciliation that is both keenly desired and frustratingly delayed. As Seymour Kleinberg notes, "Society has not acted as the surrogate family in which we all develop our loyalties and moral sense. In fact, too often it acts just like the families of gay men: filled with contempt and indifference."[14]

The voices of the family emerge from the various articles, speeches, and essays contained in *Reports from the Holocaust*. I detect at least three major strains: the grating soprano of the enraged child, the wounded contralto of the guilt-inducing mother, and the rasping bass of the humiliating father. Because I hear these voices coming not only from Kramer's page but also from my own head, I respond to them with an unusual intensity. Kramer's ability to address the subconscious of gay readers accounts in large part for the power he exerts on and the anger he arouses from readers.

The enraged child is perhaps the most obvious and embarrassing of his voices. A self-conscious profanity peppers his articles as though Kramer were a teenager trying to shock his respectable parents. He calls Dr. Anthony Fauci, for example, a "FUCKING SON OF A BITCH OF A DUMB IDIOT" (*RH*, 194) and Mayor Koch a "cocksuck[ing], . . . heartless, selfish son of a bitch" (*NH*, 90). He dares us to be offended (*RH*, 171), admitting that he sounds like "an asshole," and warns us that we had better "get up off of [our] fucking tushies and fight back" (*RH*, 172–73). The childishness of this rage can be measured by the word "tushies," which deflates his jeremiad with baby talk.

If Kramer often sounds like a child, he even more often strikes the note of a whining Jewish mother. During his running feud with the GMHC, he wrote its then director Tim Sweeney: "I love GMHC as much as, if not more than, most. After all, it was founded in my living room, I gave it its name (for better or worse), . . . and I gave it two years of my life, full time. . . . If I have pain and anger and frustration as well, it is very much like that of a parent toward a wayward and unfocused child who is not growing up the way I want it to" (*RH*, 119). In another open letter, this time to Richard Dunne, the executive director of GMHC, he writes as though the organization's existence was a personal labor: "I did not spend two years of my life fighting for your birth to see you turn into a bunch of cowards" (*RH*, 110). The basic strategy of Kramer's Jewish mother voice is to spread guilt liberally, especially in reference to his own suffering. He prefaces an invitation for others to join him in meaningful action by announcing: "I don't know how much longer I have to live" (*RH*, 146). Usually, however, the tone is less lachrymose, as when he tells the readers of the *Native* of his anger, frustration, and tortured sleep (*RH*, 49). Although Kramer's personalization of guilt is a useful way to keep his attacks from becoming vague, abstract, and distant, it is a dangerous rhetorical ploy since many gay men, subjected to it from birth, resist being made to feel guilty.

Moreover, the effectiveness of Kramer's guilt-tripping is offset by his compulsion to humiliate his gay readers with familiar fag-baiting terms. He often sounds like a football coach rousing the team by insulting its manhood, or like a father striking out at his effeminate son. He repeatedly calls the leadership of the GMHC "sissies" and "wimps" (*RH*, 106, 110, 113). In *The Normal Heart*, Ned Weeks yells at one character, "Bruce, for a Green Beret, you're an awful sissy!" (*TNH*, 91). He attacks others for being "cowards" and for growing "weak" (*RH*, 109, 112). What makes Kramer's recourse to this homophobic language particularly odd is his clear understanding of its insidiousness. In his concluding essay in *Reports from the Holocaust*, he writes, "The concept of 'manliness' is the stereotypical straight expectation for all males; somehow, all gay men are therefore 'sissies.' (How gay men hate this word!)" (*RH*, 236). Yet Kramer cannot resist using such stereotypes and regretfully acknowledges that he is unable to inspire people without punishing them (*RH*, 186). His need to provoke gay men as sissies comes from a very deep source: his awe of power and the powerful, and his anger over his perceived powerlessness (*RH*, 135). These twin obsessions—the awe of power and the shame of weakness—generate some of the most bizarre episodes of Kramer's AIDS activism.

The episode I find the most disturbing is his break with GMHC, a break that not only occasioned much of his journalism, but also forms a large part of *The Normal Heart*. According to Kramer, he was maneuvered into resigning from the board when he was excluded from a meeting with Mayor Koch because of his abrasive and confrontational manner. After he quit, he tried several times to rejoin but was repeatedly rebuffed. In frustration, Kramer wrote a series of open letters in which he argued that GMHC had forsaken its original path and succumbed, in Kramer's suggestive phrase, to "the 'fuck the founding father' syndrome" by committing itself to patient services instead of political action (*RH*, 138–39). In his open letter to Richard Dunne, he insists that Gay Men's Health Crisis was not founded to help those who are ill but to protect the living to go on living (*RH*, 103). In the same letter he writes, "GMHC has also placed itself in thrall to forces other than its Board. Somewhere along the line, the organization was completely taken over by Professional Custodians—social workers, psychologists, psychiatrists, therapists, teachers—all of whom have vested interests in the Sick, in the Dying, in establishing and perpetuating the Funeral" (*RH*, 112). The passage distorts the history of GMHC, which by Kramer's own account began in reaction to Dr. Friedman-Kein's request for funds for several patients without medical insurance and for research (*RH*, 12), and thus, as a form of patient services. But the most disturbing element in this passage is Kramer's rejection of the sick and dying, his the-dead-should-bury-the-dead attitude. For a man who insists that gays take responsibilities for their own lives, he has a strangely cavalier attitude to those with AIDS (*RH*, 128). Kramer is not really as cold hearted as he makes himself appear—he meticulously records the names of his dead friends on index cards—yet he seems compelled to deny his concern by striking a tough-guy attitude.

Part of the explanation for Kramer's attitude toward people with AIDS is what Judith Wilson Ross has called "the Death Metaphor"—that to be diagnosed with AIDS is to be dead already. According to Ross, we come to think of AIDS as death because it alleviates the pain of watching others die, and because "it better fits the drama that we have constructed about the coming of and the meaning of AIDS."[15] But Kramer's attitude also derives from his notions of masculinity: care of the sick is "women's work," a sign of weakness. In *The Normal Heart*, Ned recounts his frustration about getting the board to take political action in sexist terms: "I thought I was starting with a bunch of Ralph Naders and Green Berets, and . . . they turn into a bunch of nurses' aides." Emma Bookner replies: "You've got to warn the living, protect the healthy, help them keep on living. I'll take care of the dying" (*TNH*, 79). Kramer, the adaptor of D. H. Lawrence, follows Lawrence's archetypal scheme: women are the devotees of Thanatos, men the celebrators of life.

Yet Kramer's attitude toward AIDS patients, I think, turns on still another part of the stereotypical code of masculinity, and the clue is found in his rejection of the "Professional Custodians." One key lesson AIDS mental health programs try to teach persons with AIDS is accepting the inevitable loss of control that comes as the disease progresses.[16] George Whitmore has caught the fear and anger of men in their thirties and forties, who are used to managing corporate and personal affairs and find themselves suddenly unable even to get out of bed: "I very much like being in control," admitted one media executive, "the control was taken away."[17]

"AIDS is about shit and blood," writes Whitmore, and the loss of bowel control is an obligatory scene in the AIDS literary drama—a horrifying moment, humiliating to the patient, as well as the care giver.[18] Whitmore writes about a nurse, opening the door to her favorite patient's room to find it "full of shit and blood. Shit and huge clots of blood covered the floor. It covered the bed. . . . [The patient's] body was twisted across the bed. Shit and blood were still pouring out of him. His feet were slipping and sliding in it" (Whitmore, 153). Kramer's obsession with bodily elimination appears even before the advent of AIDS. *Faggots* opens with Fred Lemish—who suffers from both constipation and a shy bladder—being peed on, and the novel ends with him defecating. In one of the most moving passages of *The Normal Heart*, Bruce speaks of his lover, Albert:

> His mother wanted him back in Phoenix before he died, this was last week when it was obvious, so I got permission from Emma and bundle him all up and take him to the plane in an ambulance. . . . Then, after we take off, Albert loses his mind, not recognizing me, not knowing where he is or that he's going home, and then, right there, on the plane, he becomes . . . incontinent. He starts doing it in his pants, and all over the seat; shit, piss, everything. I pull down my suitcase and yanked out whatever clothes were in there and I start mopping him up as best I can . . . and I sit there holding his hand, saying, "Albert, please, no more, hold it in, man, I beg you, just for us, for Bruce and Albert."
> (*TNH*, 105–6)

Caring for the sick and dying means confronting in the most graphic ways the loss of control and with it the loss of masculinity.[19] Kramer, who is in awe of power, fears that GMHC's attention to patient services will make it and him weak. Kramer suffers from a fairly common reaction among those who work with the terminally ill—what Horstman and McKusick have identified as "Helper Helplessness Syndrome."[20] One would be mistaken, however, to see Kramer as heartless. Kramer flirts with losing control even as he argues for the need for discipline and power; he is drawn to the dying even as he speaks of devoting himself to the living. What makes a Kramer performance fascinating to watch is the drama of his attempts to yoke contradictory forces, and the extremes to which he is driven in this mad attempt.

Kramer's rhetoric is filled with binary oppositions: masculine/feminine, living/dead, gay/straight, love/sex, relationships/promiscuity, friends/enemies. In this respect, his language differs little from the general rhetoric of AIDS (Treichler, 63–64). But whereas most writing on AIDS maintains these oppositions, Kramer constantly conflates them. Kramer distinguishes between the "living" and the "dying," but his refusal to be tested for HIV infection derived not so much from his fears that the test would exclude him from the "living" but from his desire to keep open the prospect that he is one of the dead. His famous dictum that *"Each and every minute of my life, I must act as if I already have AIDS and am fighting for my life"* conflates the categories even as it insists upon them (*RH*, 91).

Kramer's difficulties with conventional categories is nowhere more apparent than in his attitude toward gay marriage and family. Kramer wants the state to allow gay marriages, and he concludes *The Normal Heart* with the symbolic marriage of Ned Weeks to Felix as though the ceremony were necessary to legitimize the relationship (*NH*, 122). Kramer argues that had gays been allowed to marry, they would not have been obliged to be promiscuous (*RH*, 178–79). For Kramer, gays achieve "respectability" by imitating the disreputable heterosexuals who deny gays their rights. Kramer holds on to the illusion that somehow marriage will protect people from AIDS even as he notes that several people he encouraged to form relationships had perhaps been infected by their partners. Kramer never quite sees that promiscuity may be as much the result of searching for a pseudospouse as avoiding the commitment of a relationship, and he only belatedly realizes that the worst enemies of homosexuals are those who act to protect their constricted notions of family:

> The Family. The family. How these words are repeated and repeated in America—from campaign rhetoric to television commercials. This is a country that prides itself on proclaiming family values, as if there were no others, as if the family was homespun and united and loving, as if it is necessary to produce a child—like a product—to justify or countenance a sexual act. . . . Well, I am a member of a family, too. Or I

once thought so. . . . How convenient for them all to have disposed
of us so expeditiously, just when we need them most. But the ranks are
closed, something is happening to gay men, and we are suddenly no
longer affiliated with *the* family. Where do they think we came from?
The cabbage patch? (*RH*, 271)

Kramer desires incorporation with the family and rejects "family values" as
hollow sloganeering. As Simon Watney has pointed out, the state has used
the family as an excuse for remaining silent about AIDS and for further
stigmatizing homosexuals.[21] Yet reading Kramer, I have the sense that he
uses family metaphorically to describe an idea of community that retains its
original idealism, purged of hypocrisy, but such a formulation would mean
abandoning the oppositional rhetoric informing not only his writing on
AIDS, but traditional political polemic.

Kramer's concern with the family, which predates the AIDS epidemic, has
taken on new urgency since the health crisis, for AIDS has forced gay men to
reconsider the relationship with their families and the nonhomosexual
community. As Frances Fitzgerald points out, gay men in the seventies were
evolving in the larger urban centers a separatist life-style (Fitzgerald, 116).
The AIDS broke the spell of gay self-sufficiency. Suddenly, gay men needed
government services and family support. But their experience of indepen-
dence has led gay men to demand help as fully enfranchized citizens and fully
accepted sons. Such changes have, in turn, altered gay political thinking and
rhetoric.

Yet what sort of rhetoric could replace traditional oppositional language?
If the sharp division of "them" and "us" is no longer useful or accurate, but
the conflation of opposites into a unified society is far from being achieved,
then it becomes virtually impossible to speak, especially in Kramer's habitu-
ally passionate way. If his pronouncements of 1987 appear, even to Kramer,
to be among his angriest and most hyperbolic, he may have been frustrated
about finding a language that is urgent without being oppositional. If he
shrilly calls for force and praises Zionist terrorist organizations (*RH*, 191), he
does so out of frustration with the diffusion of gay politics. In this respect
Kramer's writings become symptomatic of problems within the gay movement, which has witnessed both its greatest successes in legitimizing itself
before the American public and its greatest failures in protecting its own
population.

Seymour Kleinberg, one of the most cogent and sensitive commentators
on homosexuality, has addressed these gay social and rhetorical problems.
"Not only must gay men refrain from what alone gave them a powerful
enough identity to make a mark on the consciousness of society, a behavior
that replaced society's contempt with the much more respectable fear and
anger," he writes, "but they must cease to think of themselves as unloved
children. And they must do both before they have evidence that society

accepts them or that their behavior has meaning for each other more nurturing than it has been" (Kleinberg, 59). In short, Kleinberg suggests that the gay movement needs a visionary polemic that will speak of the desired changes in social structure as though they have already occurred.

How does one integrate the social role of gay people into a culture that has not yet accepted them? In her study of the gay movement in the Castro district of San Francisco, Frances Fitzgerald notes the changes in the way various gay groups communicate among themselves and to the heterosexual population. Gone is the "verbal terrorism" that marked the debate on whether to close gay bathhouses. Replacing it has been a rational discussion of issues "without discovering 'enemies' and building up factions." Kramer hints that a possible model for the relationship between hetero- and homosexuals may be found in the relationship between gentiles and Jews. As the title of his collection states, Kramer compares the AIDS epidemic and the Holocaust. Borrowing from Hannah Arendt's analysis of the Holocaust, Kramer argues that gay people can avoid genocide only by demanding their political rights. By capitulating to hostile authority because they trusted its essential benevolence, Jews sealed their downfall; and by believing in the responsiveness of the Federal government, gays allowed AIDS services and research to be ignored, underfunded, or subject to unconscionable delays. Gays must force heterosexuals to accommodate homosexuals. And just as Jews have preserved their ethnic, cultural, and spiritual difference, even as they have found a place within the American polity, so must homosexuals preserve their cultural and social identity even as they keep a sharp eye out for homophobia.

A nonseparatist political action is already emerging. Its most astounding success has been the NAMES Project, an ongoing activity about which Kramer and other radical gay theorists have remained remarkably silent. The NAMES Project has encouraged individuals and groups to create fabric pieces as memorials for those who have died of AIDS, and it assembles and exhibits these pieces as the "Quilt," an enormous patchwork of grief and hope. Despite its grassroots reputation and folksy appearance, it serves as a highly sophisticated piece of political symbolism, engineered for the hard realities of both media exposure and backroom politics. Its first appearance on the Washington Mall in October 1987 created a picture that made all of the networks and front pages of the major newspapers. At once extremely personal and utterly public, the Quilt integrates personal grief and public outrage, the fear of the closeted and the aggression of the activist, the solidarity of gay friends and the sympathy of straight family, individual continuity and communal loss. Unlike so many public protests, the Quilt is quiet, and those who come to witness it are hushed by its magnitude, its seemingly unlimited detail, and its inescapable unity of effect. Stretched out between the rows of autumnal trees, the Quilt turned Washington into both a bed and a grave. Beyond the lines of people weeping or with bowed heads, the Capitol rises small and grand, solid and toylike, distant and inescapably connected. The NAMES Project has struck a new chord in the American psyche: it is a way to incorporate gay people into the fabric of society while recognizing—even commemorating—their contributions and sufferings. It forms the type of statement gay writers are only beginning to stitch together with words.

15

The Rhetoric of the NAMES Project AIDS Quilt: Reading the Text(ile)

JUDY ELSLEY

In October 1988, a quilt containing almost nine thousand hand-made panels, each one in memory of a person who had died of AIDS, was spread out on the Ellipse, south of the White House. The 375,000-square-foot quilt with panels from 50 states in the United States (as well as from Canada, Germany, Italy, Mexico, The Netherlands, New Zealand, and Sweden), attracted thousands of people to mourn those who had died. Before its final display in Washington D.C., the quilt, which weighed 11,510 pounds, completed a 20-city, 12,000 mile, four-month national tour, raising $500,000 for care and services for people with AIDS.

In October 1990, the NAMES Project put on one of its displays—a simultaneous five-city show. The weekend displays began with reading and unfolding ceremonies at each of the five sites. At noon in Atlanta and Washington D.C., 11:00 A.M. in Chicago and Houston, and 9:00 A.M. in Los Angeles, an electronic audio linkup permitted each of the cities to share in a national reading of the names, dramatizing the common threads of the epidemic. Cleve Jones, founder of the NAMES Project, wrote in September 1990, "It has been three years since the quilt was first displayed on the mall in Washington D.C. Since then the number of dead have grown from 27,000 to nearly 100,000 and the quilt has grown from 1,920 panels to over

12,000."[1] These statistics lead us to ask why the quilt has proved such a popular and effective way to respond to the AIDS epidemic. I will attempt to answer that question, focusing, in particular, on reading the quilt as a textile text.

In part, the panels provide a way for survivors to make a difference. Because caretakers feel particularly helpless in terms of healing those afflicted with the disease, the quilt is something concrete and lasting over which they do have control. A disease that eliminates life so mercilessly is, in small part, counteracted by the creation of a commemorative quilt panel, as Cleve Jones suggests when he says that "this quilt is a gift from the hands and hearts of thousands of Americans who have not despaired. It stands as a statement of hope and remembrance."[2]

Making a panel provides the grievers with a way to begin to deal with their loss. "These are not stories of an illness," writes Cindy Ruskin. "Rather, they are stories of courage, fear and anger, and mostly, they are stories of love."[3] The displayers of the NAMES Project recognize the need to express loss and consciously provide an appropriate and supportive context for grief in a public place: stewards walk around with boxes of kleenex, offering them to those who come to the viewing. Attenders are expected to weep. The coffin-shaped panels representing so many dead enact an immense quilted funeral. "The quilt is not offered as entertainment. It's supposed to be *excruciating*," says Cleve Jones.[4] Grief is, to some extent, formalized and ritualized so that it becomes if not manageable at least acceptable.

The quilt shows us that the dead are not so much numbers as, quite literally, names. Like the Vietnam War Memorial, with which it is often compared, the NAMES Project quilt focuses on the individuality of the tragedy of AIDS. We can no longer keep the horror of AIDS at arm's length by using statistics, the Project suggests; the individual names bring AIDS home. The NAMES Project thus seeks to restore individuality, and by extension dignity, to those who have died of AIDS. Each panel tells several stories, all of them about human love and suffering; first, the story of the person who died of AIDS, and then the story of the person or people who made the block. Indeed, each panel is accompanied by a letter from the maker, explaining the thoughts and feelings of the survivors. "What they do," says Cleve Jones, speaking of the survivors, "is they come to the quilt, and they cry, and then they empty their pockets, and then they sign up and get to work. We've seen that over and over" (Bellm, 35).

This is a remarkable response when we consider the aversion the disease so often invokes, encompassing as it does a particularly toxic set of fears: fear of homosexuality, of a plague striking young people, and of death. As Phil Nash astutely observes, "AIDS threatens the ideals on which all our cultural values are balanced: the quest for love and the fear of death. . . . The stunning and paradoxical reality of AIDS is that death—for many the greatest fear—has found its way into our most passionate and tender moments."[5] Because AIDS embodies our worst fears, it is much easier to marginalize, through disgust and rejection, than to face directly. But what we cast out is also what defines us. Our disgust bespeaks our desire, as Peter Stallybrass and Allon White argue in *The Politics and Poetics of Transgression*: "The 'top' attempts to reject and eliminate the 'bottom' for reasons of prestige and status, only to discover, not only that it is in some way frequently dependent upon that low-Other, but also that the top *includes* that low symbolically. . . . The result is . . . a psychological dependence upon precisely those Others which are being rigorously opposed and excluded at the social level. It is for this reason that what is *socially* peripheral is so frequently *symbolically* central."[6]

The quilt acts as a perfect symbol of the issues it raises for, like the issues themselves the quilt embodies both disgust and desire. A quilt traditionally represents the comfort and security of domestic life. Moreover, it lies on a bed, which is the most intimate place in the home. The NAMES Project, by analogy, brings this disease we would like to keep at a distance into the most intimate parts of our lives. There is a subtle interplay between what we most fear—death from AIDS—and a quilt that we associate both with domestic security and comfort, and with the bed, a place of procreation. Life and death meet in the AIDS quilt. That commingling helps both to dissipate the fear and to remind us that no one is immune. By employing a quilt, the NAMES Project brings AIDS literally and metaphorically home.

Although the quilt offers no solution to the physical virus, it does attempt to cure the psychological virus of prejudice and fear: "As a nation, we have struggled not only against a disease, but also against the equally destructive enemies of ignorance, hysteria and bigotry" (*National*, 4) After seeing these panels, we can no longer dismiss the victims as promiscuous perverts who got what they deserved. The Academy Award–winning documentary film of the quilt, "Common Threads," consciously works to the same end by focusing on a child, a heterosexual man, and several gay couples in stable, longterm relationships, thus challenging our stereotypical assumptions of who gets AIDS.[7]

The quilt, then, works as a symbol, but it also works as rhetoric. This quilt quite literally invites a reading—the panels are the leaves of an enormous textile text. Speaking its complex visual, verbal, and nonverbal language, the NAMES Project quilt sets about claiming power for people with AIDS by creating a story of their own making, for the victims, the panel makers, and even those who come to see the quilt.

"Language is not limited to words," says Carroll Smith-Rosenberg in *Disorderly Conduct*. She continues: "If by 'language' we mean symbolic communication, then a host of nonverbal forms can be adopted. Dress and food codes, religious rituals, theories of disease etiology, the varied forms of sexuality, all function in societies around the world in highly expressive ways."[8] The NAMES Project quilt acts in just such a highly expressive way.

Women have long used quilts to speak the unspeakable; here we see men doing just that.

The quiltmakers are well aware that he who possesses the rhetoric possesses the power. One way to begin claiming the rhetoric is to provide a way to speak about AIDS that avoids the harmful language of difference and discrimination, for as Susan Sontag argues in *AIDS and Its Metaphors*, "much in the way of individual experience and social policy depends on the struggle for rhetorical ownership of the illness: how it is possessed, assimilated in argument and in cliché."[9] She goes on to point out that AIDS has been "possessed" by political and military metaphors that have set up an opposition between "we" who are healthy and "they" who are sick. According to Sontag, such an opposition is dangerous because the "non-us" are also constituted as foreign, wrong, guilty (Sontag, 48). Us and them, winners and losers, healthy and sick—these dualities represent the binary oppositions that lead ultimately to the underlying pair: "superior" and "inferior."

Feminist theorists have long exposed such dualism as one of the ways that women have traditionally been denied power. AIDS, like women, threatens the patriarchy and is therefore reduced to a place of inferiority on the binary grid. Even apparently innocent language can bear sinister implications. "Risk group," for example, is a "neutral-sounding, bureaucratic category which also revives the archaic idea of a tainted community that illness has judged" (Sontag, 46). The NAMES Project, well aware of the power of rhetoric, suggests in its press releases that journalists employ the phrase "Person with AIDS" rather than "victim" because "the use of 'victim' creates the false impression that people with AIDS are distinct from everybody else" (*National*, 6). The quilt provides an opportunity for People with AIDS (PWA) to repossess the rhetoric and thus reinscribe their stories so that they can claim dignity and status for themselves rather than be marginalized into mere victims.

Even the audience that comes to view the quilt is invited to participate in rewriting the story: "In the corner of the quilt is a large square that visitors can write on. . . . First a person looks at the fabric, takes off his or her shoes before kneeling to write on the square. Then the person gets up, in tears. You see drying teardrops all over the cloth" (*National*, 8). The ephemeral tears speak along with the signatures. Love and grief are stitched in and worked out in every panel. The inexpressible finds expression.

The quilt creates an opportunity to counter prejudice by endlessly repeating itself: "part of making an event real is just *saying* it, over and over," says Cleve Jones. The repetition of a message for sympathy and support that would have turned people off is transformed, through the quilt, as panel after panel is set out in a visual display that reinforces the message. "One of the most moving moments to me during Thursday's unfurling of the quilt," says journalist Rob Morse, "was listening to a woman I know talk about the ceremonial reading of the nearly 3,000 names."[10] The repetition of names and panels, a seemingly endless list, moves the listeners and viewers in a way that logical arguments could not.

Not only does the NAMES Project quilt work as a text, it operates as a particular kind of text. Open ended, protean, populist, cultural critique, the quilt most resembles the novel. M. M. Bakhtin's theory of that genre, as he sets it out in *The Dialogic Imagination*, helps us understand more clearly this textile text. Both novel and quilt refuse definitive definition because they exist in a continual state of change. The novel, "this most fluid of genres,"[11] resembles the mutability of the AIDS quilt, which literally changes shape as more panels are added to it, increasingly becoming the "baggy monster" Henry James defined as the novel.

Moreover, both novel and quilt develop from a grassroots movement, drawing on the individual experience of actual people. The novel is "characterized by a deliberate and explicit autobiographical and memoirist approach" (Bakhtin, 27), for "at its core lay personal experience and free creative imagination" (Bakhtin, 39). Like the novel, each quilt panel expresses, through free creative imagination, the personal experience of the remembered person. Indeed, the NAMES Project grew out of the personal frustration of Cleve Jones, who was initially motivated by his own sense of helplessness after his friend Marvin Feldman died of AIDS in October 1986. Like Jones, the NAMES Project provides a way for many others to transform the facelessness and hopelessness of AIDS into respect for individual men and women; for "each of these quilt panels bears the name of someone who has died of AIDS . . . ; each embodies the love and grief of the family, friends and lovers who created it" (Ruskin, 9). What could be more autobiographical and memoirist in approach?

At the same time the NAMES Project affirms individuality, it also, paradoxically, builds community. Miriam Schapiro points to this interplay between the personal and the communal in the AIDS quilt in a discussion of contemporary quilting when she describes the project as "Eloquent contemporary testimonies that the collaborative, satisfying, embracing traditions of female domestic art still enable people to connect and express personal grief, political rage, and joy."[12] We can go further to say that the success of the project depends directly on community cooperation and cocreation, as Cleve Jones recognizes only too well: "I may veto things now and then, but I really don't own this project. I could get hit by a car tomorrow and these people around me wouldn't falter" (Bellm, 35).

The NAMES Project, with its emphasis on individuality in community, practices in textiles the heteroglossia Bakhtin identifies as essential to the novel. Bakhtin's sense of heteroglossia as "a *system* of languages that mutually and ideologically interanimate each other" describes precisely the multivocal nature of these quilt groups (47). Heteroglossic language shifts the focus from individual author to a concatenation of voices within and outside of the text(ile). Individual voices are heard in the context of community, not in competition with each other, not necessarily in harmonious concert, but jostling together in a celebration of separate voices.

Bakhtin identifies heteroglossia as the central "art" of the novel. As journalist Phil Nash points out, heteroglossia also defines the art of the AIDS quilt: "It may better be seen as a new art form—one that has risen from the depths of our collective awareness as Americans, as a tribe, as a people yearning to express our common sorrow and hope, as warriors against a culture where power and profit depend on dividing people into 'markets,' 'minorities,' 'risk groups,' or other convenient parcels that can be bought, sold or ignored. The Quilt weaves these pieces back together" (Nash, 12). By focusing on community and emphasizing relationships—between people, panels, fabric—the quilt offers more than aesthetic values; it dissipates a monolithic and prejudicial central power into a myriad of individual voices, each claiming power for itself without setting up competition with others. Moreover, the many voices resist the silencing that constitutes the culture's most effective way to marginalize AIDS and PWAs.

Heteroglossia works at every level of these groups' work. Within each quilt the individual pieces, the layers of fabric, the different makers, and the audience, create a continuous polylogue that does not privilege any one component. The author/maker, in particular, is toppled as king of creation. As Bakhtin says of the novel, "The author participates in the novel (he is omnipresent in it) with almost no direct language of his own" (Bakhtin, 47). The reader/audience becomes an active participant in the novel/quilt, changing the text and changed by it in a complex and continual interplay; for "we ourselves may actually enter the novel (whereas we could never enter an epic or other distanced genre)" (Bakhtin, 32).

We see the dynamic of interactive multivocality worked out when we trace one panel made for the AIDS quilt. Gary Baker died of AIDS in Tucson, Arizona, on July 3, 1989. His support group, particularly his mother, Jean, decided to make a panel for him. Together with a friend, Miles, who is HIV positive, she selected fabric and started the panel. Jean called a dinner party for many of Gary's friends to work on the panel, and she sent pieces of fabric to family and friends for their contribution. Even Gary himself contributed posthumously in that his photograph and the cover of LAN Magazine, which he edited, was reproduced on fabric and incorporated in the quilt. Jean said, "It just grew . . . a bit of a hodge-podge, I guess. But that was the kind of panel that most interested people to see when the quilt was displayed."[13] About 30 to 40 people were involved in making this hodgepodge, this polylogue of voices, this quilt panel. Creating the panel changed the participants, because they began to move through their grief as they worked: "It was very hard to do alone—too painful. Doing it with the support of other people was very important" (Baker). This panel of many voices was then connected to other panels, speaking their own voices.

The panels, attached together in groups of eight, are arranged to make space for people to walk between them, so that the viewers also become part of the quilt, adding their presence and voices to the composition of the quilt.

This heteroglossic interplay has the effect of undermining neat borders and distinctions, and of course, this undermining is the central purpose of the NAMES Project. Borders keep us immune from AIDS and its impact, but as Michael Smith, general manager of the NAMES Project, observes, "there are no casual observers. We all suffer from the devastation of AIDS in our lives" (*National*, 8). The NAMES Project claims power for itself, not through one more set of binary opposites, but in an alternative, heteroglossic way that leaves no one marginalized.

Heteroglossia in the novel, Bakhtin argues, undermines the myth we hold that language is completely unified (Bakhtin, 68). In a parallel fashion, the AIDS quilt shifts the consciousness of a whole society from a single, fearful view of AIDS to multivocal diversity, and by doing so enables us to begin to face our fear. There are many ways to speak about AIDS, the quilt tells us; each one valid. Acting as a critique of our cultural construction of AIDS, the quilt fulfills the same purpose as the novel: " 'Novel' is the name Bakhtin gives to whatever force is at work within a given literary system to reveal the limits, the artificial constraints of that system."[14]

The anticanonical nature of the novel parallels the countercultural activity of the NAMES Project as the quilt sets about upsetting the cultural status quo. Bakhtin's description of the novel as "the leading hero in the drama of literary development in our time precisely because it best of all reflects the tendencies of a new world still in the making" (Bakhtin, 7), could also apply to this quilt, because it encourages us to rethink the ways we view AIDS.

Like the novel, the quilt is meant for popular consumption, reaching beyond those participating in the quilt-making to a wide, nonprivileged, diffuse audience: the more people the better, regardless of who they are. Inherent in a focus on such an all-inclusive audience is the belief that, even though we would like to dissociate from them, we are intimately implicated in the issues the quilt raises. The NAMES Project reminds us that we are all involved; we are all responsible. "AIDS cannot be stopped in any country unless it is stopped in all countries," declared the retiring head of the World Health Organization, Dr. Hafdan Mahler, at the Fourth International Conference in Geneva on AIDS (Sontag, 91). Susan Sontag, summing up AIDS as "one of the dystopian harbingers of the global village" (Sontag, 93), says: "the AIDS crisis is evidence of a world in which nothing important is regional, local, limited; in which everything that can circulate does, and every problem is, or is destined to be, worldwide" (Sontag, 92).

Inclusive audience bears the corollary of inclusive participation: no one is excluded on the grounds of insufficient knowledge or skills. Hawthorne's 1855 complaint against that "damned mob of scribbling women" who were threatening the exclusivity of his art as a novelist, finds its twentieth-century parallel in this quilt group.[15] Anyone can pick up a needle and start stitching.

Cleve Jones's concern with including everyone spreads naturally enough to the language the NAMES Project employs: "We want the grandmother from Iowa who hand-stitched her boy's flannel shirts together to be comfortable enough with us to come and see the panel. We don't use the rhetoric of the gay liberation movement or the Left or the 'New Age.' We don't allow ourselves to be defined in a way that will exclude anyone" (Bellm, 35). "Everyone belongs there, everyone is transformed," journalist Rob Morse commented on the display he attended ("AIDS Quilt," B5).

The novel, Bakhtin tells us, began as a marginalized genre: "The enormous success of the novel in the nineteenth century has obscured the fact that for most of its history it was a marginal genre, little studied and frequently denounced" (Holquist, xxvi). Through its very popularity, the quilt seeks to disturb the marginalized cultural status of AIDS. Sewing is a particularly effective way to counter that marginalization if we accept Ozzie Mayers's interpretation of the craft in "The Power of the Pin: Sewing as an Act of Rootedness in American Literature." He argues that we can view sewing as a kind of rootedness, as a symbolic act of survival, which suggests "an urge not to flee but to pin oneself down in order to discover the unconscious, unarticulated, and private modes of expression buried within."[16] Although he does not mention them by name, Mayers describes here the intentions of the NAMES Project to root itself and its issues in cultural consciousness.

That rootedness takes place in the present, for both novel and quilt, for it is "the spontaneity of the inconclusive present . . . that keeps the genre from congealing" (Bakhtin, 27). This present is all open-endedness: "The present is something transitory, it is flow, it is an eternal continuation without beginning or end; it is denied an authentic conclusiveness and consequently lacks an essence as well" (Bakhtin, 20). The quilt relies on that transitory present for the efficacy of its work. The AIDS quilt is designed entirely for display, not at a museum, but as a one- or two-day event, a temporary performance, in cities all over the United States; thus it reflects a belief in the immediacy, the pressing presentness of AIDS issues. Situated primarily in the present, neither novel nor quilt reaches a conclusion but exists in a continual state of becoming. The novel, says Bakhtin, "is the sole genre that continues to develop, that is as yet uncompleted" (Bakhtin, 3). Likewise, the work of the NAMES Project has no conclusion until AIDS itself has been eliminated.

Focused though it is on the present, the NAMES Project is not imprisoned by it. It reaches back into the past and forward into the future. From the vantage point of that insistent present, the AIDS quilt reevaluates, rewrites, and reintegrates past and future. Sontag observes that AIDS ties the act of sex, which is very much situated in the present, to an ominous past and future: "The fear of AIDS imposes on an act whose ideal is an experience of pure presentness (and a creation of the future) a relation to the past to be ignored at one's peril" (Sontag, 72). Displaying the AIDS quilt in the present serves not only as a poignant way to grieve for the past, but also as a way to raise money and hope for the future. Fear of past and future is transcribed into reconciliation with the one and hope for the other.

This direct, physical, present contact takes place, both in the quilt and in the novel, in a rather surprising place: the world of carnival. Carnival, for Bakhtin, makes a space for the reversal of cultural norms in a playful way so that a challenge of status quo that would otherwise seem too threatening becomes, through laughter and play, acceptable. Carnival "celebrates temporary liberation from the prevailing truth of the established order; it marks the suspension of all hierarchical rank, privileges, norms and prohibitions. Carnival was the true feast of time, the feast of becoming, change and renewal. It was hostile to all that was immortalized and complete" (Bakhtin, 109). The idea of carnival works at several levels in the AIDS quilt. First, in its colorful profusion, the AIDS quilt can be read quite literally as creating a carnivalesque space. Moreover, rooted in the domestic, a quilt, through its very ordinariness, symbolically draws the issues out of distant seriousness into carnivalesque proximity. The quilt allows us to play with horrifying ideas, making an amalgam of fear of death with the material pleasure of color and fabric. Like the novel, the quilt brings us into "a zone of direct and even crude contact . . . where one can finger it familiarly on all sides, turn it upside down, inside out, peer at it from above and below, . . . expose it, examine it freely and experiment with it" (Bakhtin, 23). Thus the AIDS quilt constitutes a kind of carnival, not only in its appearance, but also in its intention to disrupt set ways of thinking, to encourage change and renewal, to open up what has been closed as complete through "symbolic inversion" (a term Barbara Babcock defines as: "any act of expressive behavior which inverts, contradicts, abrogates, or in some fashion presents an alternative to commonly held cultural codes, values and norms be they linguistic, literary or artistic, religious, social and political"[17]).

The NAMES Project aims to change attitudes not by setting itself apart from society, but through the infiltration of quilt and carnival. There can be little doubt that the NAMES Project aims to make permanent changes in the way we see ourselves. Once again, the quilt parallels the novel: "Finally, in a novel the individual acquires the ideological and linguistic initiative necessary to change the nature of his own image" (Bakhtin, 38).

How effective is the quilt? Cleve Jones says, "I used to take some pride in the fact that I could move people to tears with my oratory. Now I find that I just get up to speak and they start weeping" (Bellm, 35). But the NAMES Project aims to do more than reduce people to tears; the quilt works towards turning around a nation's thinking about homosexuality and AIDS. This constitutes an unlikely goal, an impossible dream, and yet the quilters strive for it regardless of the apparent impracticability.

That transformation, however, is a long-term, ongoing process, one that takes precedence over any finished product. The sewing itself is more a means than an end. "Sewing, with the rootedness it connotes, becomes an expression of creativity and a means of revolutionizing a conventional female act into a source of endurance and vision," says Ozzie Mayers (Mayers, 673). The NAMES Project shows that we can go further to say that the sewing itself, the finished quilt, the material product, is of secondary importance to the process of healing, community, and transformation it represents.

16

The Way We Teach Now: Three Approaches to AIDS Fiction

ANNIE DAWID

"(H)e doesn't seem different from me. He's not."
—*Susan Sontag, "The Way We Live Now"*

In the fall of 1990, I taught a short story class in which—among the more than 40 stories we read—three dealt with the topic of AIDS. These stories—"Nothing to Ask For," by Dennis McFarland; "The Way We Live Now," by Susan Sontag; and "Philostorgy, Now Obscure," by Allen Barnett—approached the subject with an array of voices and from diverse points of view. All contained fictional characters of breadth and depth. Some were more successful than others in reaching my students; by the end of the course, several said they had had enough of the subject. What did not vary, however, was the clear need that students have to read fiction about an issue that directly impinges upon their lives each and every day, as college students constitute one of the highest risk categories for AIDS. The years of college are, for many, the first ones in which they fully explore their sexuality, approaching the issue both in practice and theory.

The first of the three, "Nothing to Ask For," allowed the students to confront a character dying of AIDS through the first-person narrative of a straight man—white, married, former alcoholic but otherwise unthreateningly middle-class. Dan feels helpless as he watches his best friend, Mack, slowly succumb to the ravages of the disease. Mack and Lester, his lover, are both gay, both angry, both grateful to Dan for his ministrations as well as a little resentful; particularly Lester, who has recently tested HIV positive. Dan spends the day on which the story takes place being the perfect caretaker: he buys Mack a new, soft toilet seat; cooks a turkey; cleans the apartment; gives his dear friend a bath. Lester, who is still healthy enough to spend energy railing against the inequities of medical research—"If it was Legionnaires dying, we wouldn't have any moratorium" on fetal tissue research—finally explodes against selfless Dan's pious housecleaning. "Oh, Dan, really," he says. "You go too far. Down on your knees now, scrubbing our toilet."[1] Dan's response: "Maybe I'm working out my survivor's guilt . . . if you don't mind" ("Nothing," 61).

This is precisely the route the student-reader takes into the heart of AIDS territory and its various manifestations in fiction. "Nothing to Ask For" allows the student a "safe entry"—not to mention a safe exit—into and out of this poignant story. By empathizing with the straight, healthy narrator, the student still identifies the AIDS sufferer as "other." Through Dan, the reader approaches the issues of homophobia and its myriad implications. Mack's parents had more or less disowned their homosexual son but have now "come around" in Mack's last months. Bitterly, caustically, Dan says, "Better late than never" ("Nothing," 56). The reader fills with righteous anger at the small-minded sister who "refused to let Mack enter her house at Christmastime—actually left him on the stoop in sub-zero cold—until he removed the gold earring from his ear" ("Nothing," 56). Yet the reader remains on the outside looking in, for we know that Mack will die, and Lester will die, but Dan will return to his home and the untainted dinner table of the nuclear family.

Student reaction to this piece was loud and heartfelt; many said they were moved to tears. Others knew people with the disease and feared for their own futures as would-be Dans. In response to his apparently unsympathetic wife's remonstrances that he is not spending enough time with his own family, her asking if it is fair that he spends his entire Saturday with Mack, Dan says, "I told her that fairness was not my favorite subject these days, given that my best friend was dying," ("Nothing," 57).

Implicit in the idea of lack of fairness is the heterosexual narrator's guilt that he, like his best friend from college, has led an unstable and unsafe life, but he, unlike Mack, will not die of it. Their friendship which has "endured the onlooking fisheyes of his long string of lovers and my two wives" (55) for over 20 years, forms the basis of the student reader's trust in the story. Dan says, "We persisted simply because we couldn't let go of the sense of *thoroughness* our friendship gave us; we constantly reported to each other on our separate lives, as if we knew that by doing so we were getting more from life than we would ever have been entitled to individually" ("Nothing," 55).

Gay and straight, the students understood what the ties of friendship are capable of supporting, and they were allowed to imagine themselves as the sacrificing and guilty Dan who will survive while this apparently discriminating disease vanquishes his best friend. Years before, however, the rescued and the rescuer occupied opposite positions, as Dan remembers: "Nine years ago, it was Mack who drove *me* to a different wing of this same hospital—against my drunken, slobbery will—to dry out." ("Nothing," 62). (Alcoholism, incidentally, is another issue with which the students can strongly identify.) What they may not identify with is the paraphernalia Dan observes in Lester's room: "movies whose cases show men in studded black leather jock-straps, with gloves to match—dungeon masters of startling handsomeness. On the floor, a stack of gay magazines. Somewhere on the cover of each of these magazines, the word "macho" appears; and inside some of them, in the personal ads, men, meaning to attract others, refer to themselves as pigs ("Nothing," 56–57). The narrator does not comment on these items, but the way in which he describes them indicates his feelings of foreignness to the materials, as if they were written in another language.

The second story, "The Way We Live Now," did not offer the student a cozy and lovable narrator/narrative in which to feel safe. Instead, Sontag's enormous cast of characters, the nameless patient dying of AIDS, the high-pressure, fast-paced life of the New York scene—all serve to keep readers at bay, challenging them to empathize with a not especially lovable person who is dying, as well as with the varied crowd of friends who now order their lives around visits to the sickbeds of friends dying of AIDS.

The center of the story, a New York denizen of the upper echelons of the artsy and monied world, has no name to distinguish him from anybody else. In this way, he remains a statistic of the disease, one of the many gay men students have read about in the sensationalistic press around the subject of AIDS. This same patient had, earlier, before his illness, failed to visit his friend Zack, who is now dead of the disease. "According to Clarice, Zack's widow, he didn't come very often, he said he hated hospitals, and didn't feel he was doing Zack any good, that Zack would see on his face how uncomfortable he was."[2] We should note that here the disease has plucked a married heterosexual man from the ranks of the well, and the story throws straight and gay friends and lovers of the patient together without distinction. One of the patient's female friends responds to the above comment with: "Oh, he was one of those, Aileen said. A coward. Like me" ("Now," 8).

The friends of the patient come to accept AIDS as part of the way they live, now, in the last cruel gasp of the twentieth century. The statistics have become their best friends, their former enemies, their old flames. "'Yes, don't you think we're more at home, here, with him, with the disease,' said Tanya, 'because the imagined disease is so much worse than the reality of him, whom we all love, each in our fashion, having it.'" Another friend says, "I know for me his getting it has quite demystified the disease," ("Now," 10).

In this way, the reader comes to identify, as in McFarland's story, with friends of the patient rather than with the patient himself. The setting changes everything, however. This time we do not get to know any of the friends particularly well, nor the environment. The sweet home of "Nothing to Ask For," with its sweet old neighbors who care for the gay couple as if they were their own children, is replaced by an urban and anonymous atmosphere in which names come and go as fast as faces on a train, seen from the perspective of a darkened suburban platform as the express whizzes by without stopping.

My students had a great deal of difficulty with the flowing omniscient narrative and fast-paced rhythm of Sontag's story. They could not keep any of the characters straight—so to speak—and they were never invited to enter into the soul of any one character because of the huge cast of extras—like bodies in a Cecil B. deMille extravaganza. More than one student linked the number of friends with the number of letters in the alphabet, concluding that Sontag had deliberately planned to exclude no one from possible linkage to the disease. "Sexuality is a chain that links each of us to many others, unknown others, and now the great chain of being has become a chain of death as well," says a straight woman character who chides a gay man for believing that she is not also at risk ("Now," 10).

The "chain of death" image frightened my group of 18 college students, all white, most of them between the ages of 18 and 22. While many have grown up with AIDS and condoms and safe sex as watchwords of their generation, they overwhelmingly continue to link AIDS with gay men and bathhouse promiscuity. Unfortunately, all three stories (all originally appearing in *The New Yorker*) do focus on gay men with AIDS, so this yoking is not challenged by these particular works of fiction. However, in Sontag's story, far more than in McFarland's, the assumption that our collective lives are permanently altered suffuses the fiction from start to finish. "Everybody is worried about everybody now, said Betsy, that seems to be the way we live, the way we live now" ("Now," 5).

Sontag's story also focuses on the ugly side of the sainted friends; while we never ever have the opportunity to judge Dan (of "Nothing to Ask For") poorly, Sontag shows us the full range of human response in the group of friends who show up at the patient's bedside. "There's always that vulgar jockeying for position around the bedside of the gravely ill," comments one friend. "It's undeniable, isn't it . . . the fascination of the dying. It makes me ashamed," says another ("Now," 11). Old feuds resurface as the disease (also unnamed) lingers and lingers. Since AIDS does not kill quickly—and decidedly mercifully—the various friends not only return to their "normal" lives but actually begin to resent the patient for his sickness: "He himself had done something to loosen the bonds of love that united the friends around him, by seeming to take them all for granted, as if it were perfectly normal for so many people to carve out so much time and attention for him" ("Now," 15).

I am reminded of Nathanael West's comment that readers do not fall in love with his characters because "there is nothing to root for in my books," he said, "and what is even worse, no rooters."[3] It is precisely this lack of "rooters" that kept the students in my class resisting "The Way We Live Now." The story resembles life, however, far more than "Nothing to Ask For," because it is more ambiguous; motives are shifty, behavior suspect. Some of the gay men in the story actively mourn the "good old days" of free-for-all sex. Eden is behind them, they seem to say, and while they are now wiser, they cannot disavow themselves of the notion that paradise was a wonderful place indeed. "Whatever happened it was over, the way he had lived until now, but . . . he did think about it, the end of bravado, the end of folly, the end of trusting life, the end of taking life for granted, and of treating life as something that, samurai-like, he thought himself ready to throw away lightly, impudently" ("Now," 14). The students, some born as late as 1972, have never known a sexual life free of the specter of AIDS. That does not prevent them from wishing for one, however, and my sense was that resentment free-floated around the room during the days when we discussed "The Way We Live Now," as if they wanted to blame characters like the unnamed patient for the frightening disease confronting them all. In this way, Sontag's view is the harshest of the three authors, the least gentle by way of assuring the readers that they can all return to their lives, business as usual.

Finally, "Philostorgy, Now Obscure," the most recent of the three, takes the "AIDS story" out of the status of the literature of disease and returns it to the larger amalgamation of the love story—love between the sexes, or between members of the same sex, or the love between friends. In this story, AIDS is not the focus but rather the impetus that charges it and sends its characters hurtling toward one another in a way that would not be as urgent or dynamic if AIDS were not part of the setting. The story deals with the friendship between one man and two women, formerly college roommates, as well as a visit the male character makes to a former lover, one who might have been "the perfect husband" for him ten years earlier, and who possibly could have altered his life forever. Lorna, Roxy, and Preston meet up, after a long absence, in the Chicago home where Roxy still lives. Preston and Roxy, who have the solidest bond among the threesome, are comfortable enough together to suffer the vagaries of the English language. "'Which reminds me, dinner won't be ready for another half hour. Can you wait or are you dying?' She dropped her head into her hand. 'I don't believe I said that.'"[4] Preston reassures Roxy, who, by way of dealing with the incursion of AIDS into the world of her dearest, closest friend, has read up on every latest nuance of the disease and its research. Her head-on confrontation with AIDS is in direct contrast to Lorna's. Seven years before, Preston himself told her about this "then unnamed disease," and she unbearably remembers herself saying, "Not you. It won't happen to you" ("Philostorgy," 38).

AIDS whets the emotions of these characters, whittling the edges of dying friendships, honing the characters' interactions to a deadly sharpness. Lorna, who has let the friendship lapse as a result of her new motherhood, rationalizes thus: "Even if there were anything she could do for him, she in Chicago and he in New York, her babies would have to take precedence" ("Philostorgy," 38).

Their friendship, once powerfully charged, has waned, as friendships commonly do, because of time and distance and new lovers or spouses taking up a space previously reserved for the closest friends. When Lorna finally breaks down and apologizes for her distance, Preston is unforgiving.

> "You're going to have another baby in three months. By the time you've weaned it, I could be dead."
>
> She started sobbing at that. "Tell me what I can do for you."
>
> "I could send you a pamphlet called, 'When Someone You Know Has AIDS.' It's filled with helpful hints for friends of the afflicted," he said. "Or better yet, why don't you continue on as if I never existed?" ("Philostorgy," 40)

This story was one of the last we covered in a 10-week quarter, and I regretted the late placement of it on my syllabus, for students wrote in their reading journals that they had tired of AIDS. Interestingly, they did not make similar comments about stories involving failed love affairs, or poverty, or depression, or racism, which were the themes of numerous other stories. "Philostorgy, Now Obscure" focuses on the lives of its characters, not on the disease. It is as if, by 1990, readers and writers both had matured to the point where they could see individuals apart from the illness and acknowledge that friendships and love affairs still thrive or die or continue in their faltering way as they did before AIDS had a name.

Of the various stories I photocopied as a supplement to the class text, students indicated which they felt essential, and which could be eliminated from the syllabus the next time I taught the class. Almost every student listed "Nothing to Ask For" as a must for the short story course. The other two did not appear on either list, though one student offered this explanation: "The AIDS issue became tiresome, but it is a pressing issue of our time." It is clear they liked the safest, most loving story of the three, and while I am disappointed they did not choose the more difficult stories as essential to the class, I cannot blame them; they are frightened.

We must now include stories like these when we teach fiction if we are to educate our college students in a broad and caring way.

"And it was encouraging," says one of the Sontag characters, that "he was willing to say the name of the disease, pronounce it often and easily, as if it were just another word, like boy or gallery . . . because . . . to utter the name is a sign of health" ("Now," 9–10).

Notes and References

CHAPTER ONE

1. Daniel Defoe, *A Journal of the Plague Year* (1722; New York and Toronto: New American Library, 1960). Subsequent references to this work will be cited in the next as *JPY*.
2. Daniel Defoe, *Due Preparations for the Plague* (London, 1722).
3. Watson Nicolson, *The Historical Sources of Defoe's Journal of the Plague Year* (Boston: Stratford Co., 1919).
4. For historical, scholarly, and medical studies of bubonic plague in the seventeenth century and AIDS in relationship to plagues, see Elizabeth Fee and Daniel M. Fox, eds., *AIDS: The Burdens of History* (Berkeley, Los Angeles, and London: University of California Press, 1988); James Leasor, *The Plague and the Fire* (New York: Avon, 1961); *The Plague Reconsidered: A New Look at Its Origins and Effects in 16th and 17th Century England* (Cambridge, England: "Local Population Studies," 1977); and Paul Slack, *The Impact of Plague in Tudor and Stuart England* (London, Boston, Melbourne, Henley: Routledge & Kegan Paul, 1985).
5. Albert Camus, *The Plague*, trans. Stuart Gilbert (New York: Vintage Books, 1948).
6. Paul Monette, *Borrowed Time: An AIDS Memoir* (San Diego, New York, and London: Harcourt Brace Jovanovich, 1988).
7. Randy Shilts, *And the Band Played On: Politics, People, and the AIDS Epidemic* (New York: St. Martin's Press, 1987).
8. Daniel Defoe, *Augusta Triumphans* (London, 1728), 45–46.
9. Larry Kramer, *The Normal Heart* (New York and Scarborough, Ontario: New American Library, 1985).

CHAPTER TWO

1. John Duffy, *Epidemics in Colonial America* (Port Washington: Kennikat, 1953), 4.
2. The nonfiction response, a considerable body of work that grows each month, offers little direction; its strategies are strikingly different from the fiction. At its simplest level, the nonfiction seeks to educate. Shelves of publications, generated largely by the medical community, try to counter the hysteria compounded by ignorance by clarifying concerns over the virus's transmission as well as by counseling the prudence of tempering life-styles. Apart from such educational functions, the nonfiction has grappled as well with incendiary public questions of gay rights, angrily assailing the dangers of the revival of homophobia (for example, Larry Kramer's *Reports from the Holocaust*). An emerging body of investigative nonfiction ventures into the politics of misdirected government policies and the adequacy (or inadequacy) of the medical community's response (for example, Randy Shilts's *And the Band Played On*). But the largest share of the nonfiction records—explicitly, graphically, and tenderly—the individual acts of raging against the premature dying of the light (for example, Paul Monette's *Borrowed Time*, Emmanuel Dreuilhe's *Mortal Embrace*, Steven Petrow's *Dancing in the Dark*, and George Whitmore's *Someone Was Here*). Such works employ the

poignancy of interviews or the immediacy of diaries and journals to give AIDS a name, an identity, a face.

3. Andrew Holleran, *Ground Zero* (New York: Morrow, 1988), 18.

4. To underscore the point, a similar argument can be made to account for the tremendous national outpouring of emotion following the April 1990, death of Ryan White, an Indiana schoolboy who was infected through a blood transfusion and who gained national attention for his determined efforts to stay in public school. Against the lurid coverage afforded other prominent deaths from the homosexual community—Rock Hudson or Liberace come to mind—the response to Ryan White's death was intensely somber and circumspect. Richard Goldstein, writing in the *Village Voice* shortly after the funeral ("Death in the Family," 12 May 1990, 67), argued that Ryan White earned such media attention because he better fit the "model of an 'innocent victim.' "

5. Alice Hoffman, *At Risk* (New York: Putnam, 1988), 202. Subsequent references to this work will be cited parenthetically in text as *AR*.

6. Robert Ferro, *Second Son* (New York: Crown, 1988), 23. Subsequent references to this work will be cited parenthetically in text as *SS*.

7. Susan Sontag, "AIDS and Its Metaphors." *New York Review of Books*, 27 October 1988, 195.

8. George Whitmore, *Nebraska* (New York: Grove, 1987), 45. Subsequent references to this work will be cited parenthetically in text as *Nebraska*.

CHAPTER THREE

1. Andrew Holleran, *Ground Zero* (New York: William Morrow, 1988), 11.

2. Alice Hoffman, *At Risk* (New York, Putnam, 1988). All subsequent references are to this edition and are included parenthetically. Crown published a paperback edition in 1989.

3. David Leavitt, "The Way I Live Now," *New York Times Magazine*, 9 July 1989, 28.

4. Charles Bazerman is Professor of English at Baruch College, and Assistant Editor of the journal *Science, Technology, and Human Values*, in which capacity he read an earlier version of this article and generously gave me permission to quote his comments.

5. David Wojnarowicz's essay "Post Cards from America: X-Rays from Hell" fiercely criticizes New York's John Cardinal O'Connor—"a fat cannibal from that house of walking swastikas up on fifth avenue," that "creep in black skirts" who "has kept safer-sex information off local television stations and mass transit advertising spaces . . . thereby helping thousands and thousands to their unnecessary deaths"—as well as North Carolina Senator Jesse Helms and California Representative William E. Dannemeyer (New York: Coalition of Artists Against AIDS, 1989, 5). Wojnarowicz's essay appeared in the brochure for a New York gallery exhibition "Witnesses: Against Vanishing" and became the focus of heated controversy over National Endowment for the Arts funding, which was first given for the exhibit, then withdrawn, and later rewarded given that the grant was not for the brochure.

6. While liberal clerics are urging compassion and an all-out effort to combat the ignorance and prejudice surrounding AIDS, some bastions of fundamentalism are claiming that AIDS is God's punishment for sin. The American Council of Christian Churches, a fundamentalist group who say they represent two million "Bible Christians," are on record that AIDS is God's punishment for homosexuals and drug addicts (P. Steinfels, "AIDS Provokes Theological Second Thoughts," *New York Sunday Times*, News of the Week in Review, 19 November 1989). At the Vatican conference on AIDS in November 1989, many Catholic clergy complained that the Church was focusing all its attention on sexual behavior and drug use, and not listening to PWAs themselves ("Vatican Meeting Splits over AIDS," [AP], *Boston Globe,* 15 November 1989). On December 10, 1987, the Church had issued a 30-page policy paper saying that it is sometimes appropriate to teach that condoms can prevent AIDS because some "people will not act as they can and should" (A. Goldman, "The Bishops: An Unseemly Battle," *New York Sunday Times*, News of the Week in Review, 3

January 1988). But conservative forces within the Church, led by New York's John Cardinal O'Connor, strongly rejected this teaching, which led to a later pronouncement in October 1989 by the American Catholic Bishop's Ad Hoc Committee on the HIV Virus forbidding teaching about condoms. The chairman, Archbishop Roger Mahony of Los Angeles, said, "There is no such thing as safe, or safer, sex. That's an illusion" ("Bishops Reject Condom Teaching," [AP], *Boston Globe,* 13 October 1989).

7. In reviewing Hoffman's most recent *Seventh Heaven* (1990) for the *New York Times,* Alida Becker writes,

> "In her previous novels, Ms. Hoffman has shown a fondness for tossing supernatural ingredients into the stew of ordinary life. Sometimes (as in 'Illumination Night,' which features a reclusive giant and a little boy who isn't growing fast enough) the effect is to open up a disorienting fissure between the normal and the fantastic, one that makes the storytelling seem a bit too self-consciously artificial. In others ('Fortune's Daughter' and 'At Risk,' both of which present us with fortune-tellers who lose faith in their powers), the results are more successful, subtly projecting the characters' emotional lives into a much more shadowy dimension. This is also the case in 'Seventh Heaven.' " (5 August 1990, Section 5, 2)

Earlier novels by Alice Hoffman are: *Property Of* (1977); *The Drowning Season* (1979); *Angel Landing* (1980); *White Horses* (1982); *Fortune's Daughter* (1985); and *Illumination Night* (1987).

8. Kay Longcope, "A Strong Link in Topsfield," the *Boston Globe,* 7 November 1989, 22.
9. Sally Jacobs, "Isolated Cases: In Suburbs, Many Keep AIDS Hidden," *Boston Globe,* 17 September 1990, 13.
10. Kay Longcope, "AIDS quilt: Stitched with Love, Bound by Tears," *Boston Globe,* 21 September 1990, 15.
11. Donna Haraway, "The Biopolitics of Postmodern Bodies: Determinations of Self in Immune System Discourse." *Differences,* 1 (Winter 1989): 3–43.
12. Shawn O'Connor, "The Big One: Literature Discovers AIDS," in *The AIDS Epidemic: Private Rights and the Public Interest,* ed. Padraig O'Malley (Boston: Beacon Press, 1989), 485–506.
13. Susan Sontag, *AIDS and Its Metaphors* (New York: Farrar Straus and Giroux, 1989), 26–27.
14. Jan Zita Grover, "AIDS Culture," reviews of *Thinking AIDS, AIDS and Its Metaphors,* and *AIDS: The Women, Women's Review of Books,* vol. 6, no. 7 (April 1989): 6.
15. *Treatment Issues: The GMHC Newsletter of Experimental AIDS Therapies.* Available from GMHC, Department of Medical Information, 132 West 24th Street, Box 274, New York, N.Y. 10011.
16. George Whitmore, *Someone Was Here: Profiles in the AIDS Epidemic* (New York: NAL/New American Library, 1988), 187. Hereafter cited as Whitmore.
17. "Out-of-kilter Health Care" (editorial), *Boston Globe,* 17 May 1990, 14.
18. Richard A. Knox, "Health Care Double Standard Cited," *Boston Globe,* 12 September 1990, 3.

CHAPTER FOUR

1. Leo Tolstoy, *The Death of Ivan Ilyich* (New York: Bantam, 1981), 93.
2. Lee Edelman, "Politics, Literary Theory, and AIDS," *South Atlantic Quarterly* 88:1 (Winter 1989): 309. Subsequent references to this work will be cited as Edelman.
3. Rüdiger Lautmann, "Categorization in Concentration Camps as a Collective Fate: A Comparison of Homosexuals, Jehovah's Witnesses and Political Prisoners," *Journal of*

Homosexuality, 19:1 (1990): 71. Subsequent references to this work will be cited in text as Lautmann.

4. Hans-Georg Stümke, *Homosexuelle in Deutschland: Eine politische Geschichte* (Munich: C.H. Beck, 1989), 102.

5. James Steakley, *The Homosexual Emancipation Movement* (New York: Arno Press, 1975), 106. Subsequent references to this work will be cited in text as Steakley.

6. Susan Sontag, "Fascinating Fascism," in *Under the Sign of Saturn* (New York: Farrar, Straus and Giroux, 1980), 105.

7. Paul O'M Welles, *Project Lambda* (Port Washington, NY: Ashley, 1979); Marty Rubin, *The Boiled Frog Syndrome* (Boston: Alyson P, 1987); and Geoff Mains, *Gentle Warriors* (Stamford, Conn.: Knights Press, 1989). Subsequent references to these works will be cited in the text as *PL, BFS,* and *GW*, respectively.

8. At the time Hitler came to power two different homosexual social identities were being contested. On the one hand, (Jewish, homosexual) sexologist Magnus Hirshfeld's Humanitarian-Scientific Committee argued for a democratic inclusion of homosexuals under the law (on grounds that they suffered from an irreversible disorder but caused society no harm). On the other, various free-thinking models, e.g. Hans Blüher's elitism or the *Gemeinschaft der Eigenen* (Society of "Self-Owners") asserted that homosexuals were a breed apart, culturally superior, or a higher form of human beings. A similar position is asserted in the American gay literature written by members of the leathersex community, namely that the leather aristocracy's virtue arises from its greater imaginative powers.

9. Klaus Theweleit, *Male Fantasies*, vol 2 (Minneapolis: University of Minnesota Press, 1989), xii–xiii.

10. Robert Jay Lifton, *The Nazi Doctors: Medical Killing and the Psychology of Genocide* (New York: Basic Books, 1986), 423–424.

CHAPTER FIVE

1. Peter Cameron, *Leap Year* (New York: Harper & Row, 1990), 3; hereafter cited in text as *LY*.

2. In Peter Cameron's *One Way or Another* (New York: Harper & Row, 1986), 116; hereafter cited in text as *OWOA*.

3. Peter Cameron, "The Secret Dog," *Kenyon Review* 9 (Fall 1987): 1.

4. Paul Monette, *Borrowed Time: An AIDS Memoir* (San Diego: Harcourt Brace Jovanovich, 1988), 5.

5. In *After the Ball*, Kirk and Madsen describe the behavior of some gays—essentially those homosexuals ("them") who are most likely to be HIV positive—as "immature, self-centered, destructive, silly, and creepy." Having dismissed the gay life-style as "the pits," the authors offer "A Portfolio of Pro-Gay Advertising" on which to model an extensive public relations campaign that would feature gay persons who are "wholesome and admirable by straight standards." Marshall Kirk and Hunter Madsen, *After the Ball: How America Will Conquer Its Fear and Hatred of Gays in the '90s* (New York: Doubleday, 1989), 183, 278.

6. Andrew Sullivan, "Gay Life, Gay Death," *New Republic*, 17 December 1990, 20.

7. A possible exception is the narrator of "The Secret Dog," but his behavior—shrouded in allegory—is difficult to address with certainty.

8. Edmund White, "Palace Days," in Adam Mars-Jones and Edmund White, *The Darker Proof: Stories from a Crisis* (London: Faber and Faber, 1987), 167.

9. Susan Sontag, *Illness as Metaphor* (New York: Farrar, Straus and Giroux, 1978), 54.

CHAPTER SIX

1. The Panos Institute, *AIDS and the Third World* (Philadelphia: New Society, 1989), 30. Subsequent references to this work will be cited in text as Panos.

2. Centers for Disease Control (CDC), figures through 31 December 1990.
3. CDC figures through 31 October 1990.
4. CDC figures through 31 October 1990.
5. Ishmael Reed, *Mumbo Jumbo* (New York: Macmillan, 1972), 6. Subsequent references to this work will be cited in text as Reed.
6. The first AIDS diagnosis was made in 1981; The Pasteur Institute in Paris isolated the virus today known as HIV-1 in 1983.
7. Henry Louis Gates, Jr., *The Signifying Monkey* (New York: Oxford University, 1988), 229.
8. For an account of the false leads regarding and current speculations on the inaugural period of the epidemic, see Panos, 70–74.
9. For an introduction to the relations between the African and New World belief systems mentioned here, see Robert Ferris Thompson, *Flash of the Spirit* (New York: Vintage, 1983). On Yoruba beliefs in Nigeria, see William Bascom, *The Yoruba of Southwestern Nigeria* (New York: Holt, Rinehart and Winston, 1969). On vodun, see Maya Deren, *Divine Horsemen* (New York: Thames and Hudson, 1953); Melville Herskovits, *Life in a Haitian Valley* (Garden City: Anchor Books, 1971); and Alfred Métraux, *Voodoo in Haiti* (New York: Oxford University Press, 1959). On *santería*, see Lydia Cabrera, *El Monte* (Havana: Ediciones C.R., 1954). On *candomblé*, see Pierre Verger, *Notes sur le culture des orisa et vodun* (Dakar: IFAN, 1957); and Roger Bastide, *Le Candomblé de Bahia* (Paris: Mouton, 1958). And on hoodoo, see Zora Neale Hurston, *Mules and Men* (New York: Harper & Row, 1970).
10. See Susan Sontag, *AIDS and Its Metaphors* (New York: Farrar, Straus and Giroux, 1989).
11. The most eloquent and precise account of spirit possession that I have encountered is in Deren, 247–62, and in the long and fascinating note 8 on pages 322–24.
12. On vodun rites and the revolution, see Deren, 61–63. For a fuller account of the political history of Haiti, see C. L. R James, *The Black Jacobins* (New York: Vintage, 1963).
13. Wade Davis, *The Serpent and the Rainbow* (New York: Warner Books, 1985), 159.
14. See Claude Lévi-Strauss, *The Savage Mind* (London: Weidenfeld & Nicolson, 1966).
15. October 24, 1986, 2199; See Daniel B. Hardy, "Cultural Practices Contributing to the Transmission of HIV in Africa," *Reviews of Infectious Diseases* 9, 6 (November–December 1987): 1109–19; and Peter Piot et al., "AIDS: An International Perspective," *Science* 5 February 1988, 573–79.
16. Alex Shoumatoff, *African Madness* (New York: Vintage, 1990), xi. Subsequent references to this work will be cited in text as Shoumatoff.
17. Harlon Dalton, "AIDS in Blackface," in *Living with AIDS*, ed. Stephen Graubard (Cambridge, Mass.: MIT Press, 1990), 244. Subsequent references to this work will be cited in text as Dalton. On race prejudice and the specific scapegoating of Haitians in the pandemic, see René Sabatier, *Blaming Others: Prejudice, Race and Worldwide AIDS* (Washington: Panos, 1988).
18. See in particular the poetry of Assotto Saint, Essex Hemphill, and Roy Gonsalves.
19. "Nonliterary" studies of and by women of color with AIDS comprise one section of ACT UP/NY Women & AIDS Book Groups, *Women, AIDS and Activism* (Boston: South End Press, 1990).
20. The CDC's "low estimate" of adult HIV infection in East Harlem is 13 percent. I note, with hope, that the New York City Board of Education has just passed a plan for condom distribution to students on demand. Of course, access is only a partial solution.

CHAPTER SEVEN

1. Ron Mooser, ed., *Dit verval. Verhalen rond een grote ziekte met een kleine naam* (Stories of a big disease with a small name) (Amsterdam: De Woelrat, 1988).
2. I. van den Bergen and R. Breed, *Is het waar dat Lefert aids heeft* (Amsterdam: Van Gennep, 1985); F. Stein, *Een half jaar AZT* (Amsterdam: Dekker, 1990).

3. For the Dutch Fassbinder-Affair, see M. Huygen and H. Vuijsji, "Oud Vuil," in *NRC-Handelsblad*, 16 January 1988.

4. Frans Kellendonk, "Ons wilde westen. Literatuur en publieke opinie," in his *De veren van de zwaan* (Amsterdam: Meulenhoff, 1987). The article first appeared in the daily *NRC-Handelsblad*, 20 October 1986.

5. For more information on his life and work, see F. de Rover, *Frans Kellendonk: Informatie* (Amsterdam: Meulenhoff, 1984), including a compilation of interviews with FK.

6. Frans Kellendonk, *Mystiek lichaam* (Amsterdam: Meulenhoff, 1986), 94; hereafter cited in text as *ML*.

7. Frans Kellendonk, *Bouwval* (Amsterdam: Meulenhoff, 1977), 46.

8. H. M. van den Brink, "God troont op het gezang van de mensen. Een gesprek met Frans Kellendonk" (God thrones on the hymns of man. An interview with FK), *NRC-Handelsblad*, 9 May 1986.

9. Frans Kellendonk, *De veren van de zwaan* (Amsterdam: Meulenhoff, 1987),148.

10. "Kardinaal Simonis en de kinderen van het Licht" (Cardinal Simonis and the children of the light), *HP*, 28 February 1987, 16–19.

CHAPTER EIGHT

1. Hervé Guibert, *A l'ami qui ne m'a pas sauvé la vie* (Paris: Gallimard, 1990), 21; subsequent references to this work will be cited in text as *Ami*.

2. Hugo Marsan, *La vie blessée: le sida, l'ère du soupçon* (Paris: Maren Sell & CIE, 1989), 101; subsequent references to this work will be cited in text as Marsan.

3. *Le Journal du sida* 24 (January 1991): 2. *Le Journal du sida*, published by ARCAT-SIDA (57 rue St-Louis-en-l'Ile, 75004, Paris) is the principal monthly AIDS publication in France.

4. See, for example, *Ami*, 58; Marsan, 95.

5. Guy Hocquenghem, *Le Gay voyage: Guide homosexuel des grandes métropoles* (Paris: Albin Michel, 1980).

6. Mirko D. Grmek, *Histoire du sida: début et origine d'une pandémie actuelle* (Paris: Payot, 1990), 278.

7. Guy Hocquenghem, *Eve* (Paris: Albin Michel, 1987), 58; subsequent references to this work will be cited in text as *Eve*.

8. Guibert never explicitly states that "Bill" is American, but most French readers and reviewers (*Magazine littéraire*, April 1990; *Le Nouvel observateur*, 8 March 1990; *Quinzaine littéraire*, 1 April 1990; *Le Journal de l'avancée médicale*, 7 May 1990) assumed so. According to a source close to Guibert, the real individual who served as Bill's model (and to whom the novel is addressed) is not American.

9. Interview, *Libération*, 1 March 1990. Several months later, in an interview with *Elle* magazine (21 May 1990), Guibert seemed to have modified his wrath: "[Bill] telephoned me after he read the book. He was shaken. The book made him more human."

    In the sequel to *A l'ami qui ne m'a pas sauvé la vie*, published in February 1991, Guibert reveals that he finally received Mockney's vaccine in Los Angeles on 27 January 1990; *Le protocole compassionnel* (Paris: Gallimard, 1991), 164. *Le protocole compassionnel*, the sequel that Guibert had vowed never to write, recounts "l'étonnement et la douleur, la rage et la tristesse d'un homme de trente-cinq ans dans lequel s'est greffé le corps d'un viellard" (the astonishment and the pain, the rage and the sadness of a thirty-five year old transplanted into the body of an elderly man). The title refers to the "compassionate use" protocol that allowed Guibert to receive the experimental drug DDI.

10. "Ecrire contre la montre," *Le Monde*, 2 March 1990.

11. Hervé Guibert, "Les Secrets d'un homme," *Mauve le Vierge* (Paris: Gallimard, 1988).

12. Interview, *Elle* magazine, 25 May 1990. In his interview with *Libération* (1 March 1990), Guibert admits that there was a time when he indeed "wished that [Adjani] had AIDS."

13. Personal interview, Paris, 1991.

14. In one memorable instance, Dreuilhe compares the pleasure he takes in discussing his doctors (New York physicians Joseph Sonnabend and Donald Kotler, to whom the book is dedicated) to Saint-Loup's obsession with the Prince de Borodino in Proust's *A la recherche du temps perdu*.

15. Alain Emmanuel Dreuilhe, *Corps à corps: journal du sida* (Paris: Gallimard, 1987), 148–49; subsequent references to this work will be cited in text as *Corps*.

16. Linda Coverdale, trans., *Mortal Embrace: Living with AIDS* (New York: Hill and Wang, 1988), 115–17; subsequent references to this translation will be cited as *Mortal Embrace*.

17. In addition to the novels of Guibert and Pancrazi, Marsan invokes Angelo Rinaldi's *La Confession dans les collines* (Paris: Gallimard, 1990); Francis Berthelot's science fiction allegory *Rivage des intouchables* (Paris: Denoël, 1990); and William Cliff's long poem *Conrad Detrez* (Paris: Le Dilettante, 1990).

18. Jean-Noël Pancrazi, *Les Quartiers d'hiver* (Paris: Gallimard, 1990); subsequent references to this text will be cited in text as *Quartiers*.

19. *Le Nouvel Observateur*, 30 October 1987. Aron restated his story in a now famous interview with French television channel Antenne 2 on 20 June 1987, two months to the day before his death.

20. Medical treatment for HIV infection is covered at the 100% level by French Social Security.

21. Dominique Fernandez, *La Gloire du paria* (Paris: Grasset, 1987), 82. The text is cited from the "Livre de Poche" edition; subsequent references to this work will be cited in text as *Paria*.

22. Copi (Raul Damonte), *Une Visite inopportune* (Paris: Christian Bourgeois, 1988), 54; subsequent references to this work will be cited in text as *Visite*.

23. Interview, *Le Parisien*, 18 October 1988.

24. Copi's complete theater (with the exception of *Une Visite inopportune*) has been published in two volumes in the series 10/18: Copi, *Théâtre* (Paris: Union Générale d'Editions, 1986). Copi's novels include *La Vie est un tango* (Paris: Hallier, 1979); *La Cité des rats* (Paris: Belfond, 1979); *La Guerre des pédés* (Paris: Albin Michel, 1982); and the posthumous *L'Internationale argentine* (Paris: Belfond, 1988).

25. *Le Monde* (29 October 1988) called the play "très rare, un sommet de théâtre." Other critics did not hesitate to compare his theatre to that of Beckett and to speak of a modern revival of the Commedia del l'arte.

26. Larry Kramer's *A Normal Heart* premiered in Paris in 1987 to less than enthusiastic reviews. William Hoffman's *As Is*, on the other hand, had been a great success in 1986 and played for a year at the Studio des Champs Elysées.

27. Michel Cressole, "Deux Copi Opportuns," *Libération*, 22 February 1988.

28. *Sainte Geneviève dans sa baignoire* (1966); *La Journée d'une rêveuse* (1968); *L'Homosexuel* (1971); *Les Quatres Jumelles* (1973); *La Nuit de Madame Lucienne* (Avignon Festival, 1985).

29. Interview, *Le Généraliste*, 26 February 1988. In an interview with another medical journal, *Impact Médecin* (12 November 1988), Lavelli elaborates: "Dans Copi, on rit de la mort . . . Copi démythifie la mort . . . Ce n'est pas morbide mais salutaire. La Mort est cocasse et ridicule. Le démarche théâtrale est plus tonique, sur ce sujet, que celle des intellectuels. Tout se passe dans un lieu artificiel, mais où il existe un contact avec le public. Cette sensualité de la présence, cette communion sont le privilège du théâtre." (In Copi's work, we laugh at death. . . . Copi demythologizes death. . . . This is not morbid but salutary. Death is laughable and ridiculous. The theatre's way of dealing with this subject is more invigorating than that of intellectuals. Everything takes place in a setting which is artificial but in which there exists a connection with the audience. This sensuality of presence, this communion, is the prerogative of the theater.)

30. Guy Hocquenghem, "Copi Soit-Il," in *Une Visite inopportune*, 81–82.

31. *Le Désir homosexuel* (Paris: J.-P. Delarge, 1972); *La Dérive homosexuelle* (Paris: J.-P. Delarge,

1977); *Race d'Ep! Un siécle d'images de l'homosexualité* (Paris: Editions Libres-Hallier, 1979); *La Beauté du métis* (Paris: Editions Ramsay, 1979).

32. Paris: Albin Michel. English translation: *Love in Relief*, Michael Whisler, trans. (New York: SeaHorse Press, 1986).

33. All published by Editions Albin Michel. *La Colére de l'agneau* and *Eve* are available in the collection Le Livre de Poche.

34. Guy Hocquenghem and René Schérer, *L'Ame atomique: pour une esthétique d'ère nucléaire* (Paris: Albin Michel, 1986).

35. Interview, Paris, 1991.

36. Interview, *Paris Match*, September 1987.

37. In a "Note épilogique," Hocquenghem documents the possibility of the extremely rare phenomenon of identical twins of different sexes (*Eve*, 317).

38. Interview, *Paris Match*, September 1987.

39. The Hôpital Claude Bernard, the site of a major Parisian AIDS ward, is also evoked in Guibert's *A l'ami qui ne m'a pas sauvé la vie*.

40. Adam had already lost the use of his own voice at the moment of Boy's murder (*Eve*, 172). Another aphasia, this one "une préparation au grand silence," had set in earlier in his hospitalization (*Eve*, 269).

41. Guy Hocquenghem, *La Colère de l'agneau* (Paris: Michel Albin, 1985), 82.

42. Interview, Paris, 1991. Hocquenghem had said several months before his death: "Je ne suis pas devenu croyant, je suis croyant. Je me situe dans la tradition gnostique, ce mouvement des débuts de l'Eglise, qui était fondé, disons, pour simplifier, sur le refus de donner une définition positive de la divinité" (*Libération*, 30 August 1988). (I haven't become a believer, I am a believer. I think of myself as belonging to the Gnostic tradition, to that movement in the history of the early Church which was founded—let's say, to simplify things—on the refusal to give a positive definition of divinity.)

43. *Les Voyages et aventures exrtraordinaires du frère Angelo* (Paris: Albin Michel, 1988), which appeared two days after Hocquenghem's death, continues his exploration of the relationship between Christianity and the birth of modernity.

44. René Schérer, "Angelus novus" in *Gai Pied Hebdo*, no. 334 (10 September 1988), 52.

CHAPTER NINE

1. Quoted by Richard Goldstein in "The Implicated and the Immune: Cultural Responses to AIDS," *Milbank Quarterly*, 68 Suppl. 2 (1990):300.

2. The chronological discussion and alphabetical filmography that follow (pp.224–26) are necessarily selective in their treatment of films dealing with AIDS. I discuss no educational films—their numbers are too great—and only three documentaries (which are also numerous), *Common Threads*, *Positive*, and *Silence = Death*. In addition, I do not discuss films whose relation to the AIDS pandemic is incidental, problematic, or troubling. Such films include the 1988 film *Heart of Midnight*, in which the main character (Jennifer Jason Leigh) inherits a nightclub from an uncle who died of AIDS; David Cronenberg's 1986 remake of *The Fly*, which many critics saw as an allegory for life and love in the age of AIDS; the 1988 film *Troma's War*, in which a group of tourists is stranded after a plane crash on a desert island where they are terrorized by a band of thugs whose number includes a man with AIDS, covered with sores, who surveys the female prisoners deciding whom he will infect with the virus; and the 1990 direct-to-video feature *Murder by Numbers*, a whodunit that has the poor taste to use the AIDS pandemic as a cheap plot device.

3. Fixing the date of the beginning of the AIDS pandemic is, of course, impossible. Randy Shilts, whose *And the Band Played On* (New York: St. Martin's, 1987) remains the pandemic's best chronicle, somewhat tongue-in-cheekly sees its seeds being planted in the United States during the Bicentennial celebration when sailors from all over the world

crammed New York City's bars for a Fourth of July bash (3). Film treatments of the AIDS crisis begin in the mid-1980s.

4. In a review of three television programs dealing with AIDS that aired during the same week in April 1991, John J. O'Connor comments that "television entertainment, it seems, has finally begun to grapple with AIDS." See "3 Shows About AIDS (Straight AIDS, That Is)," *New York Times*, 11 April 1991, C22.

5. Larry Kramer maintains that negotiations for the long-discussed film version of his play *The Normal Heart* dragged on and on thanks to the "selfish and exceedingly inhumane" action of Barbra Streisand, who had bought the exclusive film rights to the play. See *Reports from the Holocaust: The Making of an AIDS Activist* (New York: St. Martin's, 1989), 92–93.

6. *Village Voice*, 26 November 1985, 70.

7. The title of an article in *TV Guide* about Aidan Quinn's role in *An Early Frost* suggests a great deal about the cautious attitude in the film and television industry toward the project. See Michael Leehy, "Why This Young Hunk Risked Playing an AIDS Victim," *TV Guide*, 26 April 1986, 34–38.

8. Tom Boxer, "Actors and Director Did Their Homework," *New York Post*, 11 November 1985, 68.

9. Stephen Farber, "A Drama of Family Loyalty, Acceptance—and AIDS," *New York Times*, 19 August 1985, sec. 2:23.

10. Jane Hall, "A Shattering AIDS TV Movie Mirrors a Family's Pain," *People*, 18 November 1985, 145.

11. Vito Russo, *The Celluloid Closet: Homosexuality in the Movies*, rev. ed. (New York: Harper & Row, 1987), 178.

12. As Richard Lippe points out in his survey of contemporary film treatments of homosexuality, "*Parting Glances* is very much a film which insists on its commitment to a homosexual audience. While the film concentrates on the gay experiences several gays have within a 24 hour period, it is equally about the broader issues of gay lifestyles, gay community and gay history. . . . *Parting Glances* places its central characters within a complex but generally supportive community that contains both gays and nongays; and, in regard to its gay members, the community includes a wide range of social types" ("Gay Visibility: Contemporary Images," *Cineaction* 7 [Winter 1986–1987], 86).

13. For an even more poignant expression of this sentiment, see the last song in William Finn's 1990 musical *Falsettoland*. In that song, "What Would I Do?" Marvin, the surviving lover, surveys the play's events and defiantly and proudly sings, "I'd do it again / and again and again and / What more can I say?"

14. *Intimate Contact* was subsequently shown in the United States on the Home Box Office Cable network (HBO) and then released on videotape. *Sweet As You Are* has been a feature film on the Arts and Entertainment Channel (A&E).

15. John Lyttle, "Blood Simple?" *City Limits*, 21 January 1988, 57.

16. *As Is* opened at New York's Circle Repertory 10 March 1985, and transferred to Broadway's Lyceum Theater on 1 May 1985. The play won three Tony nominations and the Drama Desk Award in 1985. The script of the play is available in a paperback edition (New York: Vintage, 1985). The adaptation was first shown on the Showtime Cable Network on 27 July 1986, and is available on videotape.

17. *Safe Sex* premiered on 8 January 1987, at the La Mama ETC and transferred to Broadway's Lyceum Theater on 19 March 1987. The teleplay of *Tidy Endings* was first shown on HBO on 14 August 1988, and is available on videotape. The script for the entire trilogy is available in paperback (New York: Atheneum, 1988).

18. *Andre's Mother* was originally part of an evening of vignettes and songs called *Urban Blight*, first presented at the Manhattan Theatre Club on 18 May 1988. For the script of the play, see *The Way We Live Now: American Plays & the AIDS Crisis*, ed. M. Elizabeth Osborn (New

York: Theatre Communications Group, 1990), 189–94. The expanded teleplay aired on PBS's American Playhouse on 7 March 1990.

19. Quoted in a review of *Andre's Mother* published in *The Advocate*, 27 February 1990, 59.

20. Bryan Bruce, "Rosa von Praunheim in Theory and Practice," *Cineaction* 9 (Summer 1987): 29.

21. *A Virus Has No Morals* is available on videotape; *Positive* and *Silence = Death*, two-thirds of a trilogy to be completed by *Asses on Fire*, are not.

22. For evidence of that kind of emotional manipulation, see the article by Judith Light and Jeff Kaye that *TV Guide* published in advance of the telemovie's airing, "Q. Why Did Judith Light Smash a Window in Anger?", *TV Guide*, 7 January 1989, 14–15.

23. The balloons do cause death among fish and wildlife, and most states have as a result banned their release. But the legitimate environmental concern does nothing to alleviate the bathos of Robert's response to the tearful Steven in the film.

24. "Evan." Review of *Men in Love, Variety*, 25 July 1990, 22.

25. Edward Guthmann, "Stranger in Paradise," *The Advocate*, 13 March 1990, 57.

26. Quoted in a review of *Longtime Companion* published in *American Film* 15 (June 1990): 49.

27. Samuel G. Freedman, "Faces and Cries from the AIDS Battleground." *New York Times*, 15 October 1989, sec. II:42.

28. *Out Front: Contemporary Gay and Lesbian Plays*, ed. Don Shewey (New York: Grove Press, 1988), xxii.

CHAPTER TEN

1. William A. Henry, III, "A Common Bond of Suffering," *Time*, 13 May 1985, 85; subsequent references to this work will be cited in the text as Henry.

2. Jack Kroll, "Going to the Heart of Aids," *Newsweek*, 13 May 1985, 87, 89; subsequent references to this work will be cited in the text as Kroll.

3. William M. Hoffman, *As Is*, in *The Way We Live Now*, ed. M. Elizabeth Osborn (New York: Theatre Communications Group, 1990), 1:12; subsequent references to this work will be cited in the text as *As Is*.

4. Larry Kramer, *The Normal Heart*, (New York: New American Library, 1985); subsequent references to this work will be cited in the text as *TNH*.

5. Paul Berman, "Theater," *Nation*, 11 May 1985, 568–70; subsequent references to this work will be cited in the text as Berman.

6. Gerald Weales, "Aids on Stage," *Commonweal*, 12 July 1985, 406–47. Subsequent references to this work will be cited in the text.

7. Frank Rich, "'As Is,' About AIDS Opens," *New York Times*, 11 March 1985, sec. 3:12.

8. John Simon, "Splash," *New York*, 6 May 1985, 91–92.

9. Frank Rich, Review of *The Normal Heart*, by Larry Kramer. *New York Times*, 22 April 1985, sec. 3:17; subsequent references to this work will be cited in the text as Rich.

10. Mel Gussow, "Stage View," *New York Times*, 28 April 1985, ll, 3, 24, 3; subsequent references to this work will be cited in the text as Gussow.

11. *The Way We Live Now*, ed. M. Elizabeth Osborn (New York: Theatre Communications Group, 1990); subsequent references to this work will be cited in text as *TWWLN*.

CHAPTER ELEVEN

1. The quotation from Auden might also be seen as providing a positive gay image, a reference point for gay men who wish to find reassuring reinforcement from a culture they created.

2. One frequently held homophobic belief is that gay men threaten society merely by virtue of being outside the family—that often cited foundation of western society and culture. The theory goes that the freedom of gay men threatens society by presenting an alternative (one

often defined as selfish or egocentric or immature) to the commitment, responsibility, and stability of creating and maintaining a family. I might hasten to point out that the nuclear family in our time and day is suffering from a wide number of ills, very few of which could be legitimately placed at the door of homosexuality. Also, the function of the family in suppressing "difference" (especially sexual difference) is noteworthy and the family is often seen as providing in microcosm a model for the functioning of society as a whole—one in which the interests and behaviors of individuals are subordinated to the power of a male leader or father figure.

3. The parallels to Nathaniel Hawthorne's *The Scarlet Letter* here are quite obvious and are probably intentional on Bowne's part but inadvertent on the part of those conservatives who in real life proposed this step. At any rate, this connection reveals a fundamentally American response to those who break gender and sexual rules: brand them so that the "innocent" and morally upright elements of society can be protected from their real or imagined contagion. Also Hawthorne's equation of religion and law in his short novel probably also plays a role in the measures proposed to mark those infected with HIV.

4. Perhaps Pintauro's inclusion of the entire spectrum of Persons with AIDS is a reaction to criticisms of the Norman Rene film *Longtime Companion*, which featured only middle-class, white males as its afflicted characters.

5. I might also note that in the Gericault painting a nude man with a beautiful body and visible genitalia is present in the foreground. Perhaps this painting might be seen as a sort of homosexual icon and thus as doubly appropriate as a partial inspiration for a gay work of art.

6. Fierstein's tripartite structure here and his movement from lyrical, antirealist practice to domestic comedy duplicate exactly the form of his Tony Award–winning Broadway success *Torch Song Trilogy*, which was criticized in some gay circles for its parallel deference to heterosexually based models of behavior. The final play of *Torch Song Trilogy* is very similar to "On Tidy Endings," because both feature a gay man trying to reestablish a "family" after the death of a male lover. Significantly, both plays end with the main male character alone on stage, seemingly catching his breath after having worked through many of his familial problems to create a "family" unit based in obvious ways on a heterosexual paradigm.

CHAPTER TWELVE

1. Erica Carter and Simon Watney, eds., *Taking Liberties: AIDS and Cultural Politics* (London: Serpent's Tail, 1989), 186.

2. Douglas Crimp, ed., *AIDS: Cultural Analysis/Cultural Activism* (Cambridge, Mass., and London: MIT Press, 1988), 7.

3. Michael Rumaker, *A Day and a Night at the Baths* (Bolinas, California: Grey Fox, 1979), 2; hereafter cited in text as *A Day*.

4. Bill Becker, "6 Sep 84," *An Immediate Desire to Survive* (Bryn Mawr, Pa.: Dorrance, 1985), 6.

5. Paul Monette, *Borrowed Time* (London: Collins Harvill, 1988), 227–28.

6. Tessa Boffin and Sunil Gupta, eds., *Ecstatic Antibodies: Resisting the AIDS Mythology* (London: Rivers Oram Press, 1990), 166.

7. There have been relatively few hetero elegies. Examples are Henry King's "Exequy on his Wife" and Alexander Pope's "Elegy to the Memory of an Unfortunate Lady." Gerard Manley Hopkins's "The Wreck of the Deutschland" was occasioned by the deaths of a group of nuns. One good recent example is Douglas Dunn's *Elegies* (London: Faber, 1985). There have also been elegies by homosexual writers that do not deal in such friendships as I have mentioned. Auden's elegy on Yeats, for instance, is an exercise in dryness. It thrives on the precision of detachment: "What instruments we have agree/ The day of his death was a dark cold day." Its ironic effects are largely achieved by its deviation from the sentimentality of the tradition: it is more a celebration of Yeats than a lament for his passing. The importance of elegy to

the gay literary tradition as a whole is briefly dealt with in Gregory Woods, *Articulate Flesh: Male Homoeroticism and Modern Poetry* (New Haven & London: Yale University Press, 1987), 83–85.

8. *The Epic of Gilgamesh*, Trans. N. K. Sandars (Harmondsworth, Middlesex: Penguin, 1960), 91. We should not forget that much of the most emotionally expressive homoerotic literature from the pre-"homosexual" world took the form of personal laments. Witness Achilles' grief for the loss of Patroclus in the *Iliad*, and Roland's for Olivier in the *Chanson de Roland*.

9. Moschus, in his "Lament for Bion," distinguishes clearly between dead plants—"they grow again, and live another year"—and humans, who, "as soon as we are dead, / at once we sleep, in a hole beneath the earth, / a sleep so deep, so long, with no end, / no reawakening." But this is a temporary mood. Only a few lines later, Moschus sings, "As once [Persephone] granted Orpheus, for the rhythms / of his harp, the return of his Eurydice, / so shall she return you, Bion, to the hills." *Greek Pastoral Poetry*, Trans. Anthony Holden (Harmondsworth, Middlesex: Penguin, 1974), 190, 191.

10. Marc Almond, *The Angel of Death in the Adonis Lounge* (London: GMP, 1988), 21–26. Many of these laments for out gay men will not, of course, be pastoral elegies, since the lost way of life is likely to have been urban. (Pastoral can, though, be written retrospectively by a poet of rural origins, as Theocritus wrote about his native Sicily while living in Alexandria.) However, while on the subject of pornography, it occurs to me that many gay American porn videos, among them some of Kip Noll's, constitute a kind of suburban pastoral: a poolside world of perfect weather, near perfect physiques, and guiltless polymorphous perversity.

11. Andrew Holleran, *Ground Zero* (New York: Plume, 1988), 23; hereafter cited in text as *GZ*.

12. Tony Harrison, *v.* (Newcastle: Bloodaxe, 1985).

13. Robert Boucheron, *Epitaphs for the Plague Dead* (New York: Ursus Press, 1985), 32.

14. *Other Countries Journal: Black Gay Voices*, 1 (Spring 1988): 51.

15. Paul Monette, *Love Alone: 18 Elegies for Rog* (New York: St. Martin's Press, 1988), 13–15; hereafter cited in text as *Love Alone*.

16. Thom Gunn, *Undesirables* (Durham: Pig Press, 1988), 11. Before the emergence of AIDS, Gunn was already an exquisite elegist. See his poem "Talbot Road" in *The Passages of Joy* (London: Faber, 1982), 80–89.

17. Martin Humphries, ed., *Not Love Alone: A Modern Gay Anthology* (London: GMP, 1985), 76.

18. Dirg Aaab-Richards, Craig G. Harris, Essex Hemphill, Isaac Jackson, and Assotto Saint, *Tongues Untied* (London: GMP, 1987) 30.

19. Sam Ambler, "After the Howl," *City Lights Journal* 2 (1988), 36–38.

20. Carl Morse and Joan Larkin, eds., *Gay and Lesbian Poetry in Our Time: An Anthology* (New York: St. Martin's Press, 1988) 224–26; subsequent references to this work will be cited in text as *Morse & Larkin*.

21. Lee Edelman gives a coherent and acute theoretical account of this slogan in his essay "The Plague of Discourse: Politics, Literary Theory, and AIDS," in Ronald R. Butters, John M. Clum and Michael Moon, eds., *Displacing Homophobia: Gay Male Perspectives in Literature and Culture* (Durham & London: Duke University Press, 1989), 289–305.

22. Simon Watney, *Policing Desire: Pornography, AIDS and the Media* (London: Methuen, 1987), 131.

CHAPTER THIRTEEN

1. This material is reconstructed from Douglas Crimp's contribution to the *October* issue on AIDS: "How to Have Promiscuity in an Epidemic," *October* 43 (Winter 1987): 237–71, see especially pages 260–61.

2. Simon Watney, *Policing Desire: Pornography, AIDS and the Media* (Minneapolis: University of Minnesota Press, 1987), 9.
3. Angus Fletcher, *Allegory: The Theory of a Symbolic Mode* (Ithaca: Cornell University Press, 1964), 3.
4. "AIDS: Cultural Analysis/Cultural Activism," *October* 43 (Winter 1987): 3.
5. Lee Edelman, "The Plague of Discourse: Politics, Literary Theory, and AIDS," *South Atlantic Quarterly* 8 (Winter 1989): n.1, 316; subsequent references are cited in the text as Edelman.
6. Dennis Altman, "Comment on Seidman," *Social Text* 19/20 (Fall 1988): 207.
7. Steven Seidman, "Transfiguring Sexual Identity: AIDS and the Contemporary Construction of Homosexuality," *Social Text* 19/20 (Fall 1988): 203.
8. Craig Owens, "The Allegorical Impulse: Toward a Theory of Post-Modernism," in *Art after Modernism: Rethinking Representation*, ed. Brian Wallis (Boston: David R. Godine, 1984), 205; subsequent references are cited in the text as Owens. The essay was originally published in 1979 and is not significantly amended in this printing.
9. James Applewhite, "Post-Modern Allegory and the Denial of Nature," *Kenyon Review* 11 (Winter 1989): n.1, 2.
10. The term in quotation marks is that of Susan Sontag, *AIDS and Its Metaphors* (New York: Farrar, Straus, and Giroux, 1989). A response to Sontag with which I share many assumptions is D. A. Miller's "Sontag's Urbanity," *October* 49 (Summer 1989): 91–101.

CHAPTER FOURTEEN

1. Paula A. Treichler, "AIDS, Homophobia and Biomedical Discourse: An Epidemic of Signification," in *AIDS: Cultural Analysis/Cultural Activism*, ed. Douglas Crimp (Cambridge, Mass.: MIT Press, 1988), 42; subsequent references to this work will be cited in the text as Treichler.
2. Rex Wockner, "Kellogg Shareholders Stunned by Gay Speech at Battle Creek Meeting," *Baltimore Alternative*, May 1989, 1, 4.
3. Susan Sontag, *AIDS and Its Metaphors* (New York: Farrar, Straus and Giroux, 1989), 93.
4. Lee Edelman, "The Plague of Discourse: Politics, Literary Theory, and AIDS." *South Atlantic Quarterly* 88:1 (1989): 315–16.
5. Frances Fitzgerald, *Cities on the Hill* (New York: Simon & Schuster, 1987), 109; subsequent references to this work will be cited in the text as Fitzgerald.
6. Larry Kramer, *Reports from the Holocaust: The Making of an AIDS Activist* (New York: St. Martin's, 1989), 146; subsequent references to this work will be cited in text as *RH*.
7. Allan M. Brandt, "AIDS: From Social History to Social Polity," in *AIDS: The Burdens of History*, eds. Elizabeth Fee and Daniel M. Fox (Berkeley: University of California Press, 1988), 152.
8. Sander L. Gilman, "AIDS and Syphilis: The Iconography of Disease," in *AIDS: Cultural Analysis/Cultural Activism*, ed. Douglas Crimp (Cambridge, Mass.: MIT Press, 1988), 107.
9. Charles A. Rosenberg, "Disease and Social Order in America: Perceptions and Expectation." *Milbank Quarterly*, 64, suppl. 1 (1986): 51.
10. Martha Gever, "Pictures of Sickness: Stuart Marshall's *Bright Eyes*," in *AIDS: Cultural Analysis/Cultural Activism,* ed. Douglas Crimp. (Cambridge, Mass.: MIT Press, 1988), 110.
11. Andrew Holleran, introduction to *The Normal Heart* (New York: New American Library, 1985), 27.
12. Larry Kramer, *Faggots* (New York: Random House, 1978), 12; subsequent references to this work will be cited in text as *F*.
13. Larry Kramer, *The Normal Heart* (New York: New American Library, 1985), 68; subsequent references to this work will be cited in text as *TNH*.
14. Seymour Kleinberg, in *AIDS: Ethics and Public Policy*, eds. Christine Pierce and Donald Van

De Veer (Belmont, Calif.: Wadsworth, 1988), 59; subsequent references to this work will be cited in the text as Kleinberg.

15. Judith Wilson Ross, "Ethics and the Language of AIDS" in *AIDS: Ethics and Public Policy*, eds. Christine Pierce and Donald Van De Veer (Belmont, Calif.: Wadsworth, 1988), 40.

16. John R. Acevedo, "Impact on Risk Reduction of Mental Health," in *What To Do about AIDS: Physicians and Mental Health Professionals Discuss the Issues*, ed. Leon McKusic (Berkeley: University of California Press, 1986), 100.

17. George Whitmore, *Someone Was Here: Profiles in the AIDS Epidemic* (New York: New American Library, 1988), 26; subsequent references to this work will be cited in the text as Whitmore.

18. Barbara Peabody, *The Screaming Room* (San Diego: Oak Tree, 1986), 94.

19. Jerome Schofferman, "Medicine and the Psychology of Treating the Ill," in *What To Do about AIDS: Physicians and Mental Health Professionals Discuss the Issues*, ed. Leon McKusic (Berkeley: University of California Press, 1986), 56.

20. William Horstman and Leon McKusick, "The Impact of AIDS on the Physician," in *What To Do about AIDS: Physicians and Mental Health Professionals Discuss the Issues*, Ed. Leon McKusic (Berkeley: University of California Press, 1986), 63.

21. Simon Watney, "The Spectacle of AIDS," in *AIDS: Cultural Analysis/Cultural Activism*, ed. Douglas Crimp (Cambridge, Mass.: MIT Press, 1988), 82.

CHAPTER FIFTEEN

1. NAMESletter: The NAMES Project Newsletter, vol. 3, no. 2, (Fall 1990).

2. National Tour Release: See The Quilt and Understand. The NAMES Project Quilt: A National AIDS Memorial, Washington DC, October 7–10, 1988. (San Francisco: The NAMES Project Foundation, September 1988), 3; subsequent references to this work will be cited in text as *National*.

3. Cindy Ruskin, *The Quilt: Stories from the NAMES Project*. (New York: Pocket Books, 1988), 13; subsequent references to this work will be cited in text as Ruskin.

4. Dan Bellm, "And Sew It Goes," *Mother Jones*, January 1989, 35; subsequent references to this work will be cited in text as Bellm.

5. Phil Nash, "The Artist as Warrior in Time of AIDS," *Muse*, (December 1989): 9; subsequent references to this work will be cited in text as Nash.

6. Peter Stallybrass and Allon White, *The Politics and Poetics of Transgression* (London: Methuen, 1986), 4.

7. *Common Threads*, video documentary. Produced by Rob Epstein, Jeffrey Friedman, and Bill Couturie. 1989.

8. Carroll Smith-Rosenberg, *Disorderly Conduct: Visions of Gender in Victorian America* (New York: Knopf, 1985), 43.

9. Susan Sontag, *AIDS and its Metaphors* (New York: Farrar, Straus and Giroux, 1988), 93; subsequent references to this work will be cited in text as Sontag.

10. Rob Morse, "AIDS Quilt: Lost Lives That Are Part Of Us All," *San Francisco Examiner*, Sunday, December 20, 1987. B5.

11. M. M. Bakhtin, *The Dialogic Imagination* (Austin: University of Texas Press, 1981), 11; subsequent references to this work will be cited in text as Bakhtin.

12. Mariam Schapiro and Faith Wilding, "Cunts/Quilts/Consciousness," *Heresies* (December 1989): 12.

13. Jean Baker, *Interview*, October 31, 1989; subsequent references to this interview will be cited in the text as Baker.

14. Michael Holquist, Introduction to *The Dialogic Imagination*, by M. M. Bakhtin. (Austin: University of Texas Press, 1981), xxxi; subsequent references to this work will be cited in text as Holquist.

15. Sandra M. Gilbert and Susan Gubar, *The Madwoman in the Attic: The Woman Writer and the Nineteenth-Century Imagination*. (New Haven, Conn.: Yale University Press, 1985), 185.
16. Ozzie J. Mayers, "The Power of the Pin: Sewing as an Act of Rootedness in American Literature," *College English*, vol. 50, no. 6, (October 1988): 667; subsequent references to this work will be cited in text as Mayers.
17. Barbara Babcock, *The Reversible World* (Ithaca: Cornell University Press, 1972), 14.

CHAPTER SIXTEEN

1. Dennis McFarland, "Nothing to Ask For," in *The New Yorker*, 25 September 1989, 55–62; hereafter cited in text as "Nothing."
2. Susan Sontag, "The Way We Live Now," in *The Best American Short Stories 1987* (Boston: Houghton Mifflin Company, 1987), 1–19; hereafter cited in text as "Now."
3. Jay Martin, *Nathaniel West: The Art of His Life* (New York: Carroll and Graf Publishers, Inc., 1970), 334.
4. Allen Barnett, "Philostorgy, Now Obscure," in *The New Yorker*, 4 June 1990, 36–46; hereafter cited in text as "Philostorgy."

Selected Bibliography

EMMANUEL S. NELSON

NON-LITERARY TEXTS

Books on AIDS continue to proliferate; the following list of non-literary texts, therefore, is necessarily a highly selective one. These works offer broad perspectives that are of some value in locating literary texts about AIDS in their medical, historical, political, and cultural contexts.

AGGLETON, PETER, et al. *AIDS: Social Representations, Social Practices*. Philadelphia: Falmer Press, 1989.

ALTMAN, DENNIS. *AIDS in the Mind of America*. New York: Doubleday, 1986.

BLACK, DAVID. *The Plague Years: A Chronicle of AIDS, The Epidemic of Our Times*. New York: Simon and Schuster, 1986.

BOFFIN, TESSA AND SUNIL GUPTA. *Ecstatic Antibodies: Resisting the AIDS Mythology*. London: Rivers Oram Press, 1990.

CARTER, ERICA AND SIMON WATNEY, eds. *Taking Liberties: AIDS and Cultural Politics*. London: Serpent's Tail, 1989.

CRIMP, DOUGLAS. *AIDS: Cultural Analysis/Cultural Activism*. Cambridge: MIT Press, 1988.

FEE, ELIZABETH AND DANIEL M. FOX. *AIDS: The Burdens of History*. Berkeley: University of California Press, 1988.

GILMAN, SANDER. *Disease and Representation: Images of Illness from Madness to AIDS*. Ithaca: Cornell University Press, 1988.

GRMEK, MIRKO A. *History of AIDS: Emergence and Origin of a Modern Pandemic*. Princeton: Princeton University Press, 1990.

MCKENZIE, NANCY F. *The AIDS Reader: Social, Political, and Ethical Issues*. New York: Meridian, 1991.

O'MALLEY, PADRAIG. *The AIDS Epidemic: Private Rights and Public Interest*. Boston: Beacon Press, 1989.

PATTON, CINDY. *Inventing AIDS*. New York: Routledge, 1990.

———. *Sex and Germs: The Politics of AIDS*. Boston: South End Press, 1985.

SABATIER, RENE. *Blaming Others: Prejudice, Race and Worldwide AIDS*. Washington, D.C.: Panos, 1988.

SHILTS, RANDY. *And the Band Played On: Politics, People, and the AIDS Epidemic*. New York: St. Martin's Press, 1987.

SONTAG, SUSAN. *AIDS and Its Metaphors*. New York: Farrar, Straus and Giroux, 1989.
WATNEY, SIMON. "Missionary Positions: AIDS 'Africa' and Race." *Critical Quarterly*, 31:3 (Autumn 1989), 45–62.
———. *Policing Desire: Pornography, AIDS and the Media*. Minneapolis: University of Minnesota Press, 1987.

FICTION

BARNETT, ALLEN. *The Body and Its Dangers*. New York: St. Martin's Press, 1990.
BARROW, JOHN. "Killing the Pope." *Christopher Street*, issue 110, 51–57.
BARRUS, TIM. *Genocide*. Stamford, CT: Knights Press, 1989.
———. "Life Sucks." In *Men on Men 2*. Ed. George Stambolian, 255–74. New York: NAL, 1988
Beattie, Ann. "Second Question." *The New Yorker*, 10 June 1991, 38–44.
BISHOP, MICHAEL. "Icicle Music." *The Magazine of Fantasy and Science Fiction*, March 1989, 6–19.
BORGMAN, C. F. *River Road*. New York: NAL, 1988.
BOULDREY, BRIAN. "Whipped Cream and Other Delights." *Christopher Street*, issue 140, 33–36.
BOURJAILY, VANCE. *Old Soldier*. New York: Donald I. Fine, 1990.
BRYAN, JED. *A Cry in the Desert*. Austin, TX: Banned Books, 1987.
BUSBY, F. M. *The Breeds of Man*. New York: Bantam, 1988.
CAMERON, LINDSLEY. "The Angel of Death." *Christopher Street*, issue 111, 43–48.
CASHORALI, PETER. "The Ride Home." *Men on Men 3*. Ed. George Stambolian, 298–314. New York: NAL, 1990.
CHAMPAGNE, JOHN. *The Blue Lady's Hand*. Secaucus, NJ: Lyle Stuart, 1988.
CURZON, DANIEL. *The World Can Break Your Heart*. Stamford, CT: Knights Press, 1984.
D'ALLESANDRO, SAM. "Nothing Ever Just Disappears." *Men on Men: Best New Gay Fiction*, ed. George Stambolian, 126–32. New York: NAL, 1986.
DAVIS, CHRISTOPHER. *Valley of the Shadows*. New York: St. Martin's Press, 1988.
———. "The Boys in the Bars." In *The Boys in the Bars*, 71–87. Stamford, CT: Knights Press, 1989.
———. "History." In *The Boys in the Bars*, 159–206. Stamford, CT: Knights Press, 1989.
DELANY, SAMUEL. *Flight from Nevèrÿon*. New York: Bantam, 1985.
FEINBERG, DAVID. *Eighty-Sixed*. New York: Penguin, 1989.
———. "The Age of Anxiety." *Men on Men 2*. Ed. George Stambolian, 32–48. New York: NAL, 1988.
———. *Spontaneous Combustion*. New York: Viking, 1991.
FERNANDEZ, DOMINIQUE. *La gloire du paria*. Paris: Grasset, 1987.
FERRELL, ANDERSON. "Why People Get Cancer." *Men on Men 2*. Ed. George Stambolian, 211–23. New York: NAL, 1988.
FERRO, ROBERT. *Second Son*. New York: Crown, 1988.
FOX, JOHN. "Choice." *Men on Men: Best New Gay Fiction*. Ed. George Stambolian, 19–36. New York: NAL, 1986.
GLETZMAN, MORRIS. *Two Weeks with the Queen*. New York: Putnam, 1991.
GRAHAM, CLAYTON. *Tweeds*. Stamford, CT: Knights Press, 1987.
GROFF, DAVID. "Labor Day." *Christopher Street*, issue 119, 36–43.
GUIBERT, HERVÉ. *A lami qui ne m'a pas sauvé la vie*. Paris: Gallimard, 1990.
HAULE, ROBERT. "Blond Wig." *Men on Men 3*, ed. George Stambolian, 48–70. New York: NAL, 1990.
HOCQUENGHEM, GUY. *Eve*. Paris: Albin Michel, 1987.
HOFFMAN, ALICE. *At Risk*. New York: Putnam, 1988.
HOLLERAN, ANDREW. "Friends at Evening." *Men on Men: Best New Gay Fiction*, ed. George Stambolian, 88–113. New York: NAL, 1986.

————. "Lights in the Valley." *Men on Men 3*, ed. George Stambolian, 321–39. New York: NAL, 1990.

HUSTON, BO. *Remember Me*. New York: Amethyst, 1990.

INNAURATO, ALBERT. "Solidarity." *Men on Men 2*, ed. George Stambolian, 87–118. New York: NAL, 1988.

JEFFERS, ALEX. "My Face in a Mirror." *Men on Men 3*, ed. George Stambolian, 275–81. New York: NAL

JOFFE, HAROLD. *Eros: Anti-Eros*. San Francisco: City Lights, 1990.

JOHNSON, TOBY (EDWIN CLARK). *Plague: A Novel About Healing*. Boston: Alyson, 1987.

LEMON, BRENDAN. "Positive Results." *Christopher Street*, issue 114, 22–24.

LEVY, MARILYN. *Rumors and Whispers*. New York: Fawcett, 1990.

MAINS, GEOFF. *Gentle Warriors*. Stamford, CT: Knights Press, 1989.

MARS-JONES, ADAM AND EDMUND WHITE, eds. *The Darker Proof: Stories from a Crisis*. London: Faber and Faber, 1987.

MARTIN, KENNETH. *Billy's Brother*. London: Gay Men's Press, 1989.

MCFARLAND, DENNIS. "Nothing to Ask For." *The New Yorker*, 25 September 1989, 55–62.

MCGEHEE, PETER. *Boys Like Us*. New York: St. Martin's Press, 1990.

MIKLOWITZ, GLORIA. *Good-bye Tomorrow*. New York: Delacorte Press, 1987.

MOFFETT, JUDITH. "Tiny Tango." *The Year's Best Science Fiction: Seventh Annual Collection*. Ed. Gardner Dozois. 2–39. New York: St. Martin's Press, 1990.

MONETTE, PAUL. *Afterlife*. New York: Crown, 1990.

————. *Halfway Home*. New York: Crown, 1990.

MOORE, PATRICK. *This Every Night*. New York: Amethyst, 1990.

NAVA, MICHAEL. *Goldenboy*. Boston: Alyson Publications, 1988.

————. *How Town*. New York: Harper & Row, 1990.

PUCCIA, JOSEPH. *The Holy Spirit Dance Club*. New York: Liberty Press, 1988.

PURDY, JAMES. *Garments the Living Wear*. San Francisco: City Lights, 1989.

REDON, JOEL. *Bloodstream*. Stamford, CT: Knights Press, 1989.

REED, PAUL. *Facing It*. San Francisco: Gay Sunshine Press, 1984.

————. *Longing*. Berkeley: Celestial Arts, 1988.

REES, DAVID. *The Wrong Apple*. Stamford, CT: Knights Press, 1989.

RUBIN, MARTY. *The Boiled Frog Syndrome*. Boston: Alyson, 1987.

SCHULMAN, SARAH. *People in Trouble*. New York: E. P. Dutton, 1989.

SONTAG, SUSAN. "The Way We Live Now." *The Best American Short Stories 1987*, 1–19. Boston: Houghton Mifflin, 1987.

UPDIKE, JOHN. *Rabbit at Rest*. New York: Knopf, 1990.

VERGHESE, ABRAHAM. "Lilacs." *New Yorker*, 14 October 1991, 53–58.

WEIR, JOHN. *The Irreversible Decline of Eddie Socket*. New York: Perennial, 1989.

WHITE, EDMUND. "An Oracle." *Men on Men: Best New Gay Fiction*. Ed. George Stambolian, 88–113. New York: NAL, 1986.

————. "Skinned Alive." *Men on Men 3*. Ed. George Stambolian, 340–68. New York: NAL, 1990.

WHITLOCK, DEAN. "On the Death of Daniel." *The Magazine of Fantasy and Science Fiction*, March 1991, 26–42.

POETRY

Among the anthologies of poetry listed below, some deal primarily with AIDS-related themes; some others treat such themes only peripherally. In addition to these volumes, individual poems that examine the impact of AIDS have appeared in a variety of journals—both gay and non-gay. *Art & Understanding: The Quarterly Journal of Literature & Art About AIDS*. This journal has prose pieces as well.

BECKER, BILL. *An Intimate Desire to Survive*. Pittsburgh: Dorrance, 1985.

BOUCHERON, ROBERT. *Epitaphs for the Plague Dead*. New York: Ursus Press, 1985.

City Lights Anthology 2, Special Issue on "AIDS, Cultural Life, and the Arts." San Francisco: City Lights, 1988. In addition to poetry, this issue contains drawings, personal narratives, and formal essays.

DIRG, AAB-RICHARDS, et al. *Tongues Untied*. London: Gay Men's Press, 1987.

GONSALVES, ROY. *Perversion*. New York: Renaissance, 1990.

GUNN, THOM. *Undesirables*. Durham, England: Pig Press, 1988.

HUMPHRIES, MARTIN, ed. *Not Love Alone: A Modern Gay Anthology*. London: Gay Men's Press, 1985.

KLEIN, MICHAEL, ed. *Poets for Life: Seventy-Six Poets Respond to AIDS*. New York: Crown, 1989.

LYNCH, MICHAEL. *These Waves of Dying Friends*. New York: Contact II Publications, 1989.

MONETTE, PAUL. *Love Alone: 18 Elegies for Rog*. New York: St. Martin's Press, 1988.

MORSE, CARL AND JOAN LARKIN, eds. *Gay and Lesbian Poetry in Our Time: An Anthology*. New York: St. Martin's Press, 1988.

O'BRIEN, PAT. *I'm Afraid This Time Love, It's Positive*. London: Oscars Press, 1989.

SCHREIBER, RON. *John*. New York: Hanging Loose Press and Calamus Press, 1989.

DRAMA

BOWNE, ALAN. *Beirut*. New York: Broadway Play Publishing, 1988.

BUMBALO, VICTOR. *Adam and the Experts*. New York: Broadway Play Publishing, 1990.

CACHIANES, ED. *Everybody Knows Your Name*. Unpublished.

CHESLEY, ROBERT. *Hard Plays/Stiff Parts: The Homoerotic Plays of Robert Chesley*. San Francisco: Alamo Square Press, 1990. The AIDS theme is central to two plays in this volume: *Jerker or the Helping Hand* (71–118) and *Night Sweat* (9–69).

COPI (RAUL DAMMONTE). *Une Visite inopportune*. Paris: Christian Bourgeois, 1988.

FIERSTEIN, HARVEY. *Safe Sex*. New York: Atheneum, 1987.

KELLEY, LOUISE PARKER. *Anti Body*. Unpublished.

KONDOLEAN, HARRY. *Zero Positive*. New York: Dramatists' Play Service, 1989.

KRAMER, LARRY. *The Normal Heart*. New York: NAL, 1985.

LUCAS, CRAIG. *Prelude to a Kiss*. New York: Dutton, 1991.

OSBORN, ELIZABETH M. *The Way We Live Now: American Plays and the AIDS Crisis*. New York: Theatre Communications Group, 1990. This volume includes William Hoffman's *As Is* and David Greenspan's *Jack*.

PINTAURO, JOE. *Raft of the Medusa*. Unpublished.

VAN ITALLIE, JEAN-CLAUDE. *Ancient Boys*. In *Gay Plays: An International Anthology*. Eds. Catherine Temerson and Francoise Kourilsky, 329–93. New York: Ubu Repertory Theatre Publications, 1989.

MEMOIRS/TESTAMENTS

DREUILHE, EMMANUEL. *Mortal Embrace*. Trans. Linda Coverdale. New York: Hill and Wang, 1988.

GUIBERT, HERVÉ . *Le protocole Compassionnel*. Paris: Gallimard, 1991.

HOLLERAN, ANDREW. *Ground Zero*. New York: William Morrow, 1988.

KRAMER, LARRY. *Reports from the Holocaust: The Making of an AIDS Activist*. New York: St. Martin's Press, 1989.

LYNCH, MICHAEL. "Last Onsets: Teaching With AIDS." *Profession 90*. New York: MLA, 1990, 32–36.

MONETTE, PAUL. *Borrowed Time: An AIDS Memoir*. New York: Harcourt Brace Jovanovich, 1988.

MONEY, J. W. *To All the Girls I've Loved Before: An AIDS Diary.* Boston: Alyson, 1987.

PETROW, STEPHEN. *Dancing Against the Darkness: A Journey Through America in the Age of AIDS.* Lexington, MA: Lexington Books, 1990.

REED, PAUL. *Serenity.* Berkeley: Celestial Press, 1990.

———. *The Q Journal: A Treatment Diary.* Berkeley: Celestial, 1990.

WHITE, RYAN (with Ann Marie Cunningham). *Ryan White: My Own Story.* New York: Dial, 1991.

WHITMORE, GEORGE. *Someone Was Here: Profiles in the AIDS Epidemic.* New York: NAL, 1988.

CRITICISM

ALEXANDER, WILLIAM. "Clearing Space: AIDS Theatre in Atlanta." *The Drama Review*, 34:3 (Fall 1990): 109–28.

BRONSKI, MICHAEL. "AIDS, Art, and Anger." *The Guide*, 10:8 (August 1990): 23–25.

———. "Make the AIDS Epidemic Manageable." *American Book Review*, 12:2 (May–June 1990): 1, 15, 22.

BRUCE, BRYAN. "Modern Diseases: Gay Self-Representation in the Age of AIDS." *CineAction* (Winter 1988/89): 29–38.

CLUM, JOHN M. "'The Time Before the War': AIDS, Memory, and Desire." *American Literature*, 62:4 (December 1990): 648–67.

CRICHTON, E. G. "Is the NAMES Quilt Art?" *Out/Look* (Summer 1988): 5–9.

CRIMP, DOUGLAS. "AIDS: Cultural Analysis/Cultural Criticism." In *AIDS: Cultural Analysis/Cultural Criticism*, 3–16. Cambridge: MIT Press, 1988.

DAWIDOFF, ROBERT. "Memorial Day, 1988." *Personal Dispatches: Writers Confront AIDS*, ed. John Preston, 172–78. New York: St. Martin's Press, 1988.

DENNENY, MICHAEL. "A Quilt of Many Colors: AIDS Writing and the Creation of Culture." *Christopher Street*, issue 141, 15–21.

EDELMAN, LEE. "The Plague of Discourse: Politics, Literary Theory, and AIDS." *Displacing Homophobia: Gay Male Perspectives in Literature and Culture*, ed. Michael Moon, et al, 289–305. Durham: Duke University Press, 1989.

GROVE, LEE. "The Metaphor of AIDS." *Boston Globe Magazine*, 28 February 1988.

GROVER, JAN ZITA. "AIDS Culture." *The Women's Review of Books*, VI: 7 (April 1989): 6.

HARAWAY, DONNA. "The Biopolitics of Postmodern Bodies: Determinations of Self in Immune System Discourse." *Differences*, 1 (Winter 1989): 3–43.

HARPER, PHILLIP BRIAN. "The Culture of AIDS: Reflection and Analysis." *American Book Review*, 12:2 (May–June 1990): 9.

KAUFMAN, DAVID. "AIDS: The Creative Response." *Horizon*, 30 (November 1987), 13–20.

LEE, JEFFREY. "No Lyrics in This." *American Book Review*, 12:2 (May–June 1990): 7.

MURPHY, TIMOTHY AND SUZANNE POIRIER, eds. *Writing AIDS: Essays on the Literature of Crisis.* New York: Columbia University Press, 1992.

NASH, PHIL. "The Artist as Warrior in the Time of AIDS." *Muse* (December 1989): 7–10.

NELSON, EMMANUEL. "AIDS and the American Novel." *Journal of American Culture*, 13:1 (Spring 1990), 47–53.

O'CONNELL, SHAUN. "The Big One: Literature Discovers AIDS." *The AIDS Epidemic: Private Rights and the Public Interest.* Ed. Padraig O'Malley, 485–506. Boston: Beacon Press, 1989.

PASTORE, JUDITH LAURENCE. *Literary AIDS: Myths, Realities & Responsibilities.* Carbondale: Southern Illinois University, 1992.

RICHARDS, DAVID. "The Theater of AIDS: Attention Must Be Paid. *New York Times*, 5 January 1992, Arts and Leisure sec. 2:1.

SEIDMAN, STEVEN. "Transfiguring Sexual Identity: AIDS and the Contemporary Construction of Homosexuality." *Social Text*, 19/20 (Fall 1988): 190–205.

SHEWEY, DON. "AIDS on Stage: Comfort, Sorrow, Anger." *New York Times*, 21 June 1987, H5.

TREICHLER, PAULA A. "AIDS, Homophobia, and Biomedical Discourse: An Epidemic of Signification." *AIDS: Cultural Analysis/Cultural Criticism*, ed. Douglas Crimp, 31–70. Cambridge: MIT Press, 1988.

WHITE, EDMUND. "Esthetics and Loss." *Personal Dispatches: Writers Confront AIDS*, ed. John Preston, 145–52. New York: St. Martin's Press, 1989.

Appendix:
An AIDS Filmography

KEVIN J. HARTY

Andre's Mother, written by Terrence McNally, directed by Deborah Reinisch, American Playhouse for PBS, 1990.

CAST: Haviland Morris, Sylvia Sidney, Richard Thomas, Sada Thompson, Richard Venture.
SELECTED REVIEWS: *The Advocate* (27 February 1990), 59–60; *New York* (12 March 1990), 70–71; *New York Times* (7 March 1990), C24; *Variety* (7 March 1990), 55, 58; *Village Voice* (15 March 1990), 55.

As Is, written by William S. Hoffman, directed by Michael Lindsay-Hogg, Broadway on Showtime, 1986.

CAST: Doug Annear, Robert Carradine, Colleen Dewhurst, Jonathan Hardary, Julia Miles, Allan Scarfe.
SELECTED REVIEWS: *Newsday* (25 July 1986), 2. 9; *New York Daily News* (24 July 1986), 81; *Variety* (20 July 1986), 56; *Village Voice* (29 July 1986), 36–37.

Buddies, directed, edited, and written by Arthur J. Bressnan, Jr., New Line Cinema, 1985.

CAST: Geoff Edholm, Billy Lux, Dave Rose, David Schacter.
SELECTED REVIEWS: *Monthly Film Bulletin* 53 (November 1986), 332–33; *New York Daily News* (15 November 1985), 15; *New York Native* (25 November 1985), 43; *New York Post* (15 November 1985), 27; *New York Times* (15 November 1985), C14; *San Francisco Chronicle* (12 September 1985), 59; *Variety* (18 September 1985), 18; *Village Voice* (26 November 1985), 70.

Common Threads: Stories from the Quilt, narrated by Dustin Hoffman, directed by Robert Epstein and Jeffrey Friedman, Telling Pictures, 1989.

CAST (of storytellers): Sara Lewinstein, Suzi Mandell, David Mandell, Sallie Perryman, Vito Russo, and Tracy Torrey.
SELECTED REVIEWS: *Chicago Tribune* (13 October 1989), E2; *Los Angeles Times* (14 October 1989), F11 and (26 January 1990), F14; *Monthly Film Bulletin* 58 (February 1991), 40; *New Statesman and Society* (7 September 1990), 34; *New York* (16 October 1989), 108; *New York Times* (24 October 1989), C26.

An Early Frost, written by Daniel Lipman and Ron Cowen, directed by John Erman, NBC, 1985.

CAST: Ben Gazarra, John Glover, Gena Rowlands, D. W. Moffett, Aidan Quinn, Sylvia Sidney, Sydney Walsh.

SELECTED REVIEWS: *New Republic* (11 August 1986), 28; *New York* (18 November 1985), 86; *New York Daily News* (11 November 1985), 62; *New York Native* (18 November 1985), 41; *New York Post* (11 November 1985), 68; *New York Times* (11 November 1985), C17; *Village Voice* (12 November 1985), 41–42; *Women's Wear Daily* (6 November 1985), 56.

Intimate Contact, written by Alma Cullen, directed by Waris Hussein, Zenith Productions for Central Television, 1987.

CAST: Claire Bloom, Abigail Cruttenden, Sally Jane Jackson, Paul Jesson, Mark Kingston, Daniel Massey, David Phelan, Maggie Steed, Sylvia Symms.

SELECTED REVIEWS: *Chicago Sun-Times* (5 October 1987), 39; *Chicago Tribune* (5 October 1987), 2. 7; *New Statesman* (27 March 1987), 27–28; *New York* (12 October 1987), 94–95; *New York Daily News* (5 October 1987), 69; *New York Times* (6 October 1987), C18; *The Stage and Television Today* (13 November 1986), 22; *Variety* (25 March 1987), 80 and (14 October 1987), 206, 208.

Longtime Companion, written by Craig Lucas, directed by Norman René, American Playhouse for PBS, 1990.

CAST: Stephen Caffrey, Patrick Cassidy, Brian Cousins, Bruce Davidson, John Dossett, Mark Lamos, Dermott Mulroney, Brad O'Hara, Mary-Louise Parker, Michael Schoeffline, Campbell Scott.

SELECTED REVIEWS: *American Film* 15 (June 1990), 49, 51; *Atlanta Constitution* (25 May 1990), D1; *Chicago Tribune* (25 May 1990), 7. 28, *Christian Science Monitor* (24 July 1990), 14; *Cineaste* 18 (1990), 47–49; *Cinema* 150 (November 1990), 126–27; *Commonweal* (13 July 1990), 120–21; *Film Comment* 29 (May–June, 1990), 11; *Los Angeles Magazine* (June 1990), 205; *Los Angeles Times* (17 May 1990), F1; *Maclean's* (9 July 1990), 12; *Nation* (29 May 1990), 752; *National Catholic Reporter* (13 July 1990), 19; *National Review* (11 June 1990), 57–58; *New Republic* (29 May 1990), 25; *New Statesman and Society* (7 September 1990), 34; *New York* (21 May 1990), 68; *New York Times* (11 May 1990), C16; *New Yorker* (21 May 1990), 71–72; *Newsweek* (14 May 1990), 74; *Rolling Stone* (31 May 1990), 38; *San Francisco Chronicle* (5 May 1990), E1, E4; *San Francisco Examiner* (18 May 1990), C3; *Time* (14 May 1990), 99; *Variety* (14 February 1990), 36; *Village Voice* (22 May 1990), 70; *Wall Street Journal* (10 May 1990), A16.

Men in Love, written by Scott Catamas and Emerald Starr, directed by Marc Huestis, Tantric Films, 1990.

CAST: Kutira Decosterd, Carlo Incerto, Doug Self, Emerald Starr, James A. Taylor, Joe Tolbe.

SELECTED REVIEWS: *Los Angeles Times* (7 May 1990), F7; *New York Times* (27 July 1990), C10; *Philadelphia Inquirer* (31 August 1990), Weekend 15; *San Francisco Chronicle* (12 January 1990), E7; *Variety* (25 July 1990), 22–23; *Village Voice* (31 July 1990), 69.

Parting Glances, directed, written, and edited by Bill Sherwood, Cinecom International Films, 1986.

CAST: Yolande Bavan, John Bolger, Steve Buscemi, Richard Ganoung, Kathy Kinney, Adam Nathan, Patrick Tull.

SELECTED REVIEWS: *Film Journal* 89 (February 1986), 39–40; *Films and Filming* 384 (September 1986); 40–41; *Los Angeles Times* (6 March 1986), Calendar 11; *Maclean's* (21 April 1986), 75; *Monthly Film Bulletin* 53 (November 1986), 340–41; *Nation* (8 March 1986), 28; *New York* (3 March 1986), 127; *New York Daily News* (19 February 1986), 41; *New York Native* (20 January 1986), 40; *New York Post* (19 February 1986), 40; *New York Times* (19 February 1986), C21; *Newsday* (19 February 1986), II. 49; *Newsweek* (9 June 1986), 80; *Variety* (29 January 1986), 19; *Village Voice* (25 February 1986), 58; *Washington Post* (14 March 1986), Weekend 27 and (15 March 1986), B7.

Positive (Positiv), written and directed by Rosa von Praunheim, First Run Features, 1989.

CAST: Emilio Cubiero, Allen Ginsberg, Keith Haring, David Wojnarowicz.

SELECTED REVIEWS: *Los Angeles Times* (25 July 1990), F8; *New York Post* (4 May 1990), 31; *New York Times* (4 May 1990), C17; *San Francisco Examiner* (29 June 1990), C5; *Variety* (14 March 1990), 24; *Village Voice* (8 May 1990), 70.

The Ryan White Story, written by Phil Penningroth and John Herzfeld, directed by John Herzfeld, ABC Monday Night Movie, 1989.

CAST: Michael Bowen, Nikki Cox, Lucas Haas, Valerie Landsburg, Judith Light, Sarah Jessica Parker, Mitchell Ryan, Peter Scolari, George C. Scott, Ryan White, Grace Zabriskie.

SELECTED REVIEWS: *Chicago Sun-Times* (16 January 1989), 29; *Chicago Tribune* (16 January 1989), 2. 5; *New York Daily News* (16 January 1989), 68; *New York Post* (16 January 1989), 65; *New York Times* (16 January 1989), C16; *Variety* (25 January 1989), 62.

Silence = Death (Schweigen = Tod), written and directed by Rosa von Praunheim, First Run Features, 1989.

CAST: Michael Callen, Larry Kramer, Phil Zwickler.

SELECTED REVIEWS: *Los Angeles Times* (25 July 1990), F8; *New York Post* (4 May 1990), 31; *New York Times* (4 May 1990), C17; *San Francisco Examiner* (3 August 1990), C3; *Variety* (7 March 1990), 28; *Village Voice* (8 May 1990), 70.

Sweet As You Are, written by Bill Nicholson, directed by Angela Pope, BBC2, 1988.

CAST: Liam Neeson, Miranda Richardon.

SELECTED REVIEWS: *City Limits* (21 January 1988), 57–58; *Listener* (21 January 1988), 28 and (28 January 1988), 34; *New Statesman* (29 January 1988), 115; *People Weekly* (6 March 1989), 11; *Radio Times* (23 January 1988), 84; *Television Today* (28 January 1988), 23.

Tidy Endings, written by Harvey Fierstein, directed by Gavin Millar, HBO, 1988.

CAST: Stockard Channing, Harvey Fierstein, Nathaniel Moreau.

SELECTED REVIEWS: *Boston Globe* (13 August 1988), 30; *Chicago Sun-Times* (12 August 1988), Weekend Plus 47; *Library Journal* (1 October 1988), 132; *Los Angeles Magazine* 33 (August 1988), 309; *New York Daily News* (12 August 1988), 108; *New York Times* (12 August 1988), C26.

A Virus Knows No Morals (Ein Virus Kennt Keine Moral), written and directed by Rosa von Praunheim, First Run Features, 1986.

CAST: Dieter Dicken, Maria Hasenaecker, Christian Kesten, Eva Kurz, Regina Rudnick, Rosa von Praunheim, Thilo von Trotha.

SELECTED REVIEWS: *New York Daily News* (19 June 1987), 43; *New York Post* (19 June 1987), 35; *New York Times* (19 June 1987), C10; *Variety* (27 August 1986), 16; *Village Voice* (23 June 1987), 67; *Women's Wear Daily* (18 June 1987), 16.

Notes on Contributors

David Bergman, professor of English at Towson State University, is the author of *Gaiety Transfigured: Gay Self-Representation in American Literature* (University of Wisconsin Press) and the editor of *Reported Sightings: Art Chronicles, 1957–87* (Knopf) and *The Story: Readers and Writers of Fiction* (Macmillan). His volume of poetry, *Cracking the Code* (Ohio State University Press), won the George Elliston Poetry Award in 1985.

Laurel Brodsley teaches in the English Department at the University of California at Los Angeles, where she recently offered a course titled "AIDS and Plagues: A View from the Humanities." In addition to a doctorate in English, Brodsley also holds a graduate degree in public health; the focus of her research is on the relationship between literature and medicine.

Barbara Browning is assistant professor of English at Princeton University. She is currently working on two projects: a study of the relationships among secular, spiritual, and martial dance forms in Brazil; an analysis of Afro-Atlantic syncretic narratives through Yoruba *Orisha* principles.

Annie Dawid received her doctorate in 1989 from the University of Denver and teaches in the Department of English at Lewis & Clark College. Her short fictions have appeared in the *Gettysburg Review*, *Quarterly West, Folio*, and *River Styx*.

Joseph Dewey is assistant professor of modern American literature at the University of Pittsburgh at Johnstown. Author of *In A Dark Time: The Apocalyptic Temper in the American Novel of the Nuclear Age* (Purdue University Press), he is currently at work on a study of the American novel of the 1980s.

Judy Elsley received her undergraduate degree from the University of Bristol, England, and her doctorate in English from the University of Arizona. Contributor to a forthcoming volume on autobiographical literary criticism, she is working on an anthology of critical essays on the quilting metaphor in literature. She teaches at Weber State University.

Kevin J. Harty is associate professor of English at La Salle University. He is the author of articles on—among other topics—Chaucer, medieval drama, and cinematic treatments of the Arthurian legend and editor of *Strategies for Business and Technical Writing, Cinema Arthuriana: Essays on Arthurian Film*, and *The Chester Mystery Cycle: A Casebook*. He co-authored with John Keenan *Writing for Business and Industry: Process and Product*.

Gert Hekma is lecturer in Gay Studies at the University of Amsterdam. Author of over 30 articles on the history and sociology of (homo)sexuality, he recently co-edited *The Pursuit of Sodomy: Male Homosexuality in Renaissance and Enlighten-ment Europe* (Haworth).

D. S. Lawson, who received his doctorate in English from the University of Tennessee, is currently assistant professor of Humanities at Lander College. He is the author of two forthcoming books—one on Joe Orton and another on intertexuality. He has published several pedagogical articles and his poetry has appeared in *The James White Review, Bay Windows, R.F.D.*, and *Amethyst*.

James Morrison is assistant professor of English and Film Studies at North Carolina State University at Raleigh. He received his Ph.D. from SUNY-Buffalo in 1988 and has taught there and at Wayne State University. His fiction and criticism have appeared in numerous journals, including *Centennial Review, New Orleans Review, Semiotica*, and *PRISM International*. He is now working on a study of gay film makers of Classical Hollywood.

Emmanuel S. Nelson received his undergraduate education in India and his Ph.D. in English from the University of Tennessee in 1983. During 1985–86 he was a Postdoctoral Research Fellow in Commonwealth Literature at the University of Queensland, Australia. Author of over two dozen articles on ethnic, post-colonial, and gay literatures, he has edited *Connections: Essays on Black Literatures* (Aboriginal Studies Press), *Reworlding: Essays on the Literature of the Indian Diaspora* (Green-wood), and *Writers of the Indian Diaspora: A Bio-Bibliographical Critical Source-book* (Greenwood). He teaches at the State University College of New York at Cortland.

Judith Laurence Pastore holds a doctorate in English from Harvard University and teaches in the interdisciplinary Technology, Society, and Values Program at the University of Lowell. She has published articles on the novels of Don DeLillo and on the literature of AIDS. She is editing a volume titled *Literary AIDS: Myths, Realities & Responsibilities* and co-authoring a textbook *The Frankenstein Dilemma: Scientific Goals and Technological Risks from an Engineering & Humanities Per-spective*.

Joel Shatzky is professor of English at SUNY College at Cortland. He has published several articles on modern drama and on the theatrical treatment of the Holocaust. He is the editor of a Holocaust memoir titled *Hitler's 'Gift' to the Jews: Theresienstadt in the Words and Pictures of Norbert Troller* (North Carolina University Press).

Myles Weber holds a graduate degree in English from Syracuse University. Most recently he is the author of an article that appears in *The Georgia Review*.

David Wetsel is assistant professor of French at Arizona State University at Tempe. He holds a master's degree from the University of Chicago Divinity School and a doctorate from Brandeis. He is the author of *L'Ecriture et le Reste: The 'Pensees' of Pascal in the Exegetical Tradition of Port-Royal* (Ohio State University Press).

Les Wright is a doctoral candidate in Comparative Literature at the University of California at Berkeley, where he is completing a dissertation titled *The Chiasmic War: AIDS Writing and Gay Counter-Memory, 1975–1990*. A gay rights activist since the mid-seventies, he is a founding member of the Gay and Lesbian Historical Society of Northern California and editor-in-chief of *OurStories*. He is the author of "Clinton, New York" which appears in *Hometown: Gay Men Write About Where They Belong* (Dutton) and has begun work on a book-length oral history titled *Castro Street: Gay Hometown, USA* for Alamo Square Press.

Gregory Woods teaches British and American literatures and creative writing at Nottingham Polytechnic, England. He is the author of *Articulate Flesh: Male Homo-eroticism and Modern Poetry* (Yale University Press). He is now writing a book on Marcel Proust; his first collection of poems, *We Have the Melon*, will be published in 1992.

Index